A TIMES BARTHOLOMEW GUIDE
NEW YORK

Author: **Hector Feliciano**
Translation, adaptation: **Lisa Davidson-Petty**
Editor: **Alexandra Tufts-Simon**
Photo credits: **Raoul Arroche**

This edition published in Great Britain by **John Bartholomew & Son Ltd.**
and **Times Books Ltd.,** 16 Golden Square, London W1R 4BN.

This guide is adapted from *à New York* published by Hachette Guides
Bleus, Paris 1988.

© Hachette Guides Bleus, Paris, 1989. First edition.
English translation © Hachette Guides Bleus, Paris, 1989.
Maps © Hachette Guides Bleus, Paris, 1989.

British Library Cataloguing in Publication Data
Feliciano, Hector
New York. — (A Times Bartholomew guide).
  1. New York (City) — Visitor's guides
  I. Title
  917.47'10443
  ISBN 0-7230-0326-2
Printed in France by Mame Imprimeurs

A TIMES BARTHOLOMEW GUIDE

NEW YORK

*Published by Times Books and
John Bartholomew & Son Ltd*

HOW TO USE YOUR GUIDE

● Before you leave home, read the sections **'Planning Your Trip'** p. 23, **'Practical Information'** p. 29, **'New York in the Past'** p. 56 and **'New York Today'** p. 63.

● The rest of the guide is for use once you arrive. It is divided into itineraries and includes sections on museums and architecture.

● A section called **'New York Addresses'** is provided at the end of the guide, p. 189. It includes a selection of hotels, restaurants, bars and shops, organized by neighbourhood.

● To quickly locate a site, a person or practical information, use the **'Index'** p. 214.

● To easily locate recommended sites, hotels and restaurants on the maps, refer to the map coordinates printed in blue in the text. Example: III, AB2.

SYMBOLS USED

Sites, monuments, museums, points of interest
★★★   Exceptional
★★   Very interesting
★   Interesting

Hotels and restaurants
See p. 189.

MAPS

CONTENTS

Areas of Manhattan

Map VI: Uptown, north
pp. 18-19

Map V: Uptown, center
pp. 16-17

Map IV: Midtown and
pp. 14-15   Uptown, south

Map III: Lower Manhattan,
pp. 12-13   north

Map II: Lower Manhattan,
pp. 10-11   south

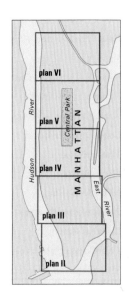

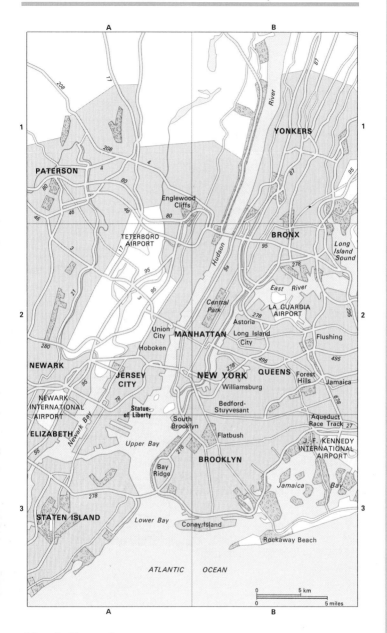

Map I: General map
New York City consists of five boroughs:
Manhattan, The Bronx, Queens, Brooklyn, Staten Island.

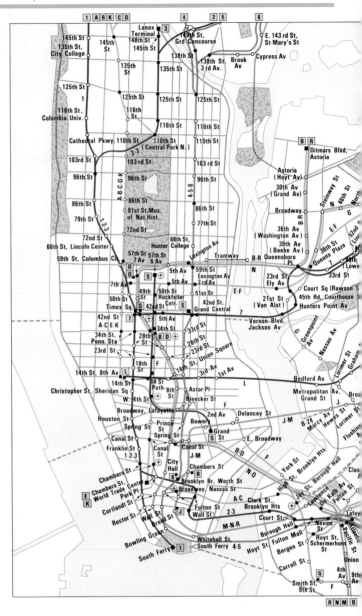

The New York subway

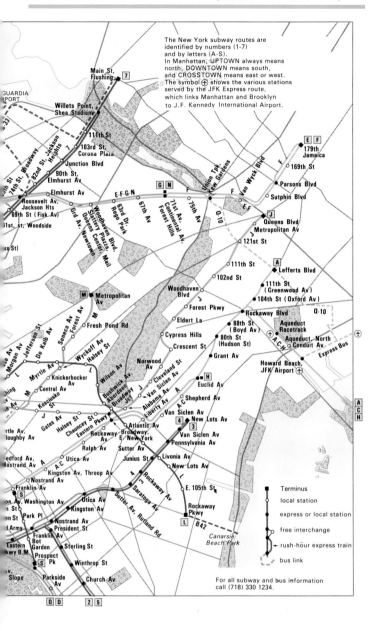

The New York subway routes are
identified by numbers (1-7)
and by letters (A-S).
In Manhattan, UPTOWN always means
north, DOWNTOWN means south,
and CROSSTOWN means east or west.
The symbol ⊕ shows the various stations
served by the JFK Express route,
which links Manhattan and Brooklyn
to J.F. Kennedy International Airport.

Terminus
local station
express or local station
free interchange
rush-hour express train
bus link

For all subway and bus information
call (718) 330 1234.

Map II: Lower Manhattan, south

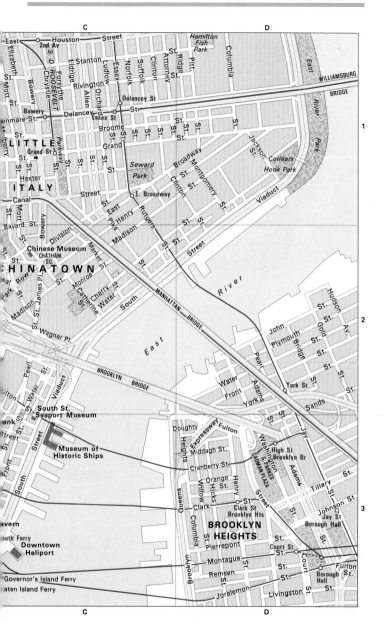

Map III: Lower Manhattan, north

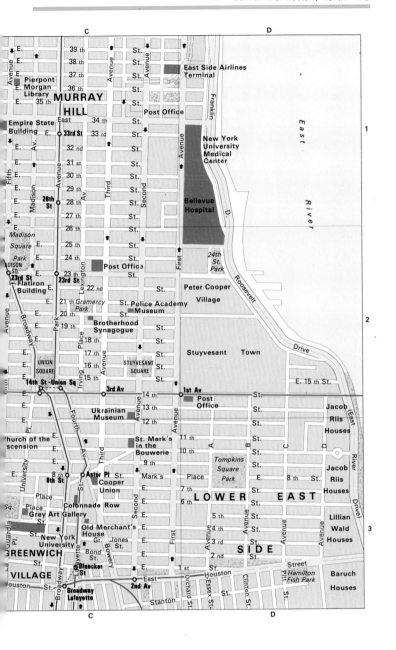

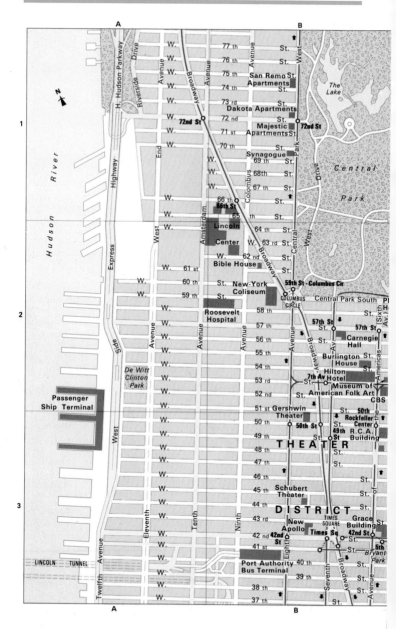

Map IV: Midtown and Uptown, south

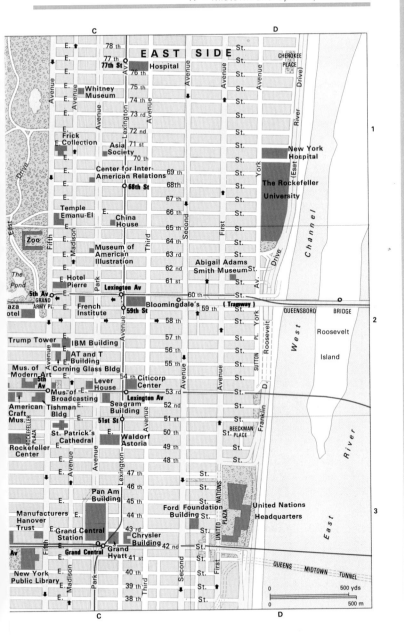

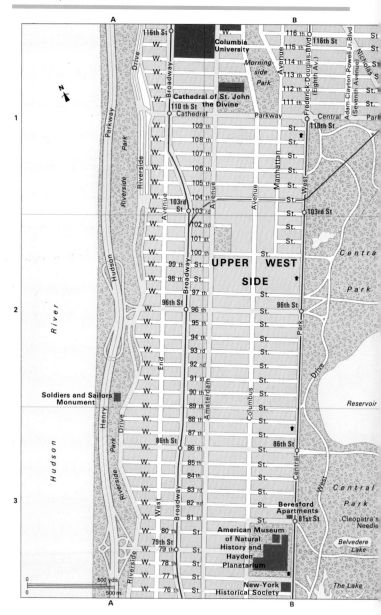

Map V: Uptown, center

Map VI: Uptown, north

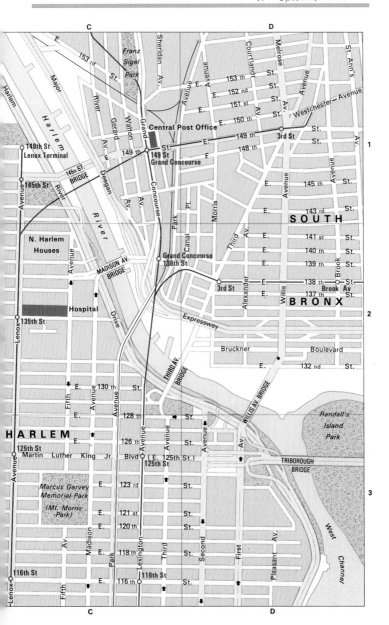

INTRODUCTION TO NEW YORK

New York is a shock of noise, movement, energy and excitement. It is a work of art on a flamboyant, giant scale.

The city has an unforgettable effect on life-long New Yorkers and one-time visitors alike. A traveler crossing the Brooklyn or Triborough bridges is confronted with the extraordinary vision of a fully upright, soaring city, like a geyser rising to the sky. Even a first-time visitor will find the dramatic Manhattan skyline a familiar sight.

The activity in New York is intense, unceasing, urgent; noise and colour permeate every aspect of city life. Indeed, the city often seems to be a world unto itself. The energy and frantic rhythm of life are evident in the rushed pace of the pedestrians and the chaotic, jerky flow of the traffic. New York is a city that never sleeps; the daylight hours are not enough for all there is to see and do.

In Manhattan, excess has become the norm where the very rich rub elbows with the very poor. You can see anything and buy anything, because everything is for sale. It is said that when they landed on this island, the Dutch didn't fall to their knees like the Quakers in Pennsylvania; instead they simply asked the first natives they met, *Hoevel?* How much? And so the island of Manhattan was sold for the first time, in 1626, for twenty-four dollars' worth of glass beads.

True or not, this story persists because the idea that the city is there for the taking lives on. As the famous song says, if you can make it here you can make it anywhere — and that's how most New Yorkers feel. Though partly a myth, the city does remain a symbol of success, and with reason — for it is the cultural capital of the nation and has attracted the brightest and most talented people from America and all over the world, including artists, writers, actors, businesspeople and scientists. Anyone can reach the top and fame and fortune are always close at hand. Your taxi driver may well be more than just a pair of shoulders behind a bulletproof screen — world-renowned composer Phillip Glass, for example, once drove a cab. Like everyone else, he was waiting for his big break. And the young waiters who serve you in restaurants are most likely actors and dancers also just waiting their turn.

The Empire State Building, symbol of New York City.

Yet, it's a city of contrasts too. Poor, run-down neighbourhoods abut opulent ones; one block is well-kept and wealthy while the next one is dirty and decaying. It's one vast melting pot where ethnic pride and neighbourhood loyalties are mixed with fervent patriotism, where poverty coexists with wealth, and callousness alternates with sentimentality.

New York has been a leading force in this century. It is a city of superlatives: It has one of the largest and most protected ports in the world, its population is more diverse than any other international city's, the New York Stock Exchange is still the major international market and it has provided the world with numerous architectural innovations.

Visitors to New York cannot help feeling that they are watching the world being created before their very eyes as new buildings go up and others are torn down, as the city flows on at a relentless pace. Only the many museums and monuments throughout the city provide a historical continuity to this constant process of construction and destruction.

Don't forget to look back over the city when you leave. The soaring New York skyline is engraved on the horizon, outlining the contours of this eternally incandescent city.

New York in brief

Location: North-east coast of the United States, at the mouth of the Hudson River. Same latitude as Naples or Madrid.

Total area: Approximately 300 sq mi/777 sq km.

Government: The city is governed by a mayor, elected for a four-year term, and the City Council.

Administrative division: Five boroughs (Manhattan, the Bronx, Brooklyn, Queens, Staten Island). The Bronx is the only borough located on the mainland; Brooklyn and Queens form the western end of Long Island.

Total area of Manhattan: 33.3 sq mi/86.3 sq km; 13.4 mi/21.5 km long; 0.8 mi/1.3 km at the narrowest point and 2.3 mi/3.7 km at the widest.

Population: All five boroughs — 7,254,00 inhabitants
1) Manhattan — 1,479,000
2) The Bronx — 1,184,000
3) Brooklyn — 2,283,000
4) Queens — 1,933,000
5) Staten Island — 373,000
The Greater New York area — 18,000,000 inhabitants.

Language: English.

Shipping activity: Second largest port in the world, after Rotterdam; 745.7 mi/1200 km of wharves on both banks of the Hudson River, with docking space for more than 200 ships at one time; 150 million tons of goods trafficked per year.

Tourism: Eighteen million visitors annually, including three million foreigners, who bring $2.5 billion to the city every year.

Nickname: The Big Apple.

Other statistics: There are more than 100,000 hotel rooms in New York, 25,000 restaurants, 300 theaters, 150 museums and 200 nightclubs. The 3500 places of worship represent over 100 religious denominations. There are close to 50 universities and higher education institutions in New York. Two hundred of the largest American companies have their headquarters in New York, as well as six of the major commercial banks. The ethnic makeup of New York is more diverse than any city in the world. Most European immigrants arrived in the United States via New York. Many stayed, and New York owes its multi-cultural heritage to them.

PLANNING YOUR TRIP

▬▬ WHEN TO GO

New York can be visited during any season. The city is at its best in the fall, when a warm Indian summer usually arrives. Late spring is also pleasant, with usually mild and sunny days.

Winters can be very cold, especially in January and February, but Christmas in the city can be entrancing and unique.

The summer heat and humidity do not seem to affect the energy of New Yorkers, although temperatures can exceed 95° F/35° C. There is always lots of action and entertainment on the streets and in the parks, with many festivals and celebrations in Central Park and elsewhere.

Temperatures (°F/°C)

	Jan	Feb	Mar	Apr	May	June	July	Aug	Sept	Oct	Nov	Dec
Maximum	41/5	41/5	50/10	64/18	75/24	86/30	91/33	84/29	75/24	64/18	54/12	41/5
Average	34/1	34/1	41/5	54/12	63/18	75/25	66/19	57/14	66/19	57/14	46/8	38/2
Minimum	27/3	27/1	30/1	44/7	55/13	68/20	75/24	71/22	59/15	50/10	39/4	34/1

▬▬ GETTING THERE

Plane

New York is probably the easiest place to get to in the world. Flights leave from all major cities. We list only a few of the many airlines that offer flights to New York.

Australia

Qantas, International Centre, International Square, Sydney 2000, ☎ (02) 236 3636.

Canada

Air Canada, 500 Dorchester Blvd., Montreal 42Z 1X5, ☎ (514) 879 7000; 75 Albert St., Ottawa, ☎ (613) 236 0689; 1040 West Georgia St., Vancouver, ☎ (604) 682 5515.

Great Britain

British Airways, 75 Regent St., London W1R 7HG, ☎ (01) 897 4000; 421 Oxford St., London W1R 1FJ, ☎ (01) 897 4000.

Pan Am, 14 Old Park Lane, London W1Y 3LH, ☎ (01) 409 0688.

TWA, 200 Piccadilly, London W1V ODH, ☎ (01) 439 0707.

Ireland

Aer Lingus, 40 Upper O'Connell St., Dublin, ☎ (01) 73 3008 or 73 3119.

Airports

New York City has three major airports:

Kennedy Airport (JFK) is located in south-east Queens, I, B3, at the southern tip of the Van Wyck Expressway, 17 mi/28 km from Manhattan. It is the largest of the three airports, with both domestic and international flights. It takes about 45 minutes to reach Manhattan by car under normal traffic conditions. Traveler information, ☎ (718) 656 4444.

LaGuardia Airport is located in north-east Queens, I, B2, on Grand Central Parkway, 8 mi/14 km from Manhattan. It primarily handles domestic flights. Regularly scheduled shuttles for Boston or Washington leave LaGuardia every hour. Travel time to Manhattan is approximately 30 minutes by car. Traveler information, ☎ (718) 476 5000.

Newark International Airport is located in Newark, New Jersey, I, A2-3, on the New Jersey Turnpike, 12 mi/20 km from Manhattan. It handles domestic and international flights and is approximately 30 minutes from Manhattan by car in normal traffic. Traveler information, ☎ (201) 656 4520.

Arrival

International passengers' passports and luggage are checked on arrival. There are usually long waiting lines at passport control and patience is recommended. Once you have stated the length and purpose of your trip, immigration officers will stamp the allowed length of stay in your passport. Non-US citizens must also show a return ticket. Contact the Immigration Bureau at least one month in advance to extend your stay, ☎ (212) 206 6500.

Transportation to the city

Taxi

This is the easiest and quickest way to reach Manhattan. The fare is indicated on the meter, but you also have to pay tolls and tip (about 20%). You can save considerably by sharing a cab with others. From JFK, it should cost between $20-25, from LaGuardia, between $10-15 and from Newark Airport between $30-40.

JFK Express (train to the plane)

This is a combination bus/subway trip. Operated by the NYC Transit Authority, this express service links JFK to seven subway stations in Manhattan and Brooklyn. The one-way fare is approximately $7. The JFK Express train stops at the following stations: Jay St./Borough Hall (Brooklyn); Broadway/Nassau St.; Chambers St./Center St.; W. 4th St./Washington Sq.; 34th St.-Herald Sq./Sixth Ave.; 47th-50th St./Rockefeller Center; 57th St./Sixth Ave.

A bus takes passengers from the various JFK airline terminals to the subway. This service operates daily from 5am to midnight, with trains every 20 minutes. The trip takes approximately one hour.

Express bus to the airport

Carey Transportation Inc., ☎ (718) 632 0500. Carey provides bus service to all three airports. There are five offices and bus stops in Manhattan: 145 Park Ave. (opposite Grand Central Terminal, between 41st-42nd Sts.; Port Authority Bus Terminal (42nd St. and Eighth Ave.); New York Hilton (W. 53rd St. and Ave. of the Americas); Sheraton City Square (Seventh Ave. and 51st St.) and Marriott Marquis Hotel (Broadway and 45th St.).

The fare from JFK to New York City is $8; from LaGuardia, $6. The same service is available from Newark to the Port Authority Bus Terminal (42nd St. and Eighth Ave.) and to the World Trade Center. Information, ☎ (212) 564 8484.

Helicopter

There is regular helicopter shuttle service between Manhattan and the three airports, from two heliports in Manhattan: E. 34th St., ☎ (800) 645 3490 (toll-free number) and E. 60th St., ☎ (800) 221 1111 (toll-free number).

From JFK: **New York Helicopter,** ☎ (800) 645 3494 (toll-free number). The fare is approximately $58. There are frequent departures from the TWA terminal to E. 34th St. One-way trip takes about 20 minutes.

From LaGuardia: same company, same telephone number as from JFK. Departures from the Main Terminal to the E. 34th St. heliport. The trip takes about 10 minutes.

Limousine rental

Telephone numbers for limousine rental companies are indicated at all the airports. Various rental possibilities are available. Limousines can also be reserved directly through a travel agent.

International Limousine Service, Airline Ticket Office, 1 E. 59th St. at Fifth Ave., ☎ (212) 355 1992 offers a minibus for 10 people by reservation only, which provides transportation to all three airports *(open Mon-Fri 8am-7pm; Sat and Sun 8am-5pm).*

Sabra Limo Service, 171 E. 88th St., ☎ (212) 410 7600. Inexpensive rates.

Ship

It is still possible to travel to New York from Europe by ship. The only transatlantic ship still in operation is the **Queen Elizabeth II,** operated by the **Cunard Steamship Company.** It makes a five-day crossing between Southampton and New York, from May through December. Crossing the Atlantic by ship is expensive. There are special fares that combine a ship crossing with return by airplane or vice versa, and youth fares (12 to 26 years old) are also available when the ship is not completely booked.

If you are lucky enough to arrive in New York by ship, you will disembark directly in Manhattan at the **Passenger Ship Terminal** on the Hudson River, between 48th-52nd Sts. For full information, contact **Cunard Steamship Company Ltd,** Southwestern House, Canute Rd, Southampton SO9 1ZA, ☎ (703) 22 9933.

Train

New York's two main railroad stations are in Manhattan: **Grand Central Terminal,** Park Ave. at 42nd St. (a National Landmark building, see p. 102), and **Pennsylvania Station,** between 31st-33rd St. and Seventh-Eighth Ave. Depending on your point of departure, trains arrive at either one or other of these stations but never stop at both.

Bus

New York's main bus terminal is the **Port Authority Bus Terminal,** on Eighth Ave. between 40th-42nd St. It is used by commuter and long-distance services. Lately expanded and renovated, it is the nation's largest and most modern bus terminal (see p. 100).

Car

Tunnels, bridges and highways lead to New York. From the north-west, the New York Thruway (routes 287 and 87) leads to Manhattan's East and West Sides and the New England Thruway (I-95) leads via connecting roads to all the boroughs. From the west, the Bergen Passaic Expressway (I-80) leads into Manhattan via the George Washington Bridge. From the south, the New Jersey Turnpike (I-95) leads into the Holland Tunnel for lower Manhattan or Brooklyn and to the George Washington Bridge for upper Manhattan or the Bronx.

▰▰ ENTRY FORMALITIES

Passport and visa

Entry formalities to the United States are subject to change. Current information can be obtained from tourism offices or embassies. A valid passport and visa are required for non-American travelers except for Canadians, who need only proof of residence, and British and Japanese citizens, who need only a passport. It usually takes two days to obtain a visa if requested in person, or three weeks to one month by mail. There is a fee for the visa. The authorized length of stay is determined by the immigration services on entry into the United States. Tourist visas are generally limited to three months.

Health precautions

No particular vaccinations or precautions are required unless you are coming from a region that has recently experienced an outbreak of a particular disease.

Insurance

Insurance is optional in the United States. However, as medical expenses are extremely high and must be paid immediately, individual insurance is highly recommended.

For a modest fee, certain airline companies offer baggage insurance, trip cancellation insurance, liability, payment of expenses in case of illness (medical care, surgery, hospitalization), accident, repatriation or death. Ask your insurance broker for information also.

Driver's license

If you would like to rent a car in the United States, you will need a valid driver's license and a major credit card. The minimum age requirement varies from state to state — it's usually 18 but in some cases may be 25.

Customs

The following items can be brought into the United States for a maximum of one year with no additional duty: clothing, toilet articles, jewelry, film or photographic equipment, binoculars, portable typewriters, portable videotape machines, televisions, radios, sports equipment and automobiles. Furthermore, adults are allowed 1/4 gal/0.946 l of alcohol, 200 cigarettes or 6 cigars or 3 lbs/1.360 kg of tobacco. Each person is allowed to bring in gifts up to a maximum value of $100 provided the stay exceeds 72 hours and this same exemption has not been used in the previous six months. The exemption cannot be accumulated among family members.

If you need to travel with medication or prescription drugs, take only enough for normal use. Make sure it is properly identified. You must also have a prescription or written declaration from your personal physician certifying that the medication is essential for your health.

A declaration must be made with the US Customs on arrival or departure for transfers of funds above $10,000. A form is supplied for this purpose.

Importing animals (cats, dogs, fish, birds), certain food products (meat and processed meat products) and some plants (cut flowers, fruit and vegetables) is subject to special, sometimes complex regulations (information available from Customs Services).

For all customs problems, check with a US embassy or *Public Information Division*, US Customs Service, Department of the Treasury, Washington, D.C. 20229.

▰▰ MONEY

The monetary unit is the US dollar ($). It is divided into 100 cents (¢). Penny = 1¢   Quarter = 25¢

Nickel = 5¢ Half dollar = 50¢
Dime = 10¢ Bills: denominations of 1, 2, 5, 10, 20, 50 and 100 dollars.

Take travelers' checks in dollars. It is easy to get reimbursed in case of loss or theft. They can be used as payment with proper identification in most stores and restaurants and can be easily cashed when presented with a passport for identification.

Credit cards

Few New York bank machines accept international bank cards. The most commonly accepted credit cards in the United States are American Express, Visa and MasterCard.

Budget

In New York, as in most places, prices go up every year. It is, however, possible to live reasonably on $50-60 per day, provided you stay in medium-category hotels and do not include the cost of travel ($15-20 for meals, $30-40 per person for shared accommodation, $5-10 for museums and getting around).

WHAT TO TAKE

Warm clothing and waterproof footwear are essential if you travel in winter. Take a raincoat (preferably with a removable lining) for April, May and November. Lightweight clothes are recommended during the summer because of the high humidity. In addition, foreign visitors need to bring an adaptor for a flat plug and to set any appliances to the correct voltage (110 and 115 V/60 Hz).

BEFORE YOU LEAVE: SOME USEFUL ADDRESSES

Australia

Embassy
Canberra, Moonan Pl., ACT 2600, ☎ (062) 70 5000.

Consulates
Melbourne, 24 Albert Rd., 3205, ☎ (613) 697 7900.
Sydney, TG Tower, Hyde Park Sq., NSW 2000, ☎ (02) 264 7044.

Canada

Embassy
Ottawa, 100 Wellington St., ONT K1P 5T1, ☎ (613) 238 5335.

Consulate
Montreal, Suite 1122, Quebec South Tower, Placedesjardins, PO Box 65, H5B 1G1, ☎ (514) 281 1886.

Great Britain

Embassy
London, 24 Grosvenor Sq., W1A 1AE, ☎ (01) 499 9000.

Consulates
Edinburgh, 3 Regent Terr., HE7 5BW, ☎ (031) 556 8315.
Belfast, Queen House, Queen St., BT1 6EQ, ☎ (0232) 228 8239.

Ireland

Embassy
Dublin, 42 Elgin Rd., Ballsbridge, ☎ (01) 68 8777.

PRACTICAL INFORMATION

▬ ACCOMMODATION

Accommodation in New York is expensive and often takes most of a traveler's budget.

Hotels

Most hotels are located in the Midtown and Uptown areas, while the Downtown area has only a few. Recommended hotels are listed by neighbourhood in 'New York Addresses' at the end of the book, p. 189.

It may be difficult to find a room in New York and it is important to reserve in advance. Many hotels offer up to 50% off on weekends.

Add 8.25% to the total to obtain the amount of your bill. Note: Telephone service in hotels may be very expensive.

Gratuities are not included for any services. For information, see 'Tipping' p. 51.

Bed and Breakfast

There are several organizations offering bed and breakfast accommodation in New York (listed below). Write to obtain a detailed brochure of their facilities and conditions. Reserve well in advance.

Prices range from $35-75 per person, $100 and up for four people. Credit cards are usually accepted.

Bed & Breakfast Group (New Yorkers at Home), 301 E. 60th St., 10022, ☎ (212) 838 7015. This group has approximately 200 apartments in Manhattan and offers a personal way to meet New Yorkers. Reservations must be made well in advance *(open Mon-Fri 9am-4pm)*.

City Light Bed & Breakfast, Ltd, PO Box 20-355, Cherokee Station, 10024, ☎ (212) 737 7049.

New World Bed & Breakfast, 150 Fifth Ave., suite 711, 10011, ☎ (212) 675 5600. Formed in 1983, this service offers close to 100 apartments in New York; it is constantly increasing its selection of apartments.

Urban Ventures, PO Box 426, 10024, ☎ (212) 594 5650. Formed in 1979, it has approximately 600 apartments available *(open Mon-Sat 9am-5pm)*.

YMCA or YWCA (Young Men's or Women's Christian Association)

This is an organization that provides simple, reasonably priced accommodation.

YMCA McBurney, 215 W. 23rd St., between Seventh-Eighth Aves., ☎ (212) 741 9210. 279 rooms, men only.

One of New York's many yellow cabs, a good way to get around the city.

YMCA Sloane House, 356 W. 34th St. between Eighth-Ninth Aves., ☎ (212) 750 5850. 1492 rooms, men only.

YMCA Vanderbilt, 224 E. 47th St. between Second-Third Aves.,☎ (212) 755 2410. 439 rooms, for men and women.

YMCA West Side, 5 W. 63rd St. between Broadway-Central Park West, ☎ (212) 787 4400. 700 rooms, for men and women.

Student housing

International House, 500 Riverside Dr. at 123rd St., ☎ (212) 678 5000. For students, researchers and professors, minimum age: 19. This is a dormitory with two beds per room, which can be rented by the day ($20 for the first night, $13 for additional nights), week or month *(open late May-Aug).*

International Student Center, 38 W. 88th St., ☎ (212) 787 7706; 210 W. 55th St., ☎ (212) 757 8030. Accommodation for foreign students. The West 88th Street address offers the additional benefit of proximity to Central Park and the Museum of Natural History. Price per day is $6, maximum stay five days.

Apartment rentals

If you plan a long stay in New York and would like the comfort of an apartment (shared or not), a good way to find less expensive accommodation is to place an advertisement in *The Village Voice.* Replies are usually serious and prompt.

▬▬ AIRLINES

Air Canada, 488 Madison Ave. at 51st St., IV, C3 , ☎ (212) 869 1900.

Air France, 666 Fifth Ave. at 52nd St., IV, C3 , ☎ (212) 315 1122.

American Airlines, Manhattan Air Terminal, 100 E. 42nd St., IV, C3 , ☎ (212) 619 6991. Same telephone number for branch offices: 120 Broadway; 875 Third Ave.

Delta, Manhattan Air Terminal, 100 E. 42nd St., IV, C3 , ☎ (212) 239 0700. Same telephone number for branch office: 1 E. 59th St. at Fifth Ave.

Eastern Airlines, Manhattan Air Terminal, 100 E. 42nd St., IV, C3 , ☎ (212) 986 5000. Shuttle service to Boston and Washington from LaGuardia Airport.

New York Air, Manhattan Air Terminal, 100 E. 42nd St., IV, C3 , ☎ (212) 839 9533.

Pan Am, Manhattan Air Terminal, 100 E. 42nd St., IV, C3 , ☎ (212) 687 2600. Same telephone number for branch offices: 600 Fifth Ave. at 18th St.; 1 World Trade Center; 1 E. 59th St. at Fifth Ave.; 166 W. 32nd St. Shuttle service to Boston and Washington from LaGuardia Airport.

Sabena, 720 Fifth Ave. at 56th St., IV, C2 , ☎ (212) 247 8880.

Swissair, 608 Fifth Ave. at 49th St., IV, C3 , ☎ (212) 484 0750 or (718) 995 8000.

TWA, Manhattan Air Terminal, 100 E. 42nd St., IV, C3 , ☎ (212) 290 2121 (for domestic flights), ☎ (212) 290 2141 (for international flights).

▬▬ BUSINESS HOURS

Banks

Banks are generally open Monday-Friday, 9am-3pm, sometimes until 4pm. Some branches remain open late on Thursday nights or open on Saturday mornings (usually savings banks only).

Offices

Most offices open at 9am and close at 5pm.

Traffic

On weekdays, rush hour lasts several hours, from approximately 7:30-9:30am and from 5-7pm. Traffic is often heavy at other times of day as well, especially during the winter holiday season, end of November through December.

Stores and shops

Department stores and clothing shops are generally open from 9am-6pm; Thursday nights until 8 or 9pm. In some of the more trendy areas, such as Greenwich Village, the East Village and SoHo, the shops and galleries may not open before noon.

Many of the shops selling electronic and photographic equipment are closed on Saturday but open on Sunday.

Restaurants

Fashionable restaurants are generally open from noon-2:30pm and from 6-11pm. Most other restaurants stay open all day and well into the evening. Many coffee shops, snack bars and delis stay open all night (see p. 203).

▬▬▬ *CHILDREN*

Various activities

Young Visitors, 175 W. 88th St., V, A3, ☎ (212) 595 8100. Excursions designed for children of all ages.

AT&T Info Quest Center, 550 Madison Ave. at 56th St., IV, C2, ☎ (212) 605 5555. Located in the AT&T building, this center offers hands-on exhibits and displays about communications, robots and computers *(open Wed-Sun 10am-6pm, Tues 10am-9pm; no admission charge)*.

Empire State Building and the Guinness World Record Exhibit Hall, Fifth Ave. at 34th St., III, C1, ☎ (212) 947 2335 *(open daily 9:30am-8pm; children under five admitted free)*.

For information about other activities for children, see 'Parks' p. 43.

Babysitters

Babysitters' Association, ☎ (212) 865 9348.

Babysitters' Guild, 60 E. 42nd St., IV, C3, ☎ (212) 682 0227. Somewhat expensive rates, four-hour minimum, arrangements available for tourists *(open daily 9am-9pm)*.

CASH, Student Employment Office, 21 Washington Pl. III, C3, ☎ (212) 598 2971. This office is part of New York University *(open Mon-Fri 9am-5pm)*.

Children's museums

American Museum of Immigration, Liberty Island, ☎ (212) 422 2150. Take the Battery Park Ferry to the Statue of Liberty. The museum includes recordings and photographs.

American Museum of the Moving Image, Zukor Theater, 31-34 35th St., Astoria, Queens, ☎ (718) 784 4742. This was the site of the first film studios on the East Coast between 1919 and 1942. Rudolph Valentino and Paula Negri worked here.

Brooklyn Children's Museum, 145 Brooklyn Museum, on Eastern Parkway and Atlantic Ave., ☎ (718) 735 4432. The museum was opened in 1899. This pioneering establishment has acquired new collections in such fields as science, technology, history and natural sciences. It includes more than 40,000 items *(open Mon, Wed and Fri 1-5pm, Thurs 1-8pm, Sat and Sun 10am-5pm)*.

Children's Museum of Manhattan, 34 W. 54th St. at Eighth Ave., IV, B2

☎ (212) 765 5904. This museum includes demonstrations in fields like history and natural sciences and encourages participation by children *(open Tues-Fri 11am-5pm, Sat noon-5pm)*.

Intrepid Air-Sea-Space Museum, Pier 86, W. 46th St., IV, A3, ☎ (212) 245 2533. This famous war ship has been transformed into a giant museum. It includes displays about the pioneers of aviation, the Apollo capsules and films on World War II *(open Wed-Sat 10am-4pm, group rates are available with a reservation)*.

Richmondtown Restoration, a New York City original, Staten Island, ☎ (718) 351 1617. From Manhattan, take the Staten Island Ferry at Battery Park, then bus n° 113 to Richmond Road and Court Place. Walk to the Courthouse Visitors' Center. This is a restored colonial village, where craftsmen work with tools using methods from the colonial period; it is a good place for a family picnic.

Staten Island Children's Museum, 1000 Richmond Terr., Snug Harbor, Staten Island, ☎ (718) 273 2060. From Manhattan, take the Staten Island Ferry at Battery Park, then bus n° 40 from Richmond Terrace to the museum. This community-oriented museum offers displays on the arts and sciences that give children a chance to participate *(open Wed-Fri 2-5pm, Sat, Sun and public holidays 11am-5pm)*.

Christmas

An immense pine tree sparkles at Rockefeller Center by the skating rink and the large department stores compete ferociously for the best window displays. Windows may feature animated scenes of old New York or fairy tales come to life. It is difficult to choose the most beautiful. Most of the major department stores are on Fifth Avenue and the windows can be easily visited in an afternoon. In the toy department of Macy's (Ave. of the Americas at 34th St., III, B1), Santa Claus himself can be visited.

Department store addresses:

B. Altman, Fifth Ave. at 34th St., III, C1 — **Lord & Taylor,** Fifth Ave. at 39th St., III, C1 — **Saks Fifth Avenue,** Fifth Ave. at 50th ST., IV, C3 — **F.A.O. Schwarz,** GM Building, Fifth Ave. at 59th St., IV, C2.

Theater

Hartly House Theater, 413 W. 46th St. at Ninth Ave., IV, B3, ☎ (212) 246 9885 *(open Sat and Sun)*.

Little People's Company, Courtyard Playhouse, 39 Grove St. at Seventh Ave., III, B3, ☎ (212) 765 9540. Children (3-8) participate in the show *(open Oct-June, Sat and Sun 1:30 and 3pm)*.

Penny Jones & Company Puppets, Greenwich Music School, 45 Barrow St., III, B3, ☎ (212) 924 4589. For children 3-8 years old *(open Sun 1 and 5pm)*.

See also 'Festivals' p. 37.

▬▬ CONSULATES

Australia, 636 Fifth Ave. at 51st St., IV, C3, ☎ (212) 245 4000.
Canada, 1251 Ave. of the Americas at 50th St., IV, B3, ☎ (212) 586 2400.
Great Britain, 845 Third Ave. at 50th St., IV, C3, ☎ (212) 752 8400.
Ireland, 515 Madison Ave. at 53rd St., 18th floor, IV, C2, ☎ (212) 319 2550.
New Zealand, 630 Fifth Ave. at 50th St., IV, C3, ☎ (212) 698 4650.

▬▬ CURRENCY EXCHANGE

You can change foreign currency into dollars at the three airports. Other useful addresses:

American Express is the largest American company for travelers' checks. It has many locations, including: 125 Broad St., II, B3, ☎ (212) 797 3900; 65 Broadway, II, B3, ☎ (212) 493 6500; 150 E. 42nd St., IV, C3, ☎ (212) 687 3700; 374 Park Ave., IV, B3, ☎ (212) 421 8240; 199 Water St., II, B3, ☎ (212) 943 6947.

Barclays Bank of New York, 300 Park Ave. at 49th St., IV, B3, ☎ (212) 418 4600; 9 W. 57th St., at Fifth Ave., IV, C2, ☎ (212) 644 0850. This British bank also changes money.

Citibank, 1 E. 59th St. at Fifth Ave., IV, C2, ☎ (212) 371 7958 *(open Mon-Fri 9am-4:30pm).*

Deak-International, at JFK Airport, ☎ (718) 656 8444 *(open Sat and Sun 8am-9pm).* Other addresses: 630 Fifth Ave. at 50th St., IV, C3, ☎ (212) 757 6915 *(open Mon-Fri 9am-5pm);* 41 E. 42nd St. at Madison Ave., IV, C3, ☎ (212) 883 0400 *(open Mon-Sat 10am-3pm).*

Reuters exchange offices, Pan Am Bldg., 200 Park Ave. at 45th St., IV, C3, 3rd floor, suite 332, ☎ (212) 661 0826. This is one of the best places to change money in New York *(open daily 8:30am-4pm).*

EMERGENCIES

Hospitals

There are many hospitals in New York. Most cost approximately $300 per night. Some of the best private hospitals in Manhattan are:

Beekman Downtown, 170 William St., II, B2, ☎ (212) 312 5300.

Beth Israel, Stuyvesant Sq. and 17th St., III, C2, ☎ (212) 420 2000.

Lenox Hill Hospital, Park Ave. and 77th St., IV, C1, ☎ (212) 794 4567.

Manhattan Eye and Ear, 210 E. 64th St., IV, C2, ☎ (212) 838 9200.

Mount Sinai, Fifth Ave. and 100th St., V, C2, ☎ (212) 650 6500.

New York Hospital-Cornell, 525 E. ·68th St. at York Ave., IV, D1, ☎ (212) 472 5454.

New York University Medical Center, 550 First Ave. at 28th St., III, D1, ☎ (212) 340 7300.

St Vincent's Hospital, Seventh Ave. at 11th St., III, B3, ☎ (212) 790 7000.

Other emergency telephone numbers

Ambulance, police, fire: 911

Assault: (212) 577 7777

Dentist: (212) 679 3966

Doctor: (212) 879 1000

Ophthalmologist: (212) 690 1875

League Against Rape: (212) 777 4000

Anti-poison center: (212) 340 4494 or 764 7667

Suicide prevention: (212) 532 2400

Loss or theft of credit cards or American Express travelers' checks: (800) 221 7282 (toll-free number).

Medication

Drugstores sell medicine, perfume, cosmetics and toilet accessories. All-night pharmacy: **Kaufman,** 557 Lexington Ave. at 50th St., IV, C3, ☎ (212) 755 2266.

ENTERTAINMENT

New York is one of the most important cultural centers in the world. Its theater, music and dance performances are among the best and it's worth seeing one of the many shows while you're in New York. *The New*

York Times, The New Yorker, New York magazine and *The Village Voice* regularly list programs and curtain times.

Theater

New York is the theater capital of America, with performances ranging from popular musical comedies to the latest avant-garde productions. The city is overflowing with successful and would-be actors and actresses.

With more than 40 theaters, Broadway offers an excellent selection of shows: musical comedies, American traditional and contemporary works and productions imported from abroad. Some of the best-known American actors and actresses first became famous in the theaters around Times Square.

Tickets for a show cost approximately $40. Same-day tickets are, however, available at half price from one of the TKTS outlets: on the mezzanine at 2 World Trade Center *(open Mon-Fri 11:30am-5:30pm, Sat 11am-3pm for evening shows only)* and at Duffy Square, Broadway and 47th St. *(open Mon-Fri 3-8pm for evening shows, Wed and Sat noon-2pm for matinees, Sun noon-8pm for matinees and evening shows)*, ☎ (212) 354 5800.

Off-Broadway refers to some 15 medium-sized theaters (100-400 seats), generally located in Greenwich Village, the East Village or on the Upper West Side. Tickets cost approximately $15. The quality of the repertory varies considerably from one theater to another; Robert DeNiro or Al Pacino may be acting in one theater, while a work-in-progress with aspiring actors is performed in another.

Off-Off Broadway refers to more than 250 theaters which offer an infinite variety of plays ranging from a classical international repertory to the most avant-garde performances. These theaters usually seat up to 100 people. Financial resources are limited, but the performances are often highly inventive and spirited.

Films

There are some very good cinemas in New York which show the best of Hollywood or experimental and art films. The Museum of Modern Art film library has regular film showings. The New York Film Festival, which screens the latest films, takes place in September and October at Lincoln Center.

Modern dance and ballet

New York has been a major center for modern dance since Martha Graham presented her work at the 92nd Street YMHA in the 1930s. The city is the undisputed international dance capital, with more than 10 modern dance and ballet companies. The most famous choreographers of the 20th century have worked here, including Alvin Ailey, Trisha Brown, Merce Cunningham, Murray Louis, Alwyn Nikolaïs and Paul Taylor. It is also possible to see some of the best visiting foreign dance companies as they almost always perform in New York during US tours.

New York is also home to two prestigious dance companies, the New York City Ballet, directed for years by the late George Balanchine, and the more classical American Ballet Theater.

Tickets are available at the theaters. Half-price tickets for same-day performances are available at the SEATS outlet in Bryant Park, 42nd St. and Ave. of the Americas, ☎ (212) 382 2323 *(open noon-7pm)*.

Classical music and opera

There are over 100 classical music concerts and recitals performed every week in New York, from October to April. The vast selection ranges from the New York Philharmonic orchestra, directed by Zubin Mehta, or the Brooklyn Philharmonic, directed by Lukas Foss, to the many concerts presented by the major orchestras, singers, ensembles or other performers visiting the city.

New York in the movies

Film-lovers have a special interest in New York. They can trace the production of their favourite movies by visiting the spots where famous scenes were shot on location. Don't forget to visit **The American Museum of the Moving Image,** 34-31 35th St., Astoria, Queens, and **The Museum of Broadcasting,** 1 E. 53rd St. (see p. 114).

On the Waterfront (Elia Kazan, 1954)
Marlon Brando and Lee J. Cobb come to blows near the old wharf of the Holland-America Line Shipping Company in Hoboken, New Jersey, right across the Hudson River from Manhattan.

The Seven-Year Itch (Billy Wilder, 1955)
The famous scene in which Marilyn Monroe's dress billows up over a subway grating was filmed at 590 Lexington Ave. (near 51st St.).

Breakfast at Tiffany's (Blake Edwards, 1961)
Audrey Hepburn has breakfast at dawn in front of the windows of the famous Tiffany jewelers (57th St. and Fifth Ave.).

West Side Story (Robert Wise, 1961)
Many scenes were filmed in the former immigrant neighbourhoods around 67th St. and 68th St. between Amsterdam Ave. and West End Ave. These neighbourhoods were razed during the construction of Lincoln Center.

Rosemary's Baby (Roman Polanski, 1968)
Mia Farrow moves into the formidable neo-Gothic apartment building, The Dakota, located at 1 W. 72nd St. and Central Park West (this building was also the scene of the tragic assassination of John Lennon in 1980; see p. 128).

Midnight Cowboy (John Schlesinger, 1969)
The scene in which Jon Voigt and Dustin Hoffman stop traffic was filmed on the corner of 58th St. and Ave. of the Americas.

The Godfather (Francis Ford Coppola, 1971, 1975)
Many scenes were filmed on the Lower East Side, on 6th St. between Ave. A and Ave. B.

Kramer vs. Kramer (R. Benton, 1979)
Dustin Hoffman's son attends PS (public school) 6 (Madison Ave. and 82nd St.).

Manhattan (Woody Allen, 1979)
Woody Allen and Diane Keaton sit on a bench in Sutton Square (Sutton Pl. and E. 58th St.). The bridge in the background is the Queensboro Bridge, which crosses the East River.

Desperately Seeking Susan (Susan Seidelman, 1985)
In the film, the discotheque (W. 21st St.) was Danceteria. It has since closed. The comedy of errors and waterfront scenes were filmed in Battery Park (Financial District). The clothes store where Madonna and Rosanna Arquette shop is called Love Saves the Day (119 Second Ave.).

After Hours (Martin Scorsese, 1986)
The all-night coffee shop where the hero takes refuge to escape his pursuers is called the Moondance Diner (Grand St. and Ave. of the Americas). It was filmed in SoHo.

Opera is very important in New York and major directors and singers are always welcomed enthusiastically at Lincoln Center. Two major companies perform for the admiring New York public, the famous Metropolitan Opera and the New York City Opera, with its more popular American repertory. Tickets are available at the theaters. Half-price tickets for same-day performances are available at SEATS at Bryant Park (see above).

FESTIVALS

January

Chinese New Year's Festival, first new moon after Jan 19, pageant and fireworks in Chinatown, II, C2.

Antique Show, end of Jan at the Armory (Park Ave. at 67th St., IV, C1).

February

National Antiques Show, Madison Square Garden (Eighth Ave. at 32nd St., III, B1) for serious antique collectors.

March

St Patrick's Day Parade, Mar 17, on Fifth Ave. More than 30 million Americans are of Irish ancestry, making this one of the most popular ethnic festivals in New York.

Ringling Bros. and Barnum & Bailey Circus Parade, late Mar, in Madison Square Garden (Eighth Ave. at 32nd St., III, B1).

April

Baseball season opens.

Easter Parade, Fifth Ave. between 48th-59th Sts., IV, C3. This parade starts near St Patrick's Cathedral around noon.

May

Ninth Avenue International Festival, street festival at Paddy's Market, between 37th-59th Sts., IV, B3. Music, food and street performers.

Martin Luther King Day Parade, May 18, Fifth Ave.

Washington Square Outdoor Art Show, late May-early June and late Aug-early Sept. Open-air art exhibition in and around Washington Sq. in Greenwich Village, III, B3.

June

Museum Mile, early June. Museums located between 82nd-106th Sts. on Fifth Ave. remain open free one night a week, 6-9pm.

Shakespeare in the Park, performances of the Shakespearean repertory in the Delacorte Theater in Central Park, V, B2.

Metropolitan Opera, free concerts, theater, dance, rock, jazz throughout the summer.

Summer Festival, concerts at the Guggenheim Museum, the Museum of Modern Art, Rockefeller Center and South Street Seaport throughout the summer.

Puerto Rican Day Parade, first Sun in June, on Fifth Ave. between 44th-86th Sts.

Feast of Saint Anthony, early June, in the Italian neighbourhood of Greenwich Village, between Houston-Spring Sts., from MacDougal-Thompson Sts., II, B1.

Lower East Side Jewish Festival, mid-June, on East Broadway, II, B3.

July

Independence Day, July 4th, fireworks presented (on southern tip of Manhattan) by Macy's department store. Regattas and music at South Street Seaport, II, C3.

Mostly Mozart Festival, mid-July-late Aug at Lincoln Center, IV, B2, open-air concerts.

Washington Square Music Festival in Greenwich Village, III, C3.

August

US Open Tennis Championships, Flushing Meadows, Queens.

Uncle Sam during one of New York's parades.

September

Book Fair, Sun in mid-Sept, on Fifth Ave. between 42nd-57th Sts., IV, C2-3.

Feast of San Gennaro, mid-Sept, the Little Italy Festival on Mulberry St., II, C1.

New York Film Festival, late Sept-mid-Oct, Alice Tully Hall at Lincoln Center, IV, B2.

October

Pulaski Day Parade, early in the month, on Fifth Ave.

Columbus Day Parade, around Oct 12 on Fifth Ave. This parade celebrates the discovery of America.

New York Marathon, on a Sun in late Oct/early Nov. This 26.2 mi/40 km race draws more than 20,000 participants who run from the Verrazano-Narrows Bridge (Staten Island) to Central Park (67th St.).

Halloween Parade, Oct 31 in the evening in Greenwich Village, Ave. of the Americas. Outlandish costumes and festivities throughout the Downtown area.

Opening night of the New York Philharmonic, at Lincoln Center, IV, B2.

November

National Horse Show, early in the month, Madison Square Garden (Eighth Ave. at 32nd St., III, B1).

Thanksgiving Day Parade, fourth Thurs in the month, sponsored by Macy's department store (Ave. of the Americas at 34th St., III, B1). Giant helium-filled Walt Disney and cartoon characters parade from Columbus Circle down Broadway to Macy's in Herald Sq.

Christmas decorations start to appear near the end of the month in the major department store windows, particularly along Fifth Ave. from 34th-59th Sts. Lord & Taylor on Fifth Ave. and 38th St., III, C1, has one of the most spectacular displays.

December

Giant Christmas tree at Rockefeller Center, IV, C3, throughout the month.

New Year's Eve, Dec 31 in Times Square, IV, B3. Tens of thousands come to celebrate the New Year in New York.

▬ FOOD AND DRINK

With more than 25,000 restaurants, New York City offers an immense variety of food. Recommended restaurants are listed by neighbourhood in 'New York Addresses' at the end of the book. Price range and type of cuisine are included (p. 189).

Americans' main meal is dinner, which is eaten usually around 7pm. Breakfast is an important meal, while lunches are often eaten on the run between engagements or at a desk. Many restaurants serve a Sunday brunch, an American tradition combining the best of breakfast and lunch.

Take-out meals are very popular and many restaurants, even certain expensive ones, allow you to purchase a meal to take home. Some establishments specialize in this type of service and don't provide any customer seating at all. Delivery service is also widespread and generally available for a small fee. Restaurant portions are often surprisingly large. Order your meals accordingly, but if you can't finish it all, ask a waiter for a doggy bag to take the remainder home.

You can eat at any time of the day or night in New York. Some restaurants stop serving for a short time between lunch and dinner and then serve late into the night. There are coffee shops or snack bars throughout the city, which serve quick meals — sandwiches or simple dishes. They are usually very busy during breakfast and lunch. The delicatessens (or delis) serve a variety of meat sandwiches and dishes that are often based on Eastern or Central European cuisine. You can either sit at a table or buy food to take out.

There are also many fine restaurants in New York. You will find that the only difficulty is deciding which type of food to eat and how much to spend. Restaurants range from the traditional steak house to gourmet establishments. You can find restaurants serving cuisines from around the world. There are a host of great chefs in New York and the competition has become increasingly fierce. In the last few years, a return to traditional American cooking has come into vogue.

Americans like drinks with lots of ice. A glass of ice water is often served as soon as you sit down in a restaurant. There is a vast selection of soft drinks, mineral waters and juices, including some which are sugar-, caffeine- or sodium-free. Iced tea or coffee is a refreshing drink on a hot summer afternoon and children and adults alike love the ice cream sodas and milkshakes.

The weak coffee in America is nothing like the expresso available in Europe but more and more restaurants have expresso machines. The 'bottomless cup' of coffee offered in many coffee shops means that additional cups of coffee are free.

American beer is surprisingly light and it is easy to develop a taste for it. American bourbon, usually from Kentucky, gin and vodka are used in many imaginative cocktails or mixed drinks. This is a domain worth exploring; try cocktail lounges, bars and taverns. It has become increasingly fashionable to drink wine in New York and, as befits a cosmopolitan city, you will be able to find any wine in the world here. Wine bars are appearing all over as well.

GETTING AROUND NEW YORK

The best way to discover the city is on foot. New York is a great place for pedestrians and the layout of the city is easy to understand. New York is divided into five boroughs: the Bronx, Brooklyn, Manhattan, Queens and Staten Island.

Manhattan Island is the heart of New York. For ease of reference, we have divided it into three main sections: Downtown, Midtown and Uptown.

Downtown is the oldest part of the city. City Hall, Wall Street and the Financial District are located here. It extends from Battery Park on the southern tip of Manhattan up to about 14th Street to the north and includes the trendy neighbourhoods of SoHo, Tribeca, Greenwich Village and the East Village, as well as Chinatown and Little Italy.

Midtown extends from around 14th Street northward to the upper 50s. It includes the neighbourhoods of Chelsea, Gramercy Park, Times Square and Rockefeller Center, among others. The two train stations, Pennsylvania Station on the west side and Grand Central Terminal on the east, are in this part of the city, as is the Port Authority bus terminal.

Uptown refers to the section of Manhattan north of around 59th Street. Central Park is the heart of this area. It is further divided into the Upper East Side, the elegant residential area of New York, and the Upper West Side, an architecturally fine residential area that includes Lincoln Center. Harlem, El Barrio and Morningside Heights (Columbia University) are located north of 110th Street.

In conversation, New Yorkers use downtown to indicate anywhere to the south and uptown anywhere to the north. In other words, when you go from Battery Park to Washington Square, you are going uptown. Going crosstown, on the other hand, means that you are going east or west.

In 1807, a zoning plan was drawn up for Manhattan, dividing the city into an organized grid of streets and avenues. This grid system starts at 14th Street and proceeds north. Below 14th Street, the layout is more complicated. Twelve avenues cross Manhattan lengthwise north to south. They are numbered from the East River to the Hudson River; 1st Avenue is therefore near the East River and 12th Avenue runs along the Hudson. Some of these avenues have names rather than numbers: Lexington Avenue, Park Avenue, Madison Avenue, Avenue of the Americas (which is also referred to colloquially as Sixth Avenue), Central Park West, Columbus Avenue, Amsterdam Avenue and West End Avenue. Broadway runs diagonally across Manhattan from the southeast to the northwest.

Traffic is generally one-way on these avenues except for Park Avenue, which is two-way.

Streets run east to west. Fifth Avenue is the dividing line between the East Side and the West Side. For example, 50 W. 14th Street is on 14th Street west of Fifth Avenue. Traffic runs west to east on even-numbered streets and east to west on odd-numbered streets.

The major crosstown streets (two-way traffic) are 14th St., 23rd St., 34th St., 42nd St., 57th St., 72nd St., 79th St., 86th St., 96th St., 110th St. and 125th St. City blocks are longest crosstown (from avenue to avenue). Blocks are the standard distance measurement and are often given in directions, for example '10 blocks north'.

▬ MEDIA

Newspapers

The New York Times is a New York institution that provides domestic and international news. Don't miss the Sunday edition which is divided into many sections — art and entertainment, business, real estate, travel, sports, book reviews, colour magazine, classified — as well as the front sections covering national and international news. It weighs several pounds.

The Wall Street Journal is another serious source of information, which is oriented towards business and financial news.

The morning *Daily News* and the evening *New York Post* are lively tabloids, featuring local news, gossip, scandals and photographs.

Weekly publications

The New Yorker has long been famous as the magazine of the New York intellectual left. It publishes short stories, poems, essays and articles by well-known writers. It also offers a good listing of cultural events.

New York magazine is interesting for its articles on New York themes and its entertainment listings which include restaurants, plays, films (without show times), concerts, museum exhibitions, gallery shows and excursions. The 'Sales & Bargains' section provides some tips on current sales.

The Village Voice is a non-conformist and contemporary newspaper. It includes listings for off-Broadway theater and avant-garde cultural events, as well as useful and amusing classified advertisements.

Foreign publications can be purchased at many, though not all, newstands throughout Manhattan.

Television

New York City has seven television stations, of which the three major networks are ABC, CBS and NBC (channels 7, 2 and 4). PBS (Public Broadcasting System) is a subsidized cultural station (channel 13), which shows excellent documentaries and theatrical presentations, often picked up from the BBC.

Cable network stations are often available in hotels for a fee. These offer a broad range of entertainment: great movies, fundamentalist religious programs, offbeat psychiatric advice, pornography, programs serving ethnic communities, intimate television confessions and telephone numbers of call girls.

MTV and channel 68 offer non-stop music programs with video clips.

The Sunday New York Times, *several pounds of newsprint and a wealth of information.*

Radio

The New York area has more than 50 radio stations, including: WNEW (102.7 FM, rock) — WLIR (92.7 FM, rock) — WCBS (100.1 FM, nostalgia) — WNCN (104 FM, classical) — WHN (105 AM, country and western) — WNYC (93.9 FM, classical) — WBGO (88 FM, jazz). Several stations broadcast only news 24 hours a day, including WINS (1010 AM).

▬ *ORGANIZING YOUR TIME*

We have included two itineraries — a weekend and a five-day tour — which cover the essential sights.

New York in one weekend

First day

Morning: Bus tour of Manhattan. **Crossroads Sightseeing**, 701 Seventh Ave. at 53rd St., IV, B2, ☎ (212) 581 2882; **Gray Line**, 900 Eighth Ave. at 54th St., IV, B2, ☎ (212) 397 2600; **New York Big Apple Tours**, 162 W. 56th St., IV, B2, ☎ (212) 582 6339.

Afternoon: Battery Park, ferry for the Statue of Liberty (see pp. 75, 171).

Evening: Dinner and evening out Downtown (see pp. 84, 89).

Second day

Morning: Empire State Building, Rockefeller Center and along Fifth Avenue (see pp. 106, 116).

Afternoon: Central Park, Metropolitan Museum (see pp. 112, 147).

Evening: Lincoln Center or Theater District for a concert, a ballet, an opera or a show.

New York in five days

First day

Morning: Financial District, World Trade Center, ferry for the Statue of Liberty (see pp. 73, 171).

Afternoon: South Street Seaport, City Hall, Chinatown, Little Italy (see pp. 73, 83).

Evening: Dinner in SoHo or Greenwich Village (see pp. 84, 89).

Second day

Morning: Circle Line cruise (three-hour) around Manhattan. Pier 83, at W. 43rd St. on the Hudson, ☎ (212) 563 3200 *(open mid-Mar to mid-Nov, from 9:45am departures every 45 minutes).*

Afternoon: Fifth Avenue, Museum of Modern Art (see pp. 106, 153).

Evening: Theater District (see p. 99).

Third day

Morning: United Nations, Park Avenue (see pp. 105, 175).

Afternoon: Central Park, Metropolitan Museum (see pp. 122, 147).

Evening: Upper West Side, Lincoln Center (see p. 126).

Fourth day

Morning: SoHo and Tribeca (see p. 84).

Afternoon: The Village (see p. 89).

Evening: Village nightclubs (see p. 208).

Fifth day

Morning: Bronx Zoo, New York Botanical Garden (see p. 182).

Afternoon: Cathedral of St John the Divine, Columbia University, The Cloisters, Fort Tryon Park (see pp. 134, 177).

Evening: Bars and restaurants of the Upper East Side (see p. 199).

Other attractions

For a view over New York City

Empire State Building, Fifth Ave. at 34th St., III, C1, ☎ (212) 736 3100. Observation platforms on the 86th and 102nd floors *(open daily 9:30am-midnight; closed Christmas and New Year's Day; half-price admission for children under 12).*

RCA Building, 30 Rockefeller Pl. (entrance on the corner of 49th St. and Fifth Ave.), IV, B3, ☎ (212) 489 2947. Observation platform on the 70th floor *(open Apr-Oct, daily 10am-8:45pm; Nov-Mar, daily 10:30am-7pm; half-price admission for children under 12).* The famous **Rainbow Room** on the 65th floor is a wonderful place to have a cocktail (see p. 119).

World Trade Center, 2 World Trade Center, II, B2, ☎ (212) 466 7397. The world's highest open-air observation platform on the 110th floor and an enclosed platform on the 107th floor *(open daily 9:30am-9:30pm; half-price admission for children 6-12, free admission for children under 6).*

The fabulous ensemble of restaurants and cocktail lounges that make up **Windows on the World** on the top floor of the North Tower is a wonderful place to stop for a cocktail (see pp. 79, 190).

Excursions with a view

Brooklyn Bridge, II, C2. The best time to visit is early in the morning or at sunset. You can walk across the bridge. Subway: Brooklyn Bridge/City Hall (lines 4, 5 or 6).

Brooklyn Heights, II, D3. A superb view of Manhattan from the Brooklyn side of the East River. Stop in at the **River Café** for a cocktail or a dinner (see p. 203). Take a taxi.

Riverside Park, V, A1-3. On the Hudson River, with views of the New Jersey Palisades and the George Washington Bridge.

▬▬ PARKS

The five New York boroughs have 26,176 acres/10,601 hectares of parkland. The Department of Parks and Recreation watches over more than 1500 properties throughout the city, including parks, malls and playgrounds. Zoos and botanical gardens have been cleverly designed and miraculously saved from the waves of construction which periodically sweep through New York. The parks offer a pleasant break from the city streets and are popular places for picnics and strolls in the spring and summer. There are often evening concerts and theater performances.

Central Park (IV, BC1-2; V BC1-2-3) is a green oasis in the center of Manhattan. During the day, do visit and take advantage of the many activities available, but do not walk through the park at night and avoid isolated areas (see 'Central Park', p. 122).

For information on city park activities, ☎ (212) 360 1333.

Central Park

Central Park Zoo, inside the park, off Fifth Ave. near 64th St., ☎ (212) 439 6500. This newly renovated zoo was re-opened in 1988. A cluster of attractive buildings surrounds a seal pool and a large variety of animals enchant adults and young people alike.

Delacorte Theater, W. 81st St. and Turtle Pond, V, B3, ☎ (212) 861 7277. In June, July and August, this theater is the site of Shakespeare in the Park, free open-air performances by Joseph Papp's Public Theater. Tickets are available at the box office on a first-come, first-served basis.

Biking

The various drives that run throughout the park are closed to motor vehicles on weekends *(Fri 7pm-Mon 6am)*, on weekdays during the summer *(10am-3pm, 7-10pm)* and on holidays. These drives are wonderful for biking.

Bicycles can be rented at **Loeb Boathouse,** 74th St., IV, C1, ☎ (212) 861 4137.

Model boats

Conservatory Pond, 74th St. near Fifth Ave., IV, C1. Even adults take this activity very seriously, spending Sunday afternoons demonstrating their navigating skills by competing in model-boat races.

Boating

Loeb Boathouse, 74th St., IV, C1, ☎ (212) 517 2233. Boat rentals *(open Apr-Oct)*.

Horseback riding in the park

Claremont Stables, 175 W. 89th St., V, B2, ☎ (212) 724 5100. This is not for beginners; must be able to ride with English saddles *(open from 6:30am)*.

Carriage rides

59th St. at Fifth Ave., IV, C2. Fare: $17 for the first 30 minutes, $5 per additional 15 minutes. Minimum of 4 people per carriage.

Ice skating

Wollman Rink, 62nd St., IV, C2, ☎ (212) 734 4843 *(open Oct 15-Apr 15, Mon, Wed and Sun 10am-5pm, Tues, Thurs and Fri 10am-5pm and 7-9pm, Sat noon-5pm and 7-9pm; reduced admission on Tues nights; skate rentals included in the price of admission)*.

For children

The Carousel, 65th St., IV, C1-2, ☎ (212) 879 0244 *(open*

10:30am-4:45pm depending on weather conditions; closed Christmas, New Year's Day and St Patrick's Day; reduced admission on Mon).

The Children's Zoo, 64th St. at Fifth Ave., IV, C1, *(open daily 10am-4:30pm).*

Swedish Cottage Marionette Theater, W. 81st St. and West Dr., V, B2, ☎ (212) 988 9093 *(open Tues-Fri for groups of 10 and more; show at noon and 3pm; special shows Dec 26-30; reservations required).*

Heckscher Puppet House, Heckscher Playground, 62nd St., IV, B2, ☎ (212) 397 3162 *(open Mon-Fri; show at 10:30am and noon for groups of 10 and more).*

Other attractions

Belvedere Castle, 79th St., on southwest corner of the large lawn, V, B3, ☎ (212) 772 0210. The Belvedere is an educational center and a weather station *(open Tues-Sun 11am-4pm, Fri 1-4pm).*

Dairy, 64th St., mid-park, IV, B2, ☎ (212) 397 3156. Tourist information center in the park *(open Tues-Fri 11am-4pm).*

The Belvedere Castle and Dairy are closed Christmas Day, New Year's Day and Jan 20, Feb 12 and Feb 17.

Botanical gardens

Brooklyn Botanic Garden, 1000 Washington Ave. Brooklyn, ☎ (718) 622 4433. Subway: Eastern Parkway/Brooklyn Museum (line 2) or Prospect Park/Empire Blvd.-Flatbush Ave. (lines D, Q, S) *(open Apr-Sept, Tues-Fri 8am-6pm, Sat, Sun and public holidays 10am-6pm; Oct-Mar, Tues-Fri 8am-4:30pm, Sat, Sun and public holidays 10am-4:30pm).* See 'The Other Boroughs', p. 183.

New York Botanical Garden, Southern Blvd. and Webster Ave., the Bronx, ☎ (212) 220 8700. Subway: Bedford Park Blvd./Grand Concourse (line D). Located in Bronx Park, the garden has 250 acres/101 hectares of trees, flowers and plants. See, 'The Other Boroughs', p. 182.

Zoos and aquariums

Bronx Zoo, Fordham Rd. and Bronx River Parkway, ☎ (212) 220 5100. Subway: Bronx Park East (line 2), E. 180th St. (lines 2, 5). Walk to the Bronxdale entrance. Not to be missed! The Bronx Zoo offers many activities and discoveries *(open Feb-Oct, Mon-Sat 10am-5pm, Sun and holidays 10am-5:30pm; Nov-Jan, daily 10am-4:30pm; free admission Tues and Thurs for children under two; children under 16 must be accompanied by an adult).* See 'The Other Boroughs', p. 182.

New York Aquarium, Surf Ave. and W. 8th St., Brooklyn, at Coney Island, ☎ (718) 266 8540 or 8500. Subway: W. 8th St./NY Aquarium (lines D, F). A footbridge leads directly to the entrance *(open Mon-Fri 10am-4:45pm, Sat and Sun 10am-5:45pm; the Children's Cove and dolphin show are closed during the winter; free admission after 2pm, Mon-Fri except holidays).* See 'The Other Boroughs', p. 183.

▬ PLACES OF WORSHIP

There are hundreds of churches and synagogues in New York. We have selected the most well-known and accessible.

Catholic churches

Church of Our Saviour, 59 Park Ave. at 38th St., III, C1, ☎ (212) 679 8166.

Holy Apostles, 300 Ninth Ave. at 29th St., III, B1, ☎ (212) 807 6799.

St Patrick's Cathedral, Fifth Ave. at 50th St., IV, C3, ☎ (212) 753 2261.

Protestant churches

Riverside Church, Riverside Dr. at 122nd St., VI, A3, ☎ (212) 222 5900 (interdenominational).

St Bartholomew's, 109 E. 50th St. at Park Ave., IV, C3, ☎ (212) 751 1616 (Episcopalian).

New York's unique identity is drawn from a diverse mix of cultures.

St Thomas, Fifth Ave. at 53rd St., IV, C2, ☎ (212) 757 7013 (Episcopalian).

Synagogues

Fifth Avenue Synagogue, 5 E. 62nd St., IV, C2, ☎ (212) 838 2122.
Spanish and Portuguese Synagogue, 8 W. 70th St., IV, B1, ☎ (212) 873 0300.
Temple Emanu-El, 1 E. 65th St. at Fifth Ave., IV, C1, ☎ (212) 744 1400.

▬ POST OFFICE AND TELECOMMUNICATIONS

General Post Office, 8th Ave. at 33rd St., III, B1 ☎ (212) 967 8585 *(open 24 hours a day).*
Grand Central Post Office, Lexington Ave. at 45th St., IV, C3 *(open Sun and holidays 11am-5pm, Sat 9am-1pm).*
Post offices are generally open Mon-Fri 8am-6pm, Sat 9am-1pm.
Postal rates: post cards, 33¢ for Europe; airmail letter, 44¢ (after 1/2 ounce rate is according to weight). Letters take about one week to reach Europe from the United States.
Stamps are available at post offices.
Telegrams: **Western Union,** ☎ (212) 962 7111.

Telephone

There are many telephone booths throughout the city. A phone call costs 25¢ for the first three minutes. All telephone booths have numbers and can receive calls.

The area code for Manhattan and the Bronx is 212; for Queens, Brooklyn and Staten Island it is 718. To call outside your area code, dial 1 + area code + seven-digit number.

Dial 0 to reach the operator. The operator can dial a number for you, but it will be more expensive. For collect calls (reverse charges): dial 0 and request a collect call or dial 0 + area code + seven-digit number.

For international calls, dial 011 (the international access code), the country code, the city code and the local number. For information on international calls (i.e., rates, country and city codes, etc.), call the following toll-free number: 1 800 874 4000.

Information: dial 411. To obtain a number outside the 212 area code, dial 1 + area code + 555 1212.

The prefix 800 indicates a toll-free number.

Free telephones to make hotel reservations are available for travelers in the three airports.

▬ PUBLIC HOLIDAYS

New Year's Day	Jan 1
Martin Luther King Day	Jan 16
Presidents' Day	third Mon in Feb
Memorial Day	last Mon in May
Independence Day	July 4
Labor Day	first Mon in Sept
Columbus Day	second Mon in Oct
Veterans' Day	Nov 11
Thanksgiving	fourth Thurs in Nov
Christmas	Dec 25

Many stores, restaurants and bars remain open during holidays in New York.

▬ SAFETY PRECAUTIONS

At first sight, New York does not seem to live up to its reputation for crime. Yet crime is widespread, despite a well-organized and efficient police force. Watch out for pickpockets on buses, subways, and in train stations and busy neighbourhoods. Pay careful attention to your bags, wallets and camera equipment. Pickpockets are professional and can spot a tourist right away.

Certain streets and neighbourhoods should be avoided. Do not go into Central Park in the evening, unless you are attending a concert; Harlem and El Barrio are not safe for walking; avoid the area around Times Square in the evening, as well as certain sections of the East Village (the Bowery, Avenues A, B, C and D).

Be careful everywhere in New York; at night, avoid isolated neighbourhoods and streets and take taxis unless you really know the subway well.

▬ SHOPPING

Shopping in New York is a unique experience. New Yorkers are great shoppers; always on the lookout for sales, they compare prices and look for discounts. There is always a sale on somewhere in the city where prices are reduced by half or even two-thirds. The best sales start right after Christmas and during July.

The first price you find may not always be the cheapest, so compare them in different stores and shops. The 'sale' price in one store may be twice the price marked in another! With its thousands of shops and businesses and more than 30 large department stores, New York is a paradise for shoppers.

Electronic and photographic equipment (stereos, computers, accessories) can be as much as one-third cheaper in New York than in Europe but, before purchasing, make sure the voltages, currents and plugs are correct. Furthermore, you can often bargain to lower the price, so be patient and know exactly what you want to buy.

Sports shops offer unbeatable prices for shirts, tennis and running shoes, pants and jeans.

Cash, travelers' checks or credit cards can be used for payment (personal checks are not accepted).

The most interesting shopping districts are:

Madison Ave. from 60th-90th Sts., IV, C1-2; V, C3. This area has the most elegant and expensive shops. Many Italian and French designer shops and prestigious art and antique dealers are located here.

Fifth Ave. at 57th St., IV, C2, is the area where the most famous jewelers are located.

Orchard and Delancey Sts., II, C1. This area specializes in high-quality discount clothes and shoes. Many of the businesses close Friday afternoon and all day Saturday, but remain open Sunday. A less prestigious, but interesting, neighbourhood.

Broadway between Canal-8th Sts., II, B1; III, C2-3. There is a large concentration of army surplus stores and jeans shops here.

Greenwich Village, mainly 8th St., III B, C-3. A multitude of shops cater to youthful styles in this area.

SoHo, II, B1, has both hip and high-fashion shops. Saturday is the most animated day, when people visit the designers, contemporary furniture shops and modern art galleries. You can find designer jeans and shoes as well as antique clothing and handmade items in many other speciality stores.

Columbus Ave. from 60th-90th Sts., IV, B1-2; B2-3, is a trend-setting area. New shops open all the time and many designers have their first boutiques here. It's a pleasant place to stroll on Sunday and mingle with the crowd.

▬▬ SIGHTSEEING SERVICES

Adventures on a Shoestring, 300 W. 53rd St., IV, B3, ☎ (212) 265 2663. Excursions with a theme: Fulton Fish Market, rehearsal of a Broadway show.

Backstage on Broadway, 288 W. 47th St., suite 346, IV, B3, ☎ (212) 575 8065. For a backstage view of a Broadway show (special rates for children).

Fulton Fish Market Tours, South Street Seaport at Fulton St., II, C3, ☎ (212) 962 1608. The New York fish market since 1837. Tours start early, from 5-8am.

Lou Singer Tours, 130 Edward St., Brooklyn, ☎ (718) 875 9084. Gastronomical tours of Manhattan; 10 tours are offered but you can arrange to visit whatever you'd like. Watch out for the portions served during the tours — they are enormous.

The Municipal Art Society, 457 Madison Ave., IV, C3, ☎ (212) 935 3960. This society offers a visit to Grand Central Station, a classic monument in the Beaux Arts style.

Museum of the City of New York Walking Tours, Fifth Ave. at 103rd St., V, C2, ☎ (212) 534 1672. A large selection of excursions planned by New York specialists.

Bus tours

Crossroads Sightseeing, 701 Seventh Ave. between 53rd-54th Sts., IV, B2, ☎ (212) 397 2600. Large program of excursions (some in foreign languages). Helicopter tours are also available.

Discount shopping and bargain stores: a New York institution.

Harlem Spirituals, Inc., 1457 Broadway, suite 1008, VI, A1, ☎ (212) 302 2594 or 2595. Lucien Corcos created the first company to offer guided tours to Harlem. There are three tours: Harlem on Sunday (gospel singing in the neighbourhood churches), Harlem on a Weekday (everyday life in Harlem) and Harlem by Night (black American cuisine and night-clubs).

Manhattan Sightseeing Bus Tours, 150 W. 49th St., IV, B3, ☎ (212) 869 5005.

New York Big Apple Tours, Inc., 162 W. 56th St., IV, B2, ☎ (212) 582 6339.

Penny Sightseeing Harlem Tours, 303 W. 42nd St. at Eighth Ave., IV, B3, ☎ (212) 246 4220.

Shortline Tours Sightseeing, 166 W. 46th St. between Sixth-Seventh Aves., IV, B3, ☎ (212) 354 4740. For groups and charters.

Helicopter tours

Island Helicopter, heliport at 34th St. on the East River, III, D1, ☎ (212) 683 4575 *(open daily except Christmas and New Year's Day 9am-9pm; $30 and up, minimum two people per flight).*

Boat tours

Circle Line, Pier 83 at W. 42nd St., IV, A3, ☎ (212) 563 3200. A three-hour cruise around Manhattan Island.

Hudson River Day Line, Pier 81 at W. 41st St., IV, A3, ☎ (212) 279 5151. One-day excursion on the Hudson, up to West Point Military Academy and back.

Staten Island Ferry, at the South Ferry Station, near Battery Park, II, B3, ☎ (212) 806 6940. Round-trip fare from Manhattan costs only 25¢.

Highly recommended for the view of lower Manhattan and the Statue of Liberty. The best time for this trip is at sunset.

Statue of Liberty Ferry, Battery Park, II, B3, ☎ (212) 269 5755.

Bicycle tours (outside New York)

Country Cycling Tours, 140 W 83rd St., V, B3, ☎ (212) 935 3960 or 874 5151. This tour includes round-trip transportation and bicycle rental for one day. It leaves on weekends at 8:30am, return by 6pm *(open Mon-Fri 9:30am-5pm, Sat noon-5pm).*

▬ SMOKING

Under the terms of a recent law, it is forbidden to smoke in most stores, restaurants, working areas and public buildings in Manhattan.

There are smoking sections in hotel lobbies and train stations.

Note to smokers: restaurants seating more than 50 people are required to reserve part of the room for non-smokers. Don't forget to state your preference. Fines for non-compliance can be expensive: up to $50.

▬ SPORTS

Some New Yorkers take sports very seriously; baseball is probably the favourite, closely followed by football and basketball. You will be able to see New Yorkers jogging, riding bikes, playing tennis, basketball and baseball in all the parks and on the streets.

New York has several professional teams which are supported enthusiastically, almost religiously. Call ☎ (212) 755 4100 for information concerning sporting events in New York.

Baseball

The season begins in spring and runs through October, ending with the famous World Series. New York has two local teams: the **Mets,** who play at Shea Stadium (subway: Willett's Point/Shea Stadium-Roosevelt Avenue, line 7), in Queens, ☎ (718) 672 3000, and the **Yankees,** based at Yankee Stadium (subway: 161st St./Yankee Stadium/River Ave., lines 4, C, D), in the Bronx, ☎ (212) 293 6000. A baseball game is a great popular event, where New Yorkers cheer loudly for their home team.

Basketball

The basketball season runs from October to April. The two local teams are the **New York Knicks** (Madison Square Garden, Eighth Ave. at 32nd St., III, B1, ☎ (212) 564 4400) and the **New Jersey Nets** (Rutgers Center, New Jersey, ☎ 201 935 8888).

Bicycle races

Apple Hap, a 47 mi/75 km race, takes place in October.

Boating

Regatta fans can attend the **Governor's Cup Yacht Race** and the **Mayor's Cup Schooner Race,** held in August and October, respectively.

Football

The season begins in early fall, culminating on Superbowl Sunday in January, which pits the two best teams in the nation. New Yorkers support the **Jets** and the **New York Giants** (Meadowlands Stadium, New Jersey, ☎ 201 935 8222).

Ice hockey

The **New York Rangers** play from October to April (Madison Square Garden, Eighth Ave. at 32nd St., III, B1, ☎ 212 564 4400).

Horseracing

The **Aqueduct Racetrack** (Ozone Park, Queens, ☎ 718 641 4700) and the **Belmont Racetrack** (Queens, ☎ 718 641 4700) offer a wide variety of races.

The **Belmont Stakes,** a thoroughbred race that is a part of the Triple Crown, the premier racing event in the US, is held every year in June. The **National Horse Show** takes place in Madison Square Garden (Eighth Ave. at 32nd St.) every year in November.

Marathon

The **New York City Marathon** is the most famous international race of its kind, with more than 20,000 participants from around the world. The 26.2 mi/40 km race begins on Staten Island and finishes in Central Park. The thousands of runners crossing the Verrazano-Narrows Bridge at the start of the race is an impressive sight. The Marathon is held in late October /early November.

For information on jogging, contact the **New York Roadrunner's Club,** 9 E. 89th St., V, C3, ☎ (212) 860 4455.

Tennis

Tournament of Champions, West Side Tennis Club, Tennis Pl., Forest Hills, Queens, ☎ (718) 268 2300.

US Open Tennis Championships, USTA National Tennis Center, Flushing Meadows-Corona Park, Queens, ☎ (718) 271 5100.

Other sports

Bowling

Madison Square Bowling Center, 4 Pennsylvania Pl., at Seventh Ave. between 32nd-33rd Sts., III, B1, ☎ (212) 563 8160 *(open Mon-Fri 9:30am-4:30pm, Sat and Sun 9:30am-midnight; admission plus shoe rental).*

Ice skating

Rockefeller Center Skating Pond, 1 Rockefeller Pl., ☎ (212) 757 5730. Romantic open-air ice skating with music right in the heart of Rockefeller Center.

Sky Rink, 450 W. 33rd St., (212) 695 6555 *(open all year; indoor rink).*

The Ice Studio, 1034 Lexington Ave., 1st floor, ☎ (212) 535 3034 *(open Thurs 8:30-10pm, Fri 5-6pm and 8:30-10pm, Sat and Sun noon-1pm and 5-6:15pm; $5 per hour, $6 for 1 1/2 hours, skate rental: $2.50; indoor skating rink).*

See also 'Parks', p. 43.

Roller skating

Roller skating is a favourite New York pastime. Go to Central Park on Sunday afternoon to watch the real professionals.

They dance, jump and break dance on surprisingly high-tech roller skates. You can try it, but watch out for cars and potholes in the roads.

To rent roller skates:

Dream Wheels, 295 Mercer St., ☎ (212) 677 0005.

US Roller World, 160 Fifth Ave., ☎ (212) 691 2680 *(open daily 9am-6pm).*

Good Skates, Central Park, northwest of Sheep Meadow, at 69th St., ☎ (212) 535 1080 *(open daily 10am-6pm).*

For horseback riding, bicycle rental, tennis and rowing, see 'Central Park', p. 123.

Swimming

New York has a large selection of beaches and bathing areas which are easy to reach from Manhattan, but very crowded during summer months.

The Atlantic Ocean is cool and doesn't warm up enough for swimming until June. Public beaches are open from May to September.

Coney Island — Brighton Beach: This was once the most popular New York beach but today is noisy, crowded and dirty. It is, however, easy to reach by subway (Stillwell Ave./Coney Island, lines B, D, F, N; Brighton Beach, line D).

Jones Beach: This is an enormous beach on the open ocean that is not as crowded as Coney Island and much cleaner. The Long Island Railroad runs a Jones Beach Special (train and bus) from Penn Station from mid-May through early September, ☎ (212) 739 4200. The trip takes about two hours.

TIME

New York is on Eastern Standard Time, which is five hours in advance of Greenwich Mean Time. During the summer months, from the last Sunday in April to the last Saturday in October, New York is on Daylight Saving Time, where clocks are advanced by one hour.

TIPPING

Tips are never included in the bill in New York; they must be calculated separately.

In a hotel, it is customary to tip the maid on the basis of approximately double the tax indicated on the bill. Porters who carry your luggage get $1 per bag and room service porters are usually given $1-2 on the spot. Hotel doormen are also given a tip when they get you a taxi — 50¢ is sufficient.

In a restaurant, tip the waiter 15-20% of the bill. One way to calculate the amount of the tip is to double the tax. The tip may be left on the table.

Taxi drivers expect tips of 15-20% of the price of the trip (they will curse you roundly if they don't receive one!); hairdressers also are normally tipped 10-15%.

There is no need to tip receptionists, elevator operators or ushers in theaters.

New York City charges an 8.25 % sales tax on meals, clothing, gifts and hotels. Do not forget to add this amount when consulting prices listed in restaurants and stores.

TOILETS

There are few public toilets in New York. Train and bus stations have toilets, but we do not recommend that you use them. They tend to be very dirty and can be unsafe as well. Restaurants, bars, hotels or department stores are the best places to try. Owners usually allow people to use the rest rooms, although in some restaurants you may have to purchase a cup of coffee or a soda.

TOURIST INFORMATION

There are many tourist information services. The New York City service is **The Convention and Visitors Bureau,** 2 Columbus Circle, IV, B2, ☎ (212) 397 8222 *(open Mon-Fri 9am-6pm, Sat, Sun and public holidays 10am-6pm).* Subway: Columbus Circle/59th St. (lines 1, A, B, C, D).

Times Square Information Center, 207 W. 43rd St. at Broadway, IV, B3.

Telephone or stop by one of these offices early in your trip. Employees are friendly and often speak several languages. Maps, brochures and tourist and entertainment information are available.

Some useful telephone numbers

Big Apple Report: (212) 976 2323 (NYC events).

City Park Information: (212) 472 1003 (concerts and events in city parks and squares).

General Tourist Information: (212) 397 8222.

Jazzline: (212) 463 0200 (New York jazz news).

Ticketron: (212) 399 4444, in Times Square (to purchase half-price theater tickets).

Time: (212) 976 1616.

Weather: (212) 976 1212.

WNCN Concert Line: (212) 921 9129 (classical music concerts).

▬ TRANSPORTATION

There are four main ways to get around in New York: bus, taxi, subway and on foot. You can also rent a bicycle or try your luck with roller skates. Renting and using a car in the city is not recommended.

Subway and bus maps are free. They are available at Grand Central Terminal and sometimes, if you're lucky, in subway stations. Exxon service stations offer road maps free of charge.

For bus or subway information, ☎ (718) 330 1234 (24 hours).

Lost and found (bus and subway), ☎ (718) 625 6200.

By bus

Buses run uptown, downtown and crosstown on streets indicated on the bus map.

Drop the exact fare ($1 at this writing) in the box next to the driver (exact change only, no bills or pennies). You may also use tokens which can be purchased in subway stations. Always request a transfer (add-a-ride) ticket to take another bus, in case you need it. These are free but can only be used to change direction for the trip you are making. For example, if you take a bus up Madison Avenue and get off at 79th Street, you can travel east or west along 79th Street free of charge. Transfers must be used immediately.

Pull on the cord or press the black strip (in newer buses) to request a stop. Buses stop every two blocks (if a stop is requested) traveling north and south and at each avenue traveling east and west. Bus stops are indicated by yellow curbs and signs which have the bus number and sometimes the bus route. Look carefully — they are not always easy to spot.

Greyhound Bus (☎ 212 971 6363) and **Trailways Bus** (☎ 212 730 7460) depart from **Port Authority Bus Terminal,** Eighth Ave. at 42nd St., IV, B3, ☎ (212) 564 8484, for destinations outside of the city.

George Washington Bridge Bus Terminal, Broadway and 178th St., ☎ (212) 564 1114, for destinations in northern New Jersey.

By subway

Most lines, both express (stopping only at major stations) and local (stopping at all stations) run north to south. There are few crosstown lines, the most important being the crosstown shuttle between Grand Central and Times Square. Certain parts of the city do not have good subway service or have only a few local stops. Some stations have separate entrances depending on the subway direction. If you want to go south (downtown), the entrance is on the west side of the avenue; to go north, enter on the east side. Directions are indicated on the subway entrances. Make sure

The New York subway

The famous New York subway was inaugurated in 1904 when the IRT line (Interborough Rapid Transit) opened linking City Hall in the south with 145th St. in the north. Several private companies, competing for the same clientele, immediately constructed tracks, often along parallel routes. This resulted in the seemingly inefficient layout of the system, which has three north-south lines on the West Side, but only one on the East Side. The city took over the subway system in 1940.

The MTA (Metropolitan Transit Authority) has recently begun to re-store the turn-of-the-century stations, decorated with multi-coloured mosaics.

In the unending battle against graffiti, the municipal authorities pur-chased trains specially designed to prevent spray paint from adhering to their surfaces.

Statistics:
— 1.5 billion users per year
— 630 trains run during rush hour on 230 mi/370 km of track (the longest system in the world) with 462 stations
— The Smith/9th St. station (Brooklyn) is the highest station in the system, 30.6 yd/28 m above the road; the 191th St. station (on Broadway) is the deepest, 60.1 yd/55 m below ground
— The fastest trains reach 53 mph/85 kph.

you are going in the correct direction because most stations do not have transfer platforms.

The subway fare is the same as the bus fare ($1). The destination and type of train, express or local, are indicated on the side of the train. Buses and subways run 24 hours a day. Rush hour is approximately from 8-9am and from 4:30-6:30pm.

By taxi

There are more than 10,000 taxis in New York. They are yellow and easy to spot. Except for a rare Checker Cab, taxis won't take more than four passengers. The fare is indicated on the meter; add 15-20% for a tip. A taxi is available if the sign for hire on the roof is lit up; if the off-duty sign is lit, the taxi driver is no longer working. Taxis can be an inexpensive means of transportation if several people are traveling together.

To lodge a complaint or to inquire about an item lost in a taxi, call **The Taxi & Limousine Commission,** ☎ (212) 825 0420.

By train

There are two train stations:

Grand Central Terminal, Lexington Ave. at 42nd St., IV, C3, ☎ (212) 736 4545. A shuttle, which is part of the subway system, links Grand Central Station to Times Square on the West Side.

Pennsylvania Station, Seventh Ave. at 33rd St., III, B1, ☎ (212) 736 4545. From Grand Central, trains head towards Connecticut, New York State and points north and west. From Pennsylvania Station, trains head towards Long Island, New Jersey, Pennsylvania and points south.

Useful telephone numbers

Amtrak, for schedule and fare information, ☎ (212) 736 4545 or (800) 872 7245 (toll-free number).

Conrail, at Pennsylvania Station, ☎ (212) 736 6000 (for New Jersey), (212) 532 4900 (for New York).

Long Island Railroad, at Pennsylvania Station, schedules and fares, ☎ (718) 454 5477; lost and found, ☎ (718) 990 8384 (for Long Island).

Lost and found, Penn Station, ☎ (212) 560 7388; Grand Central Station, ☎ (212) 560 7534.

Metroliner (express trains), ☎ (212) 736 3965.

Metro North, at Grand Central Station, schedule and fare information, ☎ (212) 532 4900; lost and found, ☎ (212) 340 2555 (for the Hudson River Valley).

MTA, at Grand Central Station, schedule and fare information, ☎ (212) 532 4900 (for Westchester County and Connecticut).

New Jersey Transit, at Pennsylvania Station, schedule and fare information, ☎ (201) 762 5100; lost and found, ☎ (201) 560 7388.

PATH or Port Authority Trans-Hudson. This is a train service between New York City and New Jersey. There are five PATH stations on Sixth Avenue with trains traveling to Hoboken and Jersey City: 33rd St., 23rd St., 14th St., 9th St. and Christopher St. Trains at the PATH station at the World Trade Center run to Hoboken and Newark. Information, ☎ (212) 466 7649; lost and found, ☎ (212) 432 1272.

Car rental

Car rental agencies are conveniently located at all three airports, as well as throughout New York. They offer various options (insurance, unlimited mileage). You will not need a car if you plan to stay in Manhattan only. Parking is costly and difficult to find, illegally parked cars are towed away, parking tickets are expensive and the traffic is often congested.

JFK Airport

Avis, ☎ (718) 656 5266.

Budget, ☎ (718) 656 6010.

Hertz, ☎ (718) 656 7600.

National, ☎ (718) 632 8300.

LaGuardia Airport

Avis, ☎ (718) 507 3600.

Budget, ☎ (718) 639 6400.

Hertz, ☎ (718) 478 5300.

Newark Airport

Avis, ☎ (201) 951 4300.

Dollar-Rent-A-Car, ☎ (201) 824 2002.

Hertz, ☎ (800) 654 3131 (toll-free number).

New York City

Avis, 217 E. 43rd St.; 460 W. 42nd St., ☎ (800) 331 1212 (toll-free number).

Budget, ☎ (212) 807 8700, for all rentals in Manhattan.

Dollar, 329 E. 22nd St., ☎ (212) 420 0870; 226 W. 56th St., ☎ (212) 399 3590.

Hertz, 150 E. 24th St.; 310 E. 48th St.; 250 W. 34th St.; 118 W. 56th St., ☎ (800) 654 3131, for all rentals (toll-free number).

National, 337 E. 64th St.; 21 E. 12th St.; 207 W. 76th St.; 148 W. 48th St., ☎ (800) 328 4567, for all rentals (toll-free number).

Rent-A-Wreck, 157 E. 84th St., ☎ (212) 628 0093; 203 W. 77th St., ☎ (212) 769 1160. The cars are not in great shape, but the rates are low.

Thrifty, 151 E. 51st St., ☎ (212) 752 8550; 149 W. 49th St., ☎ (212) 586 5680.

Parking information

General information, ☎ (718) 937 8445.

Municipal parking, Eighth Ave. at 53rd St.

Municipal lot, Leonard St. at Lafayette St.

Private parking lots are available throughout the city. The hourly rate varies from $7-15.

Note that, in New York, cars parked illegally are not only ticketed, but are also towed away. If you are unlucky enough to find yourself in this situation, you can recover your car from the lot at the West Side Highway and 36th St. The fee is very expensive — $100 plus the cost of the parking violation ticket (usually $50).

Bicycle rental

On weekdays, New York traffic is too chaotic and dangerous to ride a bike comfortably, except for New York's famous messengers, who weave in and out of traffic at full speed. On the weekends, certain areas such as Wall Street and along Park Avenue are great for bike excursions. Central Park is also ideal for cyclers.

Useful addresses

A&B Bicycle World Inc., 663 Amsterdam Ave. between 92nd-93rd Sts., ☎ (212) 866 7600. *(open Mon-Fri 10am-7pm, Sat and Sun 9am-6pm).*

Andy's Bicycles in the Park, 72nd St., Boathouse in Central Park, ☎ (212) 861 4137.

Bicycle Habitat, 244 Lafayette St. at Spring St., ☎ (212) 431 3315.

Pedal Pusher, 1036 Second Ave. between 68th-69th Sts., ☎ (212) 288 5592.

6th Avenue Bicycles, 546 Ave. of the Americas at 15th St., ☎ (212) 255 5100.

Take two pieces of identification and cash for the deposit. Many bicycle stores also rent bicycles; you must have a credit card.

NEW YORK IN THE PAST

Initially, there was no reason to believe this fertile island would become one of the greatest cities in the world. Populated by Algonquin Indians who farmed and fished in the area, Manhattan was discovered by Europeans during the spice-trading era. Merchant seamen looking for the legendary northwest passage to Asia discovered the island and immediately appreciated its sheltered site.

The first was Giovanni da Verrazano in 1524. An Italian explorer aboard the *Dauphine,* he named the territory 'Land of Angoulême'. Returning to Europe, he reported his discovery to his commander, François I, but the French sovereign wasn't interested in this distant country or its deep bay. The following year, Portuguese Estéban Gómez explored the region for Charles V. Manhattan had entered Western history.

NEW AMSTERDAM

In the early 17th century, Henry Hudson, an English sailor working for the Dutch East India Company, traveled up the river which today bears his name. He returned to Europe with enthusiastic reports about this island nestled in its splendid bay.

Dutch merchants were, however, more preoccupied with finding the trading route to Asia than with colonizing virgin territory and they remained indifferent to Hudson's descriptions. Several years later, in 1614, a Dutch sailor forced to spend the winter on the island drew up the first map of Manhattan. When he returned to Holland, his account of the Indians' friendliness and the abundant furs convinced his compatriots to set up a trading post in this region of North America.

Colonization of the New Netherland province (which included the present-day states of New York and New Jersey) began in 1623, when it was formally established as a province of the West India Company. Dutch merchants opened a trading post at the southernmost tip of the island (in what is now Wall Street) to better organize the fur trade with local Indians. The young colony was named New Amsterdam.

The first years of colonization brought Dutch families,

French-speaking Walloons and the first black slaves. In 1626, the provincial governor, Peter Minuit, bought Manhattan from the Indians for the famous sum of 60 florins, the equivalent of 24 dollars. Three years later, the new colony included close to 300 Europeans and 1000 Indians. Its main resource was the fur trade with Europe. Promoted by its governors, New Amsterdam rapidly developed into a major trading center. Neighbouring English colonists were drawn to New York, where religious and political tolerance reigned. In 1641, a French traveler reported that he had heard 18 different languages spoken by its variegated population of Indians, Dutch, English, Walloons, Scandinavians, Huguenots, Africans and Germans. The relationship between the colonists and the Indians was, however, deteriorating and there were bloody uprisings from 1643 to 1655.

From 1647 to 1664, Peter Stuyvesant, the last Dutch governor, drew up the municipal code and created a police force and fire brigade. To protect the city from English raids, he constructed a fortified palisade, which crossed Manhattan from east to west on the site of present-day Wall Street (thus the derivation of its name).

NEW YORK

The English captured Manhattan in 1664, ending Dutch control of New Amsterdam. The city was promptly renamed New York in honour of the Duke of York. Manhattan remained under English control except for one short interruption from 1673 to 1674 when the Dutch recaptured the city and renamed it New Orange. It was returned to the English in exchange for Surinam, which the Dutch believed held more commercial promise for future trading ventures.

English became the official language of the colony, although a large majority of the population continued to speak Dutch until the middle of the 18th century. Contacts with other areas of North America increased. The number of French Protestants grew considerably after the revocation of the Edict of Nantes in 1685. Trading links with England were reinforced and local entrepreneurship flourished. The palisade at Wall Street, which had become unnecessary, was demolished in 1699 and the city continued its expansion to the north. In 1734, the journalist John Peter Zenger, who had criticized the government in his newspaper, was tried for libel. His acquittal was the first test of freedom of the press in the colonies. Also about this time the first theater opened in Maiden Lane. King's College (later Columbia University) was also founded, becoming the city's first higher education establishment.

In 1763, the Treaty of Paris confirmed the loss of Canada by the French and reinforced English supremacy in North America. English rule was challenged in 1776 when the American War of Independence broke out. New York was not able to participate directly in the revolutionary effort as it was occupied by the English throughout the war. The Americans finally drove the English troops out of New York in 1783 with the aid of the French.

This effort caused devastation to the city, destroying many buildings from the Dutch period. From 1784 to 1790, New York, which by this time had reached Grand Street and numbered 20,000 inhabitants, was capital of the young nation. In 1789, George Washington was inaugurated President of the United States of America in this capital city.

GATEWAY TO AMERICA

Despite successive epidemics of yellow fever New York's population reached 60,000 by the early 19th century. In 1811, a city plan was adopted to prevent uncontrolled growth. The current layout of New York dates from this era, with streets running east and west and avenues north and south. To simplify addresses, these new roads were given numbers.

When the Erie Canal opened in 1825 linking the Great Lakes to the East Coast, New York became the obligatory stopover point between Europe, the Midwest and the Atlantic coast. New York then overtook its two traditional rivals, Boston and Philadelphia, becoming the major manufacturing center. Labour was provided by massive immigration, a determining factor that guaranteed New York the leading role in industry throughout the century. In 1830, 14,000 immigrants reached New York. Five years later, the number had more than doubled to 32,000, and in 1860, 212,000 people arrived. The great Irish famines and the 1848 workers' revolts increased the ranks of the newcomers. From 1840 to 1860, the population of New York rose from 300,000 to 800,000 people.

By the early 19th century, this small port had become the most populated urban center in the United States. Housing problems and real estate speculation took on enormous proportions and were aggravated by the narrowness of the island. The cycle of construction and demolition, still characteristic of New York, began at this period.

A CITY BECOMES A METROPOLIS

From 1861 to 1865, during the American Civil War, New York confirmed its position as the leading port and major economic and manufacturing center in the country. In 1863, the city was paralyzed for three days following serious riots protesting the methods used to draft soldiers into the Northern army. After the war, spectacular and steady urban development began to transform New York into the city we see today. Prospect Park in Brooklyn was inaugurated in 1867, the first large park of its kind in New York. New Yorkers had to wait until 1880 for one of the city's greatest achievements, Central Park.

Communications and public transportation systems continued to improve and the first elevated train was put into service in 1868. With the development of this system, areas once considered too distant were quickly urbanized. Developers built up the Upper West Side and Harlem.

During the 1880s and 1890s, 5 million European immigrants arrived in the port of New York. During this same period, the Metropolitan Opera House was created, Carnegie Hall staged its first performance and the Metropolitan Museum of Art was opened. Technical achievements paralleled cultural developments with the construction of Edison's first electrical power plant and the first tall buildings, precursors of today's skyscrapers. The Brooklyn Bridge was opened, establishing the first overland link between Manhattan and Long Island. In 1886, France gave the Statue of Liberty to the United States and it was erected at the entrance to the most active harbour in the world.

In 1898, New York reached its current city limits by annexing the neighbouring municipalities of Brooklyn, the Bronx, Queens and Staten Island. These five boroughs constitute the city of New York. With 3.4 million inhabitants, the city became the second largest in the world, after London. Unfortunately, New York was ill-equipped to properly house this large population and many people lived in poor conditions.

The end of the 19th century and the early 20th century were marked by the rise of the famous 'robber barons'. Vanderbilt, Whitney, Carnegie, Morgan and Rockefeller amassed immense fortunes from the gigantic real estate and economic developments in the city and country. Yet these multimillionaires returned some of their wealth to the city through philanthropic works, adding to the city's rich heritage. Carnegie Hall, the Frick Collection, the Public Library, the Morgan Library and the Cooper-Hewitt Museum owe their existence to these benefactors. The great New York philanthropic tradition dates from this period.

In 1904, the first underground subway line linking City Hall to 145th Street was opened. Around the same time, Harlem became the main neighbourhood for New York's black population. It experienced a renaissance in the 1920s and 1930s, and people flocked there to hear jazz at such famous nightclubs as the Cotton Club and on the stage at the Apollo Theater.

The construction of Grand Central and Pennsylvania railway stations improved transportation links with the rest of the country and was the final development in the urban railway network. In 1913, the population numbered more than 5 million inhabitants.

In 1920, following the end of World War I, Congress voted for Prohibition, outlawing alcoholic beverages. An enormous black market network dominated by powerful gangs based in New York City sprang up to provide illegal alcohol. The streets of Manhattan produced such notorious gangsters as Al Capone, Lucky Luciano and Dutch Schultz.

The 1929 stock market crash marked the beginning of the Great Depression. Bankruptcies multiplied, half the working population was unemployed and industrial production collapsed. In 1933, Fiorello LaGuardia was elected mayor of New York to fight this unprecedented crisis and the corruption that was rife in municipal government. Nicknamed 'The Little Flower',

Battery Park on the southern tip of Manhattan: a breath of fresh air in the heart of the Financial District.

LaGuardia was able to centralize municipal power and implement extensive economic reforms.

NEW YORK, CAPITAL OF THE WORLD

Activity at the port of New York increased considerably when the United States entered World War II in 1941. Also,

thousands of European intellectuals fleeing Nazi persecution escaped to New York, thereby contributing to the city's intellectual development. New York welcomed such celebrities as Albert Einstein, Fernand Léger, Thomas Mann, Claude Lévi-Strauss, Salvador Dalí, Igor Stravinsky, André Breton, Arturo Toscanini, Saint-John Perse, Bertolt Brecht and Darius Milhaud.

By 1939, New York had already begun to rival European cultural and economic centers. In 1945, New York was the only great center of culture and finance unscathed by the war, and it took its place as the undisputed capital of the world.

In the 1950s, the United Nations established its headquarters in New York, along with many multinational companies and banks. Immigration from South and Central America and Puerto Rico began in the 1950s and soon exceeded European immigration. The population of the five boroughs rose to more than 7 million people.

BANKRUPTCY AND RECOVERY

The 1960s were difficult years for New York City. Problems were created by the exodus of the middle and wealthy classes to the suburbs, the departure of many businesses and the deterioration in municipal services.

In 1974-1975, the city was unable to meet its debt payments or pay its employees. The state government, banks and unions developed a joint plan to avoid bankruptcy and created the MAC (Municipal Assistance Corporation) to manage city affairs and to restore a balanced budget. Financial recovery was achieved by 1976. Despite this economic recovery, New Yorkers nevertheless had to face some of the most worrisome aspects of contemporary urban society when a 25-hour power blackout in the summer of 1977 brought looting and vandalism to the city's poorest areas.

In November 1977, Edward I. Koch was elected mayor of New York on a platform promising to clean up the city finances. The building sector recovered and unemployment decreased as a gentrification process began to change the face of the city. The naturally optimistic New Yorkers once again gained confidence in their city.

Despite New York's economic recovery, specialists issued warnings about the increasing gap between rich and poor, partially caused by government cuts in social welfare spending.

In 1986, New York celebrated the centennial of the Statue of Liberty. Hundreds of sailing vessels from around the world sailed into the bay for the festivities which culminated in a magnificent fireworks display. By commemorating the hundred years of the Statue of Liberty, New York paid tribute to its millions of immigrants, who made the city the symbol of a free society in the modern world.

NEW YORK TODAY

A city of great contrasts and amazing diversity, New York is also a city of excess and extremes. In many ways, New Yorkers think their city is the center of the world. With more than 8 million inhabitants of all nationalities, it is still the classic melting pot of American culture. It is the leading international business and economic center, a Mecca for the art world and a trend-setter in the fashion world. New York boasts about its many accomplishments, dubbing itself the city that has everything — the tallest buildings, the greatest talents, the most museums — yet it also contains some of the most disinherited and destitute of America's poor. Even so, it has been and remains the symbol of the great American dream.

EMPIRE OF THE GREENBACK

In New York, the cliché 'time is money' is probably more true than anywhere else in the world. At the end of World War II, New York overtook London as the international financial center. Ever since, market trends have been dictated by Wall Street brokers. The multitude of books, films and articles about these golden boys has transformed them into media stars. Despite the stock market crash of 1987, New York continues to handle the world's financial interests.

EXTRAVAGANCE AND CONSUMERISM

Except for Los Angeles, nowhere else in America is the consumer mentality as all-pervasive as in New York. Shrewd businesspeople remain open for business 24 hours a day, 365 days a year. There is a grocery store open late at night on practically every street corner. New Yorkers live and work according to their own rhythms; weekends are no longer sacrosanct and nights are not necessarily for sleeping. You can find anything at any time of day or night.

Newspapers have full-page advertisements devoted to the daily specials in various stores, with detachable coupons for discounts on certain items. Discount is the magic word for the New York shopper, who is always on the lookout for a good deal. New York, with its multitude of stores, is a good place to shop; prices are extremely competitive and bargains abound.

The impressive skyline of Midtown Manhattan, viewed from the Empire State Building.

THE WORLD IN AN APPLE

New York owes much of its diversity to the successive waves of immigrants to the Big Apple. It is one of the most heterogeneous cities in America with its Italian, Russian, Hispanic-American, German, Austrian, Polish, Scandinavian, Chinese, Vietnamese, Korean and Indian populations. New York has

often been called the largest Jewish city in the world. Close to one-fifth of the city is black and the influx of Hispanic-Americans has made Spanish the second language in New York.

Each nationality has created its unique neighbourhood, resulting in areas such as Little Italy, El Barrio in East Harlem and Chinatown. Racial boundaries are still visible in Harlem and the Bronx. Nevertheless, the ethnic makeup of most neighbourhoods is fluid and the city changes with each group of new arrivals.

Tips from Edward I. Koch, Mayor of New York

Ed Koch is a New York chauvinist. A true New Yorker, he loves his home town and will boast about it to anyone willing to listen.

'New York never stops moving. The architecture changes every year. Teachers are welcome here and it's not too difficult to become a naturalized American citizen. In fact, 30% of New Yorkers were born abroad.

'This diversity creates an energy, a kind of electrical current which doesn't exist anywhere else. All nationalities, religions, ethnic backgrounds and races of the world are represented here.

'New York is both loved and detested by the rest of America. Why? Because people don't appreciate its frenzied rhythm. New Yorkers walk, talk and think faster than everyone else. You don't have to be born in New York to be a New Yorker! You become one. It's a state of mind. In fact, only 25% of the population was born here.

'My three favourite neighbourhoods are SoHo, the South Street Seaport and Greenwich Village. In SoHo, I stop at the **Broome Street Bar** or the **Manhattan Brewery** for a snack. At the South Street Seaport, near the Financial District, I'll watch the boats and stop at the **Liberty Café** on the waterfront. In Greenwich Village, I walk around Washington Square Park, 4th Street, 8th Street and Sheridan Square.

'You know, the food in our ethnic restaurants is often better than what's available in the original countries. The quality of our products is superior.

'My favourite restaurants are **Marcello's,** where I often go, and **Il Mulino,** a very popular restaurant where it's best to reserve ahead.'

THE WORK ETHIC

New York is not an easy place to live and hard work is the rule. Social mobility comes to those who are not afraid to work. Most people who move to New York intend to succeed in their chosen field.

The excitement of New York City comes directly from the creative energy of its inhabitants, their feverish desire to undertake new projects and the constant feeling of urgency that they generate. New Yorkers are tireless and fast-moving. Yuppies (Young Urban Professionals) are part of this New York phenomenon reflecting the desire to earn money, live well and enjoy the benefits of hard work.

CHAOS AND ORDER

The regimented skyscrapers and the orderly grid of streets belie the exuberant and chaotic landscape of city life, complete with traffic jams and deafening screaming sirens. It can take more than one bumpy hour to drive the 2.5 mi/4 km of potholed streets separating the East River and the Hudson. Mondrian superbly recorded this dynamic energy in his painting *Broadway Boogie-Woogie* (exhibited at the Museum of Modern Art), a lyrical composition formed by vertical and horizontal lines vibrating with a multi-coloured electrical current.

Martin Scorsese likes to compare the city's vitality to that of ancient Rome. The apparent confusion of New York masks a subtle order, similar to jazz compositions. The syncopated movement appears to be improvised but is, in fact, the product of extensive experience and meticulous practice. The city's subway system is a good example of this phenomenon. It provides very efficient service yet appears to be in severely dilapidated condition.

UPTOWN/DOWNTOWN

New York is divided into two main cultural centers: Uptown and Downtown, the north and the south.

Uptown represents tradition, established values, elitism and wealth. The major museums, famous restaurants, wealthy homes, jewelers and prestigious stores are located here on Fifth and Madison Avenues. Downtown, south of around 34th Street, is more cozy. It is home to numerous artists, actors, trendy cafés, fashionable restaurants and nightclubs. Many of the city's most famous painters, sculptors, dancers, designers, musicians and writers live in lofts in Chelsea, SoHo and Tribeca.

These two often contradictory centers have together created New York's international and cultural fame.

Central Park is the meeting ground between Downtown and Uptown, bohemia and the bourgeoisie, an oasis in New York for sports, leisure activities and entertainment. It is the one geographical and social element that joins the elegant and the rundown, the conservative and the liberal neighbourhoods. Immensely popular since its creation over 100 years ago, the park is a skillful blend of natural and man-made elements — the heart of Manhattan.

THE CHANGING FACES OF THE CITY

This controversial city, which has often been called a new Babylon, is currently undergoing a process of gentrification. After an exodus to the suburbs, many of the young and wealthy are returning to Manhattan, transforming neighbourhoods and causing real-estate prices to skyrocket. Older inhabitants, small businesses and young artists have been forced out of the city in search of more reasonable rents. Working-class streets and neighbourhoods have been transformed overnight as bulldozers move in and high-rise buildings sprout up. It has become a privilege to live in Manhattan. While promoters make a fortune, New Yorkers worry about the identity of their city, as entire neighbourhoods disappear and are replaced by huge residential towers.

NEW YORK'S ARCHITECTURE

O nly a few architectural examples from the Dutch and English colonial styles remain. Dyckman House, with its overhanging eaves and porch, is a typical example of a 17th- and 18th-century farm. St Paul's Chapel in Lower Manhattan, inspired by St Martin's-in-the-Fields in London, is the most beautiful example of Georgian architecture (1714-1830), along with the Morris-Jumel Mansion and Fraunces' Tavern.

The Federal style (1789-1825) developed along with the new Republic in reaction to the Georgian style, which was a reminder of British domination. Austerity and simplicity were the rule. The Corinthian columns and pediments were replaced with flat roofs and Doric columns. City Hall and Gracie Mansion are two of the few public buildings remaining from this period. There are more private residences in this style, including the James Watson House on State Street, the Hamilton Grange and the Abigail Adams Smith House.

THE REVIVALS

The architectural revivals, inspired by the Classical and Gothic periods, were popular throughout the entire 19th century. One of the most important, the Greek Revival, was widespread in the 1830s. New York merchants were attracted to the elements and proportions of Classical architecture, with its pediments, columns and porticos. A good example of this style can be seen in the row of private homes on Washington Square North in Greenwich Village and in the ground-floor of the Citibank building, at 55 Wall Street.

Asymmetrical planes characterized Gothic Revival buildings; circular rooms alternated with square ones and façades were highly decorated. Trinity Church, Grace Church and St Patrick's Cathedral are marvelous examples of this neo-Gothic style.

The neo-Italian Renaissance style was fashionable from 1845 to 1860. Many of the rows of brownstones, constructed from

The IBM Building (left) and the sleek Trump Tower (center) overshadow the elegant Crown Building on W. 57th Street.

brownstone from New England quarries, date from this period. Originally built as individual residences, most have now been transformed into apartments. In Manhattan, there are some beautiful examples in Greenwich Village, Chelsea, Gramercy Park, the Upper East Side and Harlem. In Brooklyn, the Park Slope and Brooklyn Heights areas also have some handsome examples.

The neo-Italian Renaissance style also spread with the development of cast-iron architecture (see 'SoHo and Tribeca' p. 84). In the second half of the 19th century, the neo-Romanesque style became popular. The Marble Collegiate Church at Fifth Avenue and 29th Street is a good example, as are the south wing of the American Museum of Natural History and the elegant De Vinne Press Building at Lafayette and E. 4th Sts. Eclecticism replaced the Revivals around 1900, with architects working in their favourite styles, including neo-Georgian (Harvard Club), neo-Classical or neo-Romanesque (old Penn Station building and the Metropolitan Museum), Beaux Arts (Custom House), neo-German Renaissance (Dakota Apartments) or Flemish (West End Collegiate Church).

THE SKYSCRAPER CENTURY

The soaring cost of land and the increasing population led architects and city planners to construct ever taller buildings, using the technical innovations of the time. In 1859, the first elevator was installed in the Haughwout Building on lower Broadway. Steel and iron construction allowed for more flexible design. The Renaissance-style Flatiron Building was constructed where Broadway joins Fifth Avenue at 23rd Street in 1902. Eleven years later, the Woolworth Building, 'a Gothic cathedral of commerce' on lower Broadway became the tallest building in the world. Manhattan's geological formation also contributed to the unique and unprecedented development of the city. The granite formation of the island provides an ideal solid foundation for the skyscrapers.

In 1916, a city zoning plan was adopted which determined the overall height and volume of buildings in relation to the neighbouring streets. As a result of this new law, buildings were constructed with successive setbacks. Fire safety measures were introduced at the same time, requiring that buildings be equipped with the now-famous metal fire escapes.

In 1925, the Exposition des Arts Décoratifs in Paris influenced many American architects and inspired the design of the Chrysler Building on Lexington Avenue between 42nd and 43rd Streets. Brick, ceramic and stone were progressively replaced by steel, glass and aluminum. The new architectural style' which tried to reveal the building structure itself can be seen in the former McGraw-Hill Building on W. 42nd Street and in the Daily News Building on E. 42nd Street. The New York skyscraper has been a model for every major city in the world, ensuring America's place in the annals of architectural history.

In recent years, post-Modernism has reacted against the functionalism of the preceding period, drawing inspiration from the Federal and Classical styles and incorporating columns, arches, brick and stone. The most representative example is the AT&T Building on Madison Avenue. The elegant corniche and enormous Classical proportions were designed by John Burgee and Philip Johnson. Still in its infancy, post-Modernism received considerable encouragement from Robert Venturi and Robert Stern.

FINANCIAL DISTRICT

Map II. — Subway: Bowling Green/Broadway (line 4); South Ferry/Battery Park (line 1); Whitehall St./South Ferry (line R). Bus: lines 1, 6.

The Financial District is centered on Wall Street at the southern tip of Manhattan. This historic neighbourhood, where the 18th-century St Paul's Chapel backs onto the 110 floors of the World Trade Center, epitomizes the ongoing transformation of New York. This has been the financial, political and judicial center of the city since the first Dutch colonists arrived in 1614. A walk through the area during business hours provides a glimpse of why Wall Street dominates the international economy.

In contrast to most of New York, which is teeming with people day and night, Wall Street is busy only during working hours. The neighbourhood is deserted at night and on weekends, except for a few strollers and cyclists meandering through the empty streets. The daytime population consists mainly of suburban commuters, whose lives are regulated by work and train schedules.

The district is nonetheless changing. Financial institutions are moving to other areas of Manhattan and to suburban neighbourhoods. Furthermore, three current city developments are transforming this area, doubling the number of residents in Lower Manhattan. The commercial and gastronomical center of South Street Seaport offers over 100 restaurants and shops. Battery Park City continues to develop on a landfill to the west of the World Trade Center. This urban complex is modeled after Rockefeller Center, with large buildings, shops and restaurants, including more than 14,000 luxury apartments. Finally, the South Ferry Tower, with 60 floors of apartments dominating the Staten Island Ferry dock, will transform the life of the neighbourhood and the famous Manhattan skyline.

The Financial District has not always belonged to businessmen. During Dutch rule, Wall Street and Trinity Church formed the northern boundary of the city. Housing, warehouses, piers, banks and shipping offices were crowded together to the south. The settlement then resembled a European city, with small winding streets which still bear their original names.

New York grew rapidly; when space was needed, the river banks on the east side of Manhattan were filled to create new land. The East River was pushed back from Pearl Street to Water

In the center of the Chase Manhattan Plaza, Jean Dubuffet's Group of Four Trees.

Street, then to South Street in 1796, by an accumulation of tree trunks, stones and old boat hulls.

At the same time, the city continued to expand to the north. In 1800, Canal Street marked the new boundary. During this time, shipping was New York's major business and the city center was bordered by Pearl Street, Front Street and South Street in the east. Sailboats were anchored in the East River where most of the piers were located. Merchants lived in elegant homes on the Battery, Bowling Green and Greenwich Street, the present-day site of the World Trade Center. Craftsmen and workers lived farther to the north, in modern-day Tribeca.

In the 1830s, the increasing port activity and the beginning of massive immigration accelerated the northward exodus of wealthy families. Beautiful homes were constructed in what was then countryside on Second Avenue (modern-day East Village), Lafayette Street and Washington Square. The former houses of affluent merchants and shippers were replaced with bank offices and insurance companies. Hundreds of thousands of immigrants crowded into the Greenwich Street and Cherry Street neighbourhoods.

Available space has always been at a premium in the Financial District. Obliged to stay near the port within a limited area, the only solution for bankers and merchants lay in constructing taller buildings. The Brooklyn Bridge was erected in 1883 to the east, providing easy access to the neighbourhood for thousands of office workers. To the west, boats brought supplies to central Washington Market warehouses. In 1889, the first 11-floor skyscraper was built at 50 Broadway, dominating the southern tip of Manhattan.

Wall Street's influence throughout the world continued to grow during the 20th century, especially after World War I. In the early 1960s, some banks and large companies decided to move Uptown, in search of available office space. At one time, it seemed that the financial community was leaving its traditional district but, with renewed confidence in Wall Street, this exodus ended. New construction projects were begun, including the Water Street Building, the twin towers of the World Trade Center and Battery Park City.

▬ *BOWLING GREEN*

Map II, B3. — Subway: Bowling Green/Broadway (line 4).

During Dutch colonial rule, the 'bowling green' was still a cattle market marking the start of Broadway, an old Indian path. According to legend, this is the exact site where the Dutch purchased Manhattan from the Indians for $24 worth of fabric and beads. In 1733, several citizens leased the site from the British Crown for the symbolic fee of one peppercorn per year to use as a bowling green. In the years preceding the American Revolution, the park gradually became a meeting place for public speakers. When the Declaration of Independence was read in 1776, crowds tore down the equestrian statue of George III, King of Great Britain. The lead was melted down and made into bullets. Fortunately, the revolutionaries saved the original fence which still encircles the park. In the early 19th century, the Green was surrounded by the most attractive homes in the city.

The **Custom House**, II, B3, was constructed in 1907 south of the square on the site of the former Fort Amsterdam, built by the Dutch in 1626. There are four sculptures on the exuberant Beaux Arts façade representing, from left to right, a meditative Asia, America confident in its future, Europe surrounded by past achievements and Africa sleeping between the sphinx and the lion. The capitals of the 44 columns surrounding the building are crowned with stone sculptures evoking Mercury, the god of commerce. The cornice is decorated with 12 marble statues which represent the 12 great commercial centers of history. Inside, the immense rotunda (135 ft/40 m high × 85 ft/25 m) of the entrance and its oval skylight make it one of the city's most beautiful public rooms. Frescos painted by Reginald Marsh below the dome depict the saga of early American explorers and the arrival of a steamship into New York harbour. Greta Garbo is recognizable among the passengers being interviewed by journalists.

There are several interesting buildings at the foot of Broadway. The former offices (1921) of the **Cunard Line** shipping company are located at n° 25. Constructed during the height of steamship travel in the euphoria of the 1920s, the Italian Renaissance façade conceals an extraordinary interior, modeled after Raphael's Villa Madama in Florence. The decoration of the entrance, the main room, which originally housed the ticket counters, and the wall frescos commemorate the boom years in transatlantic steamship travel. The Postal Service took over the building when the Cunard company moved out in 1976 and added uninspiring fluorescent lights and a suspended ceiling.

The former building of the **Standard Oil Corporation** (1922), founded by John D. Rockefeller, is across the street at 26 Broadway. The curved façade mirrors the contours of Broadway, while the tower, best seen from Battery Park, follows the north-south alignment of the streets and buildings Uptown. Oil lamps decorate the façade and top of the tower. Inside, the names of the company founders are engraved in the marble of the Renaissance-style lobby.

▬ *BATTERY PARK*

Map II, B3. — Subway: South Ferry/Battery Park (line 1); Bowling Green/ Broadway (line 4); Whitehall St./South Ferry (line R).

One of the last **subway kiosks** dating from the inauguration of the IRT line in 1904 stands at the entrance to Battery Park, between State Street and Battery Place.

Located on the southernmost tip of Manhattan Island, Battery Park originally was no more than a rocky island which had a row of cannons for the city's defense. Successive landfills closed the gap separating it from Manhattan and it is today one of the most animated parks in the city. Office workers fill the park during the lunch hour to enjoy a moment of tranquility from the busy Financial District. Musicians often play on weekends for the many families enjoying the park and there is a superb view of the Statue of Liberty from the west edge of the park.

Castle Clinton National Monument, II, B3, was constructed in 1807 during the War of 1812 to defend the city against British attackers *(open June-Aug, daily 9am-5pm; Sept-Dec and Mar-May, Mon-Fri 9am-5pm)*.

Named Castle Clinton in honor of De Witt Clinton, who served as mayor of New York and as governor of New York State, the fort was abandoned in 1824 and leased by the city. Renamed Castle Garden, it was used as an opera and entertainment center until 1854 when it was transformed into a center for arriving immigrants. As the direct precursor of Ellis Island, more than 7 million new arrivals passed through its gates between 1855 and 1890. Finally, it was remodeled in 1896 and housed the New York Aquarium until 1941. Today, Castle Clinton is a museum devoted to the history of the fort and the park.

There is an excellent view*** of New York harbour from the Dewey

Promenade, near the **statue of Giovanni da Verrazano** (see 'New York in the Past' p. 56). The Hudson River and the East River converge at this point. From here, you can admire, from left to right: Brooklyn Heights, II, D3; Governor's Island, I, A2; Staten Island, I, A3; Liberty Island and the Statue of Liberty, I, A2; Ellis Island, I, A2, and, finally, New Jersey, I, A2. Opposite, the **Verrazano-Narrows Bridge**, I, A3, is the world's longest suspension bridge (0.75 mi/1,2 km). The ticket counters and ferry docks for the Statue of Liberty and Ellis Island are located at the end of the promenade.

▄▄ PEARL STREET

Map II, B3. — Subway: South Ferry/Battery Park (line 1); Bowling Green/ Broadway (line 4); Whitehall St./South Ferry (line R).

Pearl Street lies to the east of Battery Park and owes its name to the oyster shells which were once strewn on the shores. In 1834, the **Seamen's Church Institute**, II, B3, on the corner of State Street, was founded to house sailors and their families. It is constructed on the site of Herman Melville's (author of *Moby Dick*) birthplace. The **James Watson House** (1800), the last surviving example from the elegant era of private homes on State Street, has a good view of the harbour. It is a beautiful example of the Federal style, with a flat balustraded roof, brick walls, fireplace and slender Ionic columns. Mr. Watson was a ship-owner who took advantage of the strategic location of this house to receive signals from one of his employees on Staten Island. He was thus the first to know of the arrival of one of his own or a competitor's ships.

The terminal on **Peter Minuit Plaza**, II, B3, serves as the ferry station for Staten Island and Governor's Island.

Fraunces' Tavern, II, B3, is located at 54 Pearl Street, on the corner of Broad Street. Etienne de Lancey, a French merchant who emigrated to New York following the Revocation of the Edict of Nantes, constructed this building in 1719 as a family residence. The modest brick building then stood on the banks of the river. Samuel Fraunces, a Frenchman from the Antilles, acquired the property in 1764 and opened the Queen's Head Tavern. His abilities did not go unnoticed and he was soon named chief steward to George Washington. His tavern became one of the favourite meeting places for the revolutionaries and leaders of the young nation. On December 4, 1783, General Washington bid farewell to his troops at Fraunces' Tavern after the departure of the English.

Sadly, fire severely damaged this historical site in the 19th century, leaving only the west wall intact. The rest of the building has been reconstructed, using various examples of architecture from the period. The ground floor houses a restaurant; the second floor a museum devoted to the War of Independence, which contains, among other exhibits, the arms carried by the Marquis de Lafayette.

Hanover Square, II, B3, to the north, between Pearl and William Streets, evokes the colonial era. Named in honour of the English Royal Family, this square was once the heart of a wealthy residential neighbourhood. The great fire of 1835, which ravaged a large part of the city, started here.

The **India House** (1837), at 1 Hanover Square, incorporates many Italian Renaissance elements. One of the first brownstone buildings in New York, it has been a private men's club since 1928.

▄▄ WALL STREET ★★

Map II, B3. — Subway: Wall St./William St. (line 2); Broad St./Wall St. (line J).

Wall Street, home of the New York Stock Exchange and major international banks, is the financial center of the world. Running from Broadway to the East River, Wall Street has an influence that extends far beyond its 1640 ft/500 m length. The Stock Exchange, leading banks and one of the largest gold reserves in the world are located here. It was once the seat of the federal government and is the site of the oldest parish in the city.

The famous wall was no more than a wooden palisade erected by the Dutch in 1653 to defend New Amsterdam against British attackers. It followed the modern-day layout of the street from the East River to the Hudson and had two doors, one on Broadway, the other on Pearl Street.

There is a superb view, from the corner of Pearl and Wall Streets, of the urban canyon formed by two rows of skyscrapers. The perspective stops at the brownstone façade of Trinity Church, II, B3, at the end of the street.

The imposing structure at 55 Wall Street houses **Citibank**, II, B3, one of Wall St.'s most famous buildings. Construction began in 1842 with a three-storey Classical temple with Ionic columns designed for the Merchants Exchange. Forty teams of oxen transported the 12 façade columns through the labyrinth of neighbouring streets. The building was renovated in 1907 and its capacity doubled. Three new floors were added above its 80 ft/24 m dome, this time incorporating Corinthian columns.

William Street to the right leads to the **Chase Manhattan Bank**, II, B3, located at 1 Chase Manhattan Plaza. In 1960, the construction of this 800 ft/243 m building signaled renewed confidence in Wall Street's future. Made of glass and aluminum and surrounded by a square plaza, the building was remarkably innovative for its time. The garden was designed by the sculptor Isamu Noguchi and the *Group of Four Trees* by Jean Dubuffet was installed in the plaza. The fifth basement of the bank (100 ft/30 m underground) contains the world's largest safe: 12,677 cu yd/10,600 cu m in volume and longer than a football field. Unfortunately, it is not open to visitors.

The **Federal Reserve Bank**, II, B3, is housed in the massive 'Fed' building at 33 Liberty Street. Largely modeled after the Palazzo Strozzi in Florence, this is the central American bank; part of the American federal reserve gold as well as gold reserves from 70 nations are stored in its five basements *(reserve in advance for a free visit to the 'Fed', Public Information Office, ☎ 212 791 6130).*

The **Downtown Annex of the Whitney Museum**, II, B3 *(open Mon-Fri 11am-3pm)*, is located nearby in Federal Plaza, 33 Maiden Lane. Concerts and films are presented to the public during lunch hours.

Nassau Street is a pedestrian mall, lined with fast-food establishments and various stores catering to the tens of thousands of office workers in the neighbourhood. The **Federal Hall National Monument**, II, B3 (1842), stands at the intersection of Nassau, Broad and Wall Streets. It is an imposing Greek Revival structure, erected on the site of the first federal government headquarters. It was originally used as a Custom House, and later as the federal Treasury. The **statue of George Washington** at the top of the stairs commemorates the investiture of the first president of the United States in 1789.

The **Morgan Guaranty Trust**, II, B3 (1913), founded by J.P. Morgan, stands on the southeast corner of the intersection. The façade still shows traces of an anarchist bombing in 1920 that killed 33 people and wounded 400. Inside, the large entrance lobby has an immense 16 ft/5 m crystal chandelier.

Finally, on the southwest corner, the famous **New York Stock Exchange**, II, B3 (entrance on 20 Broad Street), is the sanctuary of high finance and American industry. One in every six Americans is a stockholder and more than 30 million shares change hands every day. The neo-Classical temple built in 1903 has a sculpted pediment depicting *Integrity Protecting the Works of Man.*

In 1789, the American Congress issued bonds to reimburse debts contracted during the War of Independence. In 1792, 24 brokers signed the agreement of Buttonwood, to trade and administer these stocks.

This marked the formal beginning of the New York Stock Exchange, even though the brokers originally met under a tree located at 68 Wall Street. The Exchange gained greater influence with the War of 1812 between the United States and Britain, but it attained real economic power over the nation during the Civil War (1861-1865). Over the next 50 years, it grew at a virtually unlimited pace due to industrialization and the country's geographical expansion west. World War I brought a period of prosperity and unbridled speculation which ended in the Crash of 1929.

To prevent the recurrence of another depression, strict monitoring procedures were drawn up to regulate the stock market and, today, the New York Stock Exchange is still the financial center of the world, although certain financial markets are dominated by the London and Tokyo stock exchanges. The shares of more than 4400 companies are traded daily by the 1366 brokers forming the Stock Exchange.

The trading floor is worth visiting to watch the frenetic energy of the brokers doing business in the immense room with its 50 ft/15 m ceiling *(the Visitors' Center is open Mon-Fri 10am-4pm)*.

The **Irving Trust Company** (1932) at 1 Wall Street contains flamboyant red, orange and gold mosaics in the Art Deco lobby. The **Bank of New York** (1927) at 48 Wall Street and **70 Pine Street** with its Art Deco design also have attractive lobbies.

There are other noteworthy features of buildings in the district, including the **cupola** of the Bank of New York, the Gothic **crown and spire** at 70 Pine Street and the **pyramidal summit** of the Manufacturers Hanover Trust (1929) at 40 Wall Street. Their profiles are an essential part of the traditional Downtown skyline.

The present **Trinity Church***, II, B3, is the third to have been built on the site; the first dated from 1698. Constructed in 1847, this Episcopal church imposed the Gothic Revival style on New York. The brownstone façade created a scandal when it was built because this stone was not considered a worthy building material. The 280 ft/85 m spire dominated the New York skyline until the advent of the first skyscrapers. Today, it appears dwarfed by the towers surrounding it. The large entrance doors were modeled after the Baptistery in Florence. Some of the first Dutch colonists are buried in the beautiful **cemetery;** the oldest tomb dates from 1681. Famous people buried here include Alexander Hamilton, financier and father of American Independence who was killed in a duel with Aaron Burr, and the painter Robert Fulton, inventor of the steamboat. There is also a cross placed in memory of Caroline Webster Astor, the formidable New York dowager who lived at the end of the 19th century. At the back is a monument to the Martyrs of the Revolution. Trinity Church has adapted to the vitality of the neighbourhood and offers concerts, films and conferences during the lunch hour and holds a choir service every Sunday at 11:15am.

The famous **Equitable Building** at 120 Wall Street, east of Broadway, occupies the entire block. The two 40-storey towers were constructed in 1915 to provide office space for 13,000 people. A public protest arose against the building's massive size, which blocked light and the circulation of air to adjacent streets. As a result, in 1916, the city adopted the first zoning law in the United States regulating the size and shape of skyscrapers. The effect of this zoning law can be seen in the Irving Trust Company Building on the corner of Broadway and Wall Street.

The **Marine Midland Bank** was constructed at 140 Broadway by Skidmore, Owings and Merrill, the architects who designed the Chase Tower. Built in 1967, the restrained building and plaza are brightened by Isamu Noguchi's orange *Cube*. The twin towers of the World Trade Center are visible to the north.

▬ *WORLD TRADE CENTER***

Map II, B2. — Subway: Cortlandt St./World Trade Center (lines 1, R); Chambers St./Church St. (line A); Chambers St./W. Broadway (line 1).

Like much of the Downtown area, the World Trade Center is built on land reclaimed from the Hudson River. The foundations for the two towers are more than 66 ft/20 m deep. The earth from the excavation was placed behind a retaining wall to the west, creating a new landfill for the Battery Park City development.

The most famous of the six buildings built around the 6 acre/2.5 hectare plaza are the twin towers (1 and 2 World Trade Center). They are 1350 ft/409 m high (110 floors), each has 21,800 windows that, for security reasons, do not open and 1.25 acres/0.50 hectares of rental space per floor. The towers can sway more than 11 in/28 cm on their bases. The 50,000 employees and 80,000 daily visitors generate 50 tons of garbage every day. Finally, the center houses more than 500 companies and commercial organizations, including the customs offices for New York and New Jersey.

The two towers are the second highest buildings in the world, after the Sears Roebuck Building in Chicago. Like the Eiffel Tower and the Empire State Building, the World Trade Center has attracted its share of risktakers seeking publicity or adventure. The most famous is Philippe Petit, a Frenchman who crossed from one building to another on a tightrope. His signature can still be seen on the observation deck. In July 1975, an unemployed construction worker parachuted from the top of the towers to protest against world poverty. Mountaineer George Willig scaled one of the faces of the South Tower (2 World Trade Center) in May 1977, using equipment specially designed for the climb. When he reached the top, after 3.5 hours of climbing, he was arrested by police. The city ultimately dropped its claim for $250,000 in damages and interest with an out-of-court settlement involving a $1.10 fee (1¢ for each floor) and a promise not to repeat the offense.

There are interesting sculptures in the center, including *The Three Red Wings*, a 25-ton Calder stabile on the west side of the North Tower (1 World Trade Center). The **concourse level** has shopping facilities, a train station, subway stations and a parking lot. There are also several fast-food establishments *(open Mon-Fri 7am-7 pm, Sat 7am-5pm)*. The top floor of the **North Tower** is one of the most elegant restaurant locales in New York. **Windows on the World** comprises **The Hors D'Oeuvrerie, Cellar in the Sky** and **The Restaurant,** each with its own special character, food and service. This ensemble also has two bars, **City Lights Bar** and **Statue of Liberty Lounge.** The view over Manhattan is spectacular. The **South Tower** has a cafeteria and the observation deck on the 107th floor offers an unbeatable panorama** of the entire New York and New Jersey region *(open daily 9:30am-9:30pm)*.

▬ *BATTERY PARK CITY*

Map II, B3. — Subway: Cortlandt St./World Trade Center (line 1); Rector St./Greenwich St. (line 1).

This most recent Manhattan complex was designed by architects Cooper and Eckstut on 117 acres/47 hectares of landfill on the Hudson River. Nicknamed the 'Rockefeller Center of the 80s', the buildings will eventually provide 14,000 apartments and much-needed office space. Several groups of architects are involved and certain specifications have been imposed for the sake of coherence: the buildings must not exceed the stipulated limit, only brick and stone can be used for construction and all buildings must incorporate cornices at the top. Battery Park City will also be integrated into the traditional architecture of the Financial District. The roads will be extensions of existing streets and 30 % of the surface area will be reserved for public use. The 0.75 mi/1 km promenade along the Hudson already attracts many New Yorkers. The 10,000 steel elements of the former restaurant in the Eiffel Tower will be reconstructed in Battery Park City as a French restaurant. This new restaurant will offer an unobstructed view of another French import, the Statue of Liberty.

CIVIC CENTER — CHINATOWN — LITTLE ITALY

Map II, B-C2. — Subway: Brooklyn Bridge/City Hall (line 4); City Hall/Broadway (line R); Park Pl./Broadway (line 2).

Located between Chinatown to the north, the Brooklyn Bridge to the east and the Financial District to the south, the Civic Center and City Hall present a vast architectural diversity. Manhattan residents usually visit this area only to renew driver's licenses or perform jury duty. Yet this monumental neighbourhood is one of the most pleasant and open parts of the city.

St Paul's Chapel★, II, B2 (1766), the oldest church in Manhattan, is on Broadway between Fulton and Vesey Streets. It was modeled after St Martin's-in-the-Field's in London. A tall spire was added to the brownstone church in 1794; few changes have been made since. The bucolic cemetery surrounding the church is often crowded during the lunch hour with employees from nearby office buildings. The main entrance of the church faces away from Broadway, which didn't exist at the time of construction. George Washington's personal pew is still preserved inside the chapel.

City Hall Park, II, B2, is formed by the intersection of Broadway and Park Row to the north. These two streets have always been important communication and transportation links for New York. Park Row runs north-east, becomes the Bowery, crosses the East Side as Third Avenue and finally turns into the old Boston Post Road, which leads to New England. Broadway runs diagonally across Manhattan, crosses the Harlem River and continues in a straight line up to Albany, the state capital.

The elegant 790 ft/240 m **Woolworth Building★**, II, B2 (233 Broadway between Barclay Street and Park Place) was the world's tallest skyscraper from 1913 until 1929. The neo-Gothic style, inspired by London's Houses of Parliament, earned it the nickname 'Cathedral of Commerce'. The gargoyles represent frogs, bats and pelicans. It was constructed by self-made millionaire Frank W. Woolworth, originator of the five-and-ten stores. The company headquarters are still located in the original building, which is rare in New York. The main entrance is interesting, with gilded marble-covered walls and blue, green and gold mosaics on the ceiling. Tucked under the side corridors are sculpted figures representing Mr. Woolworth counting his money, the architect Cass Gilbert holding a model of the skyscraper in his hands and the building manager negotiating a rental. Mr. Woolworth's former offices on the 24th floor have been turned into a museum.

City Hall Park has been successively an apple orchard, a parade ground and a hanging ground. On July 9, 1776, the Declaration of Independence was read here in the presence of George Washington.

New York's animated Chinatown.

The park is today dotted with patriotic monuments. A plaque dedicated to journalist Joseph Pulitzer is a reminder that Park Row, which runs along the park, was the journalistic center of the city up to the late 19th century.

The elegant profile of **City Hall****, II, B2 (1802), in the middle of the park, was designed by Joseph-François Mangin and integrates the refinement of a French style with the Federal style. The current building replaced the Dutch City Hall, formerly on Pearl Street, and the British City Hall, on Wall Street.

Originally, the front and sides of the building were faced with Massachusetts marble. Nobody lived on the northern side at the time, so the city fathers decided to economize by using brownstone. In 1858, the dome, roof and upper floors burnt down during a fireworks display. Much later, in 1956, in disrepair due to faulty maintenance and weather damage, the façade had to be entirely renovated. The original marble was replaced with granite and brownstone.

City Hall has welcomed numerous visitors and celebrities to New York. Kings, princes, baseball players and astronauts have all been warmly received. More than 125,000 people came here to pay tribute to President Lincoln, lying in state after his assassination in 1865.

City Hall is a Classical building divided into three sections — a central body with a west and east wing. The granite base contrasts with the upper floors which are faced with brownstone. A wide staircase leads to the ground floor, now occupied by the Mayor's Office, at the end of the corridor to the left, and the City Hall press room, to the right. In the central lobby, a beautiful curved staircase with a wrought-iron handrail is surrounded by 10 Corinthian columns supporting an elegant dome. The staircase leads to the Governor's Room, an apartment which was formerly used by the state governor on visits to New York. It was transformed into a museum which contains portraits of American politicians painted by John Trumbull and antique furniture, including George Washington's desk.

The **Civic Center,** II, B2, comprises a host of buildings that deal with the administration of New York City.

The **Surrogates Court** (1911) or Hall of Records was built in the Beaux Arts style at 31 Chambers Street, to the north-east of City Hall. It houses all the official records for New York City residents. The sumptuous interior has been compared to the hall of the Garnier Palace in Paris.

The enormous **Municipal Building,** II, B2, on the other side of Lafayette Street, is one of the landmarks of the Civic Center. Constructed in 1914 by the architectural firm of McKim, Mead and White, this building houses 40 floors of office space. The massive white building straddles Chambers Street and the southern wing is supported by huge pillars which delimit a vast pedestrian area. A gold-leafed statue of a female figure, *Civic Fame*, gleams at the top of the building.

Police Plaza and **Police Headquarters,** II, B-C2, designed by the Gruzen firm, were constructed behind the Municipal Building in 1973.

The **US Courthouse,** II, B2(40 Centre Street), headquarters of the federal district court, was constructed in 1936 according to a design by Cass Gilbert, architect of the Woolworth Building. It appears to be a Classical temple topped with a 32-storey tower. Another Classical building, the **New York County Courthouse,** stands at 60 Centre Street. This grandiose edifice was designed in 1912; construction wasn't completed until 1926. The enormous exterior staircase is 105 ft/32 m wide.

Foley Square, II, B2, the pivot of the Civic Center, is formed by the intersection of Centre, Pearl, Duane and Lafayette Streets. During the 18th century, this spot was still a 66 ft/20 m deep pond called 'The Collect'. The pond was drained in the early 19th century and, by 1840, the area had become the Five Points slum, one of the most sordid in New York.

The **Criminal Courts Buildings,** II, B1-2 (1939), at 100 Centre Street, between Leonard and White Streets, incorporates an Art Deco design with four large blocks and towers. The north tower was occupied by the legendary municipal prison, The Tombs, until 1974. This had an overhead passageway to the courthouse called the 'Bridge of Sighs' after the famous Venetian landmark.

▬ CHINATOWN*

Map II, C1-2, D1. — Subway: Canal St./Centre St. (line J); Canal St./Broadway (lines D, N).

Chinatown is an active, bustling neighbourhood. To visitors, it seems to be a world of its own. With hundreds of restaurants, grocery stores and shops, this area offers a unique ambience, especially on Sundays when the neighbourhood is particularly crowded and lively. A great many of New York's 150,000 Chinese live in this area. Until the mid-20th century, the Chinese community was concentrated in the district bordered by Canal Street to the north and the Bowery to the east. Today, Chinatown has grown well beyond this area.

The community is a flourishing one, with eight daily newspapers. The ideal time to visit is during Chinese New Year, when the neighbourhood celebrates with a parade, complete with dragons, firecrackers and fireworks, held on the first full moon following January 21.

The most authentic area of Chinatown extends to the east of the Bowery. There are fewer tourists on East Broadway and Catherine Street and the daily life of the area's residents is less hectic.

Worth Street leads directly from Foley Square to **Chatham Square,** II, C2. This was a very elegant area in the early 19th century but, by the 1840s, the affluent homes were gradually replaced by lower-class housing for the many immigrants. This intersection is today one of Chinatown's main landmarks. The arch with a pagoda roof located in the center of the square is a monument to the memory of Americans of Chinese descent who died in combat. The large pagoda-shaped building on the square is a branch of the Manhattan Savings Bank.

South of Chatham Square on St James Place is the oldest Sephardic cemetery in the city, with a gravestone dating from 1683. The restaurants, cinemas and businesses east of Chatham Square on East Broadway, II, C-D1, attract large crowds. A Chinese pharmacy at n° 26 is a source of hard-to-find remedies which include ginseng, starfish, dried deer antlers and more traditional herbal medicines.

The **Bowery,** II, C1-2, starts north of Chatham Square. The oldest pharmacy in New York, **Olliffe's Apothecary** at n° 6, dates from 1803. At n° 18 of the same street, the **Edward Mooney House,** II, C2 (1785), on the corner of Pell Street, is one of the oldest residences in New York City, dating from the beginning of the Federal style.

Pell Street leads to **Mott Street,** Chinatown's main street, lined with restaurants and shops. The **Chinese Museum,** II, C2 *(open daily 10am-6pm)*, is located at n° 8. The Catholic **Church of the Transfiguration** at n° 25 dates from 1801.

LITTLE ITALY

Map II, BC1. — Subway: Prince St./Broadway (lines N, R).

Mulberry Street, to the west of Mott Street, was once the main street of Little Italy. Before the war, the neighbourhood had more than 150,000 residents of Italian descent; today there are no more than several thousand. As they became more affluent, many Italians left the traditional neighbourhood and moved to the suburbs. Two festivals revive the spirit of Little Italy, the **Feast of Saint Anthony of Padua** (first half of June) and the **Feast of San Gennaro** (around September 19). These festivals are worth a visit. Food stands, carnival rides and games attract thousands of New Yorkers. Walk up Mulberry Street and turn on Grand Street to reach Centre Street. The former **Police Headquarters,** II, B1, a handsome building constructed in 1909, is located at n° 240. The building was divided into apartments after the police moved to newer quarters in 1973.

Old St Patrick's Cathedral, II, C1, on Mulberry and Prince Streets, is the predecessor of the Fifth Avenue cathedral. Constructed in 1815 by French architect Joseph-François Mangin, it was the main church for New York's Catholics until 1879. It marked the birth of the Gothic Revival style in the United States. **St Michael's Chapel,** II, C1, at 266 Mulberry Street was constructed in 1850 according to James Renwick's plans.

The **Puck Building,** II, BC1 (1885), on the corner of Mulberry and Houston Streets, is a fine example of the Romanesque Revival. It is in very good condition and originally housed the offices of the famous satirical magazine *Puck*. The gilded and tophatted figure of Puck overlooks the main entrance of the building on Lafayette Street.

SOHO AND TRIBECA

▬ SOHO ★★

Map II, B1. — Subway: Canal St./Broadway (lines D, N, R); Canal St./Ave. of the Americas (lines A, C, E). Bus: lines 1, 6.

SoHo is bordered by Canal Street, Broadway, Sullivan Street and Houston Street (SoHo is an acronym for 'South of Houston'). The architecture here is essentially industrial; many warehouses and industrial workshops were renovated in the 1960s by artists seeking light, space and inexpensive rents. Uptown galleries and fashionable shops followed artists to the area, driving rents up and transforming SoHo into an international contemporary art center.

During the Dutch occupation of New York, SoHo was a hilly area separated from the southern tip of Manhattan by a stream near present-day Canal Street. Divided into parcels after Independence, SoHo became the city's most populated area by 1825. In the 1840s and 1850s, prestigious stores and luxury hotels lined Broadway. Starting in 1860, industry began to move into the area. Most of the present-day cast-iron industrial buildings were constructed in the late 19th century, transforming SoHo from a desirable residential neighbourhood into a grim industrial district. Sweat shops on the upper floors of these buildings employed immigrants who often worked more than 12 hours a day. In the 1950s, the industrial buildings no longer met the demands of modern technology and businesses began to leave the area. The city contemplated tearing down some of the warehouses to make way for a highway linking the East River to the Hudson. Fortunately, artists had already formed associations to purchase and renovate the vast unoccupied lofts. In 1979, to prevent further destruction by developers, residents successfully petitioned to have the area designated a historic district.

Cast-iron

SoHo has the highest concentration of cast-iron buildings in the world. This construction process was developed in England in the 18th century, then perfected in the early 19th century. The metal structure supports the weight of the building, allowing the construction of lighter buildings, with vast open spaces and large windows. This new technique was the precursor to today's prefabricated buildings; certain construction elements could be mass-produced, including columns, windows and façades. The building owner simply used a catalogue to choose a warehouse façade, which provided a selection of Renaissance or Greek Revival styles in imitation stone. In the United States, James Bogardus perfected the cast-iron technique and added considerably to the technology which led to the development of the skyscraper. The oldest remaining cast-iron façade graces the Haughwout Building, constructed in 1856 at 488 Broadway. The most recent, at 550 Broadway, dates from 1901.

On SoHo's West Broadway, modern sculpture adorns the entrance to one of the fashionable boutiques.

The 1970s were SoHo's most exciting years. Artists, fledgling gallery owners and young shop owners formed a coherent community. Dozens of exhibitions, theater performances and avant-garde movies were presented every month, attracting people from all over the city. SoHo still is an art center, but the galleries are now well established, drawing a moneyed clientele. The streets are crowded on weekend afternoons with visitors enjoying the galleries, shops and charming restaurants.

Cast-iron buildings are scattered throughout SoHo. This itinerary outlines a tour of the most representative. Guided tours are available from the **Friends of Cast-Iron Architecture**, 235 E. 87th St.

Go north on Broadway at Canal Street. The **Roosevelt Building**, II, B1 (1873) at n° 480 was designed by Richard Morris Hunt, a favourite architect of many Fifth Avenue millionaires and architect of the Metropolitan Museum of Art and the pedestal of the Statue of Liberty. The narrow columns on the façade left enough space for wide windows, which were essential at a time when there was no electric lighting. The original façade was multi-coloured.

The magnificient **Haughwout Building** at n° 488 (corner of Broome Street) was constructed in 1856. The harmonious façade was modeled after the Sansovino St Mark Library in Venice. This building was one of the first in New York to use a cast-iron frame-supporting structure, pioneering a technique later used for modern-day skyscrapers. The windows and frame are repeated 92 times on the two façades. The building, designed by John P. Gaynor for a major glass and porcelain importer, included an innovation for the time: the first passenger elevator, invented by Mr. Otis. In its current state of disrepair, it is difficult to imagine that when inaugurated, the façade was painted a beautiful cream colour.

The vestiges of the legendary **Hotel St Nicholas** stand at 521-523 Broadway, on the corner of Broadway and Spring Street. During the 19th century, this hotel occupied the entire block south of Spring Street and was the center of the elegant residential neighbourhood between Canal and Houston Streets. During its inauguration in 1854, the luxurious carpets, chandeliers, mirrors and porcelains made a considerable impression on New York journalists.

The charming **Little Singer Building** (1904) at n° 561-563, designed by Ernest Flagg, was so named because a larger, more imposing Singer Building already existed in the Financial District. Located on the corner of Prince Street and Broadway, the building creatively uses a profusion of wrought-iron and ceramic elements.

Prince Street, II, BC1, is one of the main commercial streets of SoHo. An amusing trompe l'œil mural at **112 Prince Street** (on the corner of Greene Street), painted by Richard Hass in 1974, reproduces a cast-iron façade on a blank wall. The former warehouses at n° 113 to n° 121 are now occupied by typical SoHo shops, including health food restaurants, handmade clothes and jewelry stores.

Prince Street leads to **West Broadway,** II, B1, SoHo's main street, which is lined with many internationally famous art galleries. Saturday afternoon is the busiest day for browsing. Two of the most influential SoHo galleries are in the building at **420 West Broadway**: Sonnabend and Castelli.

Spring Street leads to **Greene Street,** II, B1, a well-preserved street that gives you a good idea of SoHo's appearance in the industrial 19th century. Both sides of the street are lined with beautiful cast-iron buildings. The granite paving stones are a vestige from the 1860s when granite was used on the most widely traveled New York streets.

The building known as the **King of Greene Street** stands at 72 Greene Street. Constructed in 1872 by Isaac J. Duckworth, it is actually two structures designed as one, joined by a central pedimented portico with a pedimented cornice on the roof. The monogram on the entrance belongs to the former owners, the Gardner Colby Company.

Go south on Greene Street to **Broome Street*,** II, B1. It was one of the main New York thoroughfares in the 19th century. The **Gunther Building** on the corner of Broome and Greene Streets is a former warehouse constructed in 1872 for furrier William H. Gunther. The handsome building is remarkable for its curved windows and restrained style.

The enormous warehouse on the corner of Greene and Grand Streets was constructed in 1873. The upper floors of the two buildings at 91-93 Grand Street were used as housing for workers, while the ground floor was reserved for business purposes. The cast-iron façade was designed to imitate stone and even reproduces the grooves of stone joints.

Take Greene Street to the south to reach the **Queen of Greene Street** at n° 28-30. This building, constructed by Isaac F. Duckworth in 1872, is one of SoHo's architectural treasures. The wealth of details, the mansard roof and the blue façade attract visitors to the neighbourhood. Another

Duckworth building constructed the following year at n° 32 is also admirable, despite the unsightly fire escape added later. This section of Greene Street and adjacent streets were notorious for their brothels. Sailors frequented the houses on the south end of the street, while to the north, similar establishments catered to a wealthier clientele.

There is a succession of commercial buildings on Canal Street towards the East River. The buildings at **313 to 327 Canal Street** were originally Federal-style houses constructed in 1825. When the residential aspect of the neighbourhood began to change, these homes were converted into businesses, and one or two floors were often added.

▬ *TRIBECA***

Map II, B1-2. — Subway: Canal St./Varick St. (line 1).

Canal Street marks the boundary between SoHo and Tribeca. In the early 19th century, this cross street was a sewage and storm drain. The canal was lined with trees and New Yorkers enjoyed walking along its banks. The canal was filled in in 1829 and the present-day road laid out. The neighbouring area quickly became residential and Federal-style houses were constructed.

Today, Canal Street links the Manhattan Bridge to the Holland Tunnel. The east end near the Bowery was the diamond center of New York until this activity moved to 47th Street. The west end of Canal Street, between Broadway and Avenue of the Americas, is lined with inexpensive shops selling used hardware. Several weekend flea markets are held on lots bordering the street.

Tribeca is an acronym for, TRiangle BElow CAnal Street. Neighbour to SoHo, it was the logical next area in Manhattan for artists seeking space and moderate rents once SoHo became too expensive in the 1970s. Now increasingly fashionable, it was originally pioneered by young artists who converted the industrial buildings into residential lofts. Tribeca is no longer limited to its original boundaries of Canal Street, Hudson Street and West Broadway. It extends as far south as the World Trade Center and west to West Street.

Tribeca is the SoHo of the 1980s, an artistic neighbourhood par excellence. Its new residents have been called urban pioneers as they are colonizing an essentially industrial neighbourhood. Many of the most popular new restaurants, nightclubs and art galleries are in Tribeca. They attract a heady mixture of young artists and affluent Uptown New Yorkers.

The land which corresponds to modern-day Tribeca originally belonged to Trinity Church. In the early 19th century, the church built private brick houses and laid out two parks. In the 1850s, business and industry took over the neighbourhood and cast-iron buildings were constructed.

The new steamboat wharves were built on the Hudson and the corresponding maritime activity was centered in this area. In the 1870s, publishing and garment industries clustered near Broadway. The Washington Street Market near the wharves continued to expand in the area. A slow decline began in the early 20th century, stopped only with the construction of the Independence Plaza development in the 1970s and the influx of artists who began to renovate the buildings.

An example of an industrial building transformed into a residential loft can been seen at **395 Broadway,** II, B1, on the corner of Walker Street. The completely renovated building incorporates a false cornice.

To the west of Broadway at 49 White Street is the **Civic Center Synagogue,** II, B1. The amusing, curved marble façade clashes with the adjacent industrial buildings.

Take Broadway south to reach the corner of **Worth Street** where the imposing **AT&T Long Lines Building,** II, B2, resembles an immense granite sculpture. This enormous tower has windows only at the roof level.

In the years following the Civil War, Worth Street became the main New York garment district. Since World War I, this activity has been centered on Seventh Avenue. There is a good view of Uptown Manhattan from the corner of Worth Street and Broadway. The Gothic Revival spire in the background belongs to **Grace Church** on 10th Street. This section of Broadway, called LowBro (an acronym for LOWer BROadway), is lined with surplus clothing shops.

Continue south on Broadway to **Thomas Street,** II, B2. A charming 1875 building at nº 8 has a cast-iron ground floor and a façade mixing Romanesque and Gothic Revival elements.

The **New York City Fire Department Museum,** II, B2, at 100 Duane Street, exhibits fire engines, engravings and documents describing the history of the major New York fires.

Duane Street leads to Church Street, center of the discount shops. Clothes, shoes, appliances and thousands of other items are available at unbeatable prices. Continue to the west on Duane Street to **West Broadway,** II, B2, which starts at the World Trade Center in the south and runs north to Washington Square Park. At **147 West Broadway** is the restrained façade of a cast-iron building constructed in 1869 by an architect who designed a meticulous imitation of a stone-finished building.

Duane Park, II, B2, on the corner of Duane and Hudson Streets, was laid out by Trinity Church in the 19th century. It is now surrounded by handsome 19th- and 20th-century industrial buildings. The co-existence of dairy wholesalers and residential lofts represents Tribeca's unique identity. There are several attractive buildings around the park: **65 Duane Street** has an interesting red brick façade, **nº 171** incorporates a remarkable cast-iron façade attached to a 19th-century house; a beautiful Romanesque building stands at **nº 163**. The façade of the Art Deco **Western Union Building,** II, B2 (1930) to the north of the park at 60 Hudson Street, includes 19 different shades of brick.

Greenwich Street, II, B1-2, and the modern towers of **Independence Plaza** are located to the west of Duane Park. Constructed in 1975, these buildings occupy the former site of the Washington Market. In the 1960s, the city decided to move the market to Hunts Point in the Bronx and construct this large residential complex.

Greenwich Street runs by Jay Street and leads to **Harrison Street** which has six handsome 19th-century townhouses, II, B2. They were moved here brick by brick and reconstructed according to the original plans.

The attractive red brick and granite façade of the **New York Mercantile Exchange** (1886) stands at 6 Harrison Street. To the north, the section of **White Street,** II, B1, between Broadway and Avenue of the Americas offers a representative sample of Tribeca building styles. Note the façades at **nº 2** and **nº 10** (constructed in 1908 and 1869, respectively) and the mansard roof at **nº 17**. Continue north to Canal Street.

THE VILLAGE

Map III, ABCD2-3. — Subway: W. 4th St./Washington Sq. (lines A, C, E, F, S); Christopher St./Sheridan Sq. (line 1); 8th St./Broadway (lines N, R). Bus: lines 2, 3, 6.

The Village covers the area stretching from East River Drive to the piers on the Hudson River to the west, and from Houston Street north to 14th Street. There are two distinct villages within this perimeter; the most famous is Greenwich Village, which includes the West Village and the South Village and is noted for its literary and artistic associations, and the other is the East Village, once the haven for Jewish immigrants from Central and Eastern Europe and, now, an increasingly trendy area with shops, galleries and a variety of ethnic restaurants.

▬ GREENWICH VILLAGE***

Map II, ABC2-3.

Nestled between Broadway and the Hudson, Greenwich Village has preserved its distinctive character. A friendly, small-town atmosphere still prevails along the streets lined with trees and brownstones. The population, which consists mainly of middle-class families, intellectuals and artists, is proud of the unique Village lifestyle.

Greenwich Village is also a diverse neighbourhood. The incessant activity in Washington Square contrasts with the calm of Commerce, Bedford and Grove Streets. Jazz clubs alternate with tea rooms and quiet cafés. The townhouses and churches near Fifth Avenue evoke the splendour of the 19th century, when this was one of the city's most distinguished areas. The former slums, warehouses and factories which have been transformed into apartments are a reminder that Greenwich Village was also an immigrant neighbourhood.

When the Dutch settled on the southern tip of the island in the 17th century, Greenwich Village was still a wooded area inhabited by Sapokanikan Indians. The earth was fertile and the newly arrived colonists soon drove out the Indians and began to cultivate the land.

In the late 17th century, official documents from the British colonial period name the site Greenwich, undoubtedly in honour of its namesake near London. This completely rural area then belonged to a handful of landowners.

Greenwich Village became part of New York as the city moved steadily north. Some of the large estates were divided into lots in the late 18th century. The Village's population increased further as residents fled Uptown to escape the successive epidemics of yellow fever and smallpox near the port. In 1881, the city drew up a zoning plan which called for the hills in the neighbourhood to be flattened. The grid system included Greenwich Village but new residents ignored the plan, building homes along well-used paths, which explains the somewhat meandering street pattern in the neighbourhood.

The population of the village quadrupled between 1820 and 1850. In the 1830s, the wealthiest New York families built mansions on Washington Square, which was transformed into a public park in 1828. This new, elegant neighbourhood extended to Fifth Avenue and the adjacent streets, from University Place to Sixth Avenue (Avenue of the Americas). Henry James was born in one of these private residences on the north edge of the square. When business and industry began to move northward, the most affluent families left Greenwich Village to build homes even farther Uptown, leaving behind middle-class families and craftsmen. Most of the private homes were converted into apartments. Several famous writers lived in apartments in the Village, including James Fenimore Cooper, Edgar Allan Poe, Walt Whitman and Mark Twain.

Warehouses and factories moved to the Hudson and businesses were set up to the east and north. Greenwich Village was therefore able to preserve its residential character. The massive immigration in the late 19th century changed the face of the district, as new arrivals sought housing in this area. In 1980, Italian families and a second wave of Irish immigrants settled near Washington Square. By 1910, the transformation of the neighbourhood was complete. Slum housing and poverty had overtaken the former affluent elegance. Due to low rents, relative isolation and traditional tranquility, Greenwich Village became a haven for young artists and bohemians seeking to escape the strict morality of early 20th-century American society.

Pacifist magazines were created and published in the district and avant-garde theaters flourished. Clubs like the 'A' Club and the Liberal Club were formed, calling for profound social reforms. Eugene O'Neill and Edna St Vincent Millay presented their first plays and Bette Davis began her career in Greenwich Village. The neighbourhood was home to many other writers, including Theodore Dreiser, Sherwood Anderson, Hart Crane, John Dos Passos and e.e. cummings.

Greenwich Village underwent another transformation after World War I. Its isolation from New York's incessant traffic ended when Seventh Avenue cut through the area and Sixth Avenue was extended south of Carmine Street. The Village was linked to the rest of the city with a connection between the IRT and IND subway lines. Nevertheless, the Village continued to attract artists and non-conformists. Painter Edward Hopper and, later, Jackson Pollock lived in the Village, along with writers Mary McCarthy, Edward Albee, Allen Ginsberg, Jack Kerouac and William Styron.

Today, the Greenwich Village literary clubs are closed, the rents are among the highest in the city and tourists crowd the small streets. Real estate promoters are desperately trying to tear down houses and replace them with apartment buildings. The area represents an enormous source of revenue for the three main property owners, Sailor's Snug Harbor, Trinity Church and New York University, and the neighbourhood associations are justifiably worried about the future of the Village.

Developers have not yet been able to move into this area and Greenwich Village so far has avoided the unfortunate fate of other parts of New York City. Every type of architecture in New York is represented in Greenwich Village, and its environment is different from anywhere else in New York. The streets are quieter, the lifestyle slightly slower. People tend to be friendlier and most stores and restaurants have a regular clientele. In other words, Greenwich Village is an exception in the frenetic world of New York City.

Eighth Street, II, BC3, between Broadway and Avenue of the Americas, is the main street through Greenwich Village. It is lined with book and record shops, clothing stores and some souvenir and poster shops for tourists. There are also a large number of shoe stores.

The **Eighth Street Playhouse,** at 52 W. 8th Street, now a cinema featuring experimental and artistic films, was created in 1920 as a showcase of technological innovations. Every weekend for the late-night screening of *Rocky Horror Picture Show* (J. Sharman, 1975) fans converge on the playhouse wearing fantastic costumes and makeup.

Picturesque **MacDougal Alley,** III, B3, leads off from the west side of MacDougal Street. In the 19th century, the homes on this private street were stables for the private mansions on Eighth Street and Washington Square. Artists moved into the homes in the 1920s and 1930s and transformed them into studios and apartments. Gertrude Vanderbilt Whitney, heiress, sculptor and founder of the Whitney Museum of American Art, occupied a studio at **Washington Square Park★,** III, BC3

Washington Square Park is the largest public park in southern Manhattan and is the heart of Greenwich Village. Once marshland, it was drained and farmed by freed slaves. It then became a hanging ground and a potter's field and was finally converted into a parade ground. The park was laid out in 1828 and became a highly desirable residential location for affluent New Yorkers.

New York University, III, C3, moved to the east side of the park in 1837. Soon after, the well-to-do families moved away and their beautiful homes were demolished. In the 1950s, after a long period of disuse, the park was virtually off-limits to pedestrians and was used as a turning area for buses. One city planner even proposed extending Fifth Avenue through the park. Fortunately, this plan was nerver carried out. During warm weather, the park is a popular spot for joggers, musicians and open-air art exhibits. A colourful crowd of weekend visitors fills the park to listen to the public speakers, watch chess players or applaud the skill of young skateboarders or roller skaters. There are also, unfortunately, many drug dealers and users.

The **Washington Arch,** III, B3 (1892) to the north of the park was designed by Stanford White to commemorate the centennial of George Washington's investiture (1889). The original wooden arch was constructed from donations made my residents. The tribute was so popular that a 82 ft/25 m high marble arch was then erected at the park entrance, marking the beginning of Fifth Avenue. The frieze has 13 stars representing the 13 original colonies and 42 stars for the number of states at the time of construction. On the east pier is a sculpted group, *Washington in War;* on the west pier is *Washington in Peace.* This second sculpture is by Alexander Stirling Calder, father of the famous sculptor, Alexander Calder.

To the south of the park lies the pool of the original fountain. Empty for many years, it now serves as a podium for the dozens of improvisational comedians, musicians and speakers entertaining the diverse crowd.

The former private homes on **Washington Square North,** III, BC3, are a good example of what New York City could have accomplished if it had adopted a coherent program of city planning determining architectural styles and building façades. In the 19th century, Washington Square was surrounded on three sides by rows of similar houses; only a few remain today. Note the design of the basement accesses, the stone steps, columned porches and beautifully worked wrought iron. The upper windows often have balconies.

Two Greek Revival townhouses stand at n° 21 and n° 23 on the west end of the street. The house at n° 20 was originally a Federal-style country house constructed in 1820. The house Henry James was born in, at n° 18, served as a model for his novel *Washington Square.* It was demolished to make room for an apartment building. On the east end of the same street is a series of houses called **The Row.** Writers Edith Wharton and John Dos Passos lived here. Dos Passos wrote *Manhattan Transfer* while living at n° 3.

The main building of **New York University** (NYU), III, C3, stands at the east of the park, between Waverly Place and Washington Place. Constructed in 1894, this building houses the administration offices. Founded in 1831 to provide an alternative to the conservative and religious education provided by Columbia University, NYU is today the largest private university in the city with more than 40,000 students. Only 13 departments are located on the Washington Square Park campus; the rest are scattered throughout New York City. The **Grey Art Gallery** occupies the first floor of the main building *(entrance at 33 Washington Place, open Tues-Sat 10am-5pm, Wed 10am-8pm)*. This university-run gallery presents temporary exhibitions.

The infamous **Brown Building** (1900) next door was declared fireproof during its inauguration. In 1911, a fire broke out on the 10th floor in the Triangle Shirtwaist Company and 146 women perished either in the blaze or by jumping out of the windows. A plaque on the entrance commemorates the tragic accident.

The **Elmer Holmes Bobst Library,** the main NYU library, occupies the south east corner of Washington Square. The enormous red sandstone building was constructed in 1972 by architect Philip Johnson. Inside, the stacks and different reading rooms are organized around an interior court or atrium rising 164 ft/50 m high. On Washington Square South are the other modern NYU buildings, including the **Loeb Student Center** and the **Holy Trinity Chapel.**

The **Judson Memorial Church,** III, B3 (1892), with its beautiful mixed Romanesque Revival and Renaissance façade, was designed by McKim, Mead and White. With amber-coloured brick and ceramic and marble decoration, it is a classic example of this purely New York style. Inside are admirable stained-glass windows by John La Farge. The church is also the home of the Poet's Theater, one of the first Off-Off Broadway theaters devoted to poetry and modern dance. The beautiful tower is now used as NYU student housing.

The **Hagop Kevorkian Center** (1973) to the west of the church was designed by Philip Johnson and Richard Foster to house the NYU Near Eastern Studies Center. The entrance is a replica of the inside courtyard of an 18th-century Near Eastern house. The prestigious **Vanderbilt Law School** has occupied the next block between Sullivan and MacDougal Streets since 1951.

Tireless chess and checker players pass their time in marathon games on the south-west corner of Washington Square, attracting large groups of onlookers.

There is a charming street, **Washington Mews,** III, C3, across the park and to the right off Fifth Avenue. Former stables and gardens were converted into studios and housing by artists in the 1930s. Virtually all the houses are now occupied by NYU.

The elegant apartment building at **One Fifth Avenue,** III, B3 (1929), occupies the corner of Fifth Avenue and Eighth Street. The Art Deco building also incorporates Gothic Revival arches and gargoyles. The beautiful row of houses from n° 6 to n° 26 were originally private Greek Revival homes constructed in the 19th century and imaginatively restored in 1916.

During the 19th century, luxurious private homes lined this part of Fifth Avenue and adjacent streets. The **Lockwood de Forest House** (1887) at 7 E. 10th Street incorporates sculpted teak elements on the façade.

Many of the churches built in the 1800s are architecturally interesting. The **Church of the Ascension,** III, BC3 (1841), on the corner of Fifth Avenue and 10th Street, was designed by Richard Upjohn, architect of Trinity Church on Wall Street. It is a good example of the Gothic Revival style and includes stained glass by John La Farge and a marble bas-relief by Augustus Saint-Gaudens. The Rectory behind the church was one of the first brownstone buildings in New York.

Between 11th and 12th Streets, the **First Presbyterian Church** (1846) is an interesting building that is only visible from three sides. This Gothic

Washington Square, a popular meeting place for students, musicians and weekend visitors to Greenwich Village.

Revival church was inspired by the Holy Saviour Church in Bath (England) and the bell tower is a replica of the Magdalen College tower at Oxford.

The elegant **headquarters of the Salmagundi Club** opposite the church at 47 Fifth Avenue is the last of the brownstones which once lined the avenue. Coal baron Irad Hawley had it built for his private use in 1853. The interior has two beautiful adjacent rooms with decorated ceilings and superb chandeliers. The Salmagundi Club, founded in 1870, included among its members the painter John La Farge, jeweler Louis Tiffany and architect Stanford White. The origin of the club's name is unknown. One suggestion is that it is a deformation of the French work 'salmigondis', meaning 'hotchpotch'.

The **Lone Star Cafe,** III, BC2 , at 61 Fifth Avenue, on the corner of 13th Street, is famous for its excellent country-and-western music and Tex-Mex cuisine. At n° 66, the highly reputed **Parsons School of Design** provides courses in visual arts, fashion design, graphic and fine arts.

Former townhouses line the side streets of the Village between Fifth Avenue and Avenue of the Americas. From W. 9th Street to the north, the neighbourhood becomes more residential and calm. There is a beautiful row of Greek Revival townhouses on **W. 11th Street.**

The townhouse at **18 W. 11th Street,** III, B3, became famous after it was used as a hideout by the Weathermen, a radical group formed during the 1960s. In 1970, the group were making bombs in the basement when one accidentally blew up, killing three people. The building was later reconstructed according to a Greek Revival design.

In 1805, the Second Cemetery of the Spanish and Portuguese Synagogue was established on W. 11th Street when the first cemetery in Chatham Square became too small. Opposite stands the **New School for Social Research,** III, B3. Since its creation in 1919 as an adult educational center, this university has been in the forefront of social and cultural research. During World War II, it became the 'University in Exile' for many intellectuals fleeing Nazi Germany. Designed by Joseph Urban, it is one of the first examples of the Bauhaus style in New York. The restrained effect of the black-and-white brick and the horizontal windows reflects the functionalism of this style. The curious oval amphitheatre deserves a visit.

Cross to the west side of Avenue of the Americas to **Milligan Place,** III, B3, between 10th and 11th Streets. The houses on this charming street were constructed in 1850 around a triangular courtyard. They were originally used as housing for Basque waiters who worked in an elegant neighbourhood hotel and for French craftsmen in the luxury millinery trade. On the corner of Avenue of the Americas and 10th Street is the remarkable **Jefferson Market Courthouse** (1877). The towers, turrets and stained-glass windows of this curious Victorian Gothic building dominate the traffic and hubbub of the surrounding neighbourhood. Built on the site of the main 19th century markets, it formerly housed a courthouse. The bell tower was designed as a fire alarm and the former women's prison is now a garden. The Jefferson Market Courthouse is today a branch of the New York Public Library. The garden is maintained by neighbourhood volunteers.

Patchin Place, on the north side of 10th Street, has no more than 10 houses dating from 1849, but over the years they have attracted such famous writers as Theodore Dreiser, Eugene O'Neill and John Reed. Poet e.e. cummings so appreciated the serenity of Patchin Place that he spent the last 40 years of this life at n° **4.**

West Village, III, B3

Christopher Street, parallel to W. 10th Street, is the center of the large New York gay community. Homosexual liberation began here in the 1960s. The symbol of the gay rights movements was 'The Stonewall', a gay bar which was the scene of a confrontation between police and New York homosexuals. National demonstrations followed and the drive for homosexual rights was launched.

Gay Street, III, B3, off Christopher Street to the left, is lined with old Federal-style houses. The street name dates back many years, long before New York homosexuals moved to the area. In the 19th century, the street was occupied by immigrant families; in the 1920s, it became a sort of miniature ghetto for Blacks from the South. During Prohibition, from 1920 to 1933, this tiny street had some of New York's most famous speakeasies.

The **Northern Dispensary,** III, B3 (1831) at the intersection of Christopher Street and Waverly Place, is the only public Federal-style building in New York. A second floor added to the initial structure in 1854 is clearly visible. The triangular form of the building gives it one façade on two streets (Christopher Street and Grove Street) and two other façades on a single street (Waverly Place). In 1837, an unknown resident of the neighbourhood, Edgar Allan Poe, was treated at the dispensary for a tenacious flu.

Sheridan Square Park, III, B3, to the west has a statue of General Philip Sheridan, commander-in-chief of the Union Army, famous for his declaration 'the only good Indian is a dead Indian'. The famous **Lion's Head Pub** to the right of the park at n° 59 is a favourite meeting place for New York politicians, journalists and writers.

Grove Street, III, B3, is a quiet residential street. There is a charming wooden house constructed in 1822 at **n° 17** on the corner of Bedford and Hudson Streets. The ivy-covered 19th-century houses between Bedford and Hudson Streets are particularly charming. **Grove Court** at n° 10 is a lovely alcove of tranquility with brick houses dating from 1853. At the time, they were inhabited by working families, who have long since been replaced by wealthy residents.

Cross Hudson Street to reach **St Luke's in the Fields** (1822), a rural church which belonged to the Trinity Church parish. It is the third oldest church in Manhattan, although the current building is new. A peaceful garden surrounds the church. The entrance is near the corner of Barrow Street.

Barrow Street to the east leads to **Commerce Street**, III, B3. This small street has two elegant houses at **n° 39** and **n° 41** called the Twin Sisters. According to legend, they were built by a father for his two constantly bickering daughters.

The **Cherry Lane Theater** at 38 Grove Street has been a famous Off-Broadway theater since 1924, when it was founded in a former brewery. To the north, at 86 Bedford Street, is the former speakeasy, **Chumley's**. During Prohibition it was frequented by many neighbourhood artists and intellectuals. As a reminder of its checkered past, the restaurant still has not posted a sign on either of the two 'clandestine' entrances on Bedford and Barrow Streets.

Lovely homes line Bedford Street to the south. The house at **n° 75 1/2** dates from 1873 and is only 9.5 ft/3 m wide. It is the narrowest building in Manhattan.

There are several beautiful 19th century houses to the west on **Morton Street,** including, at **n° 59,** an interesting Federal-style entrance. Follow Hudson Street to **St Luke's Place,** one of Manhattan's most prestigious streets, with elegant Greek Revival townhouses from the 1850s. Many artists have lived in these houses, including Theodore Dreiser, Sherwood Anderson and Marianne Moore. The two lanterns at **n° 6** mark the former residence of James J. Walker, a well-known New York mayor.

Take Leroy Street to Bleecker Street, which crosses Avenue of the Americas and leads to the South Village.

South Village, III, BC3

Bleecker Street is the main street in this section of Greenwich Village. It is lined with nightclubs, theaters and cafés. **Minetta Street**, III, B3, at the north-east corner of Bleecker Street and Avenue of the Americas, follows the course of the old Minetta stream which ran through the Village to the Hudson.

The section of MacDougal Street between Bleecker and 3rd Streets was the heart of New York bohemia in the early 20th century. The **Minetta Tavern** at n° 113 was frequented by illustrious Village residents. The **Liberal Club** at n° 137 was a meeting place for social reformers. Eugene O'Neill and Edna St Vincent Millay presented their first plays in the famous **Provincetown Playhouse** at n° 133.

The **Borgia** and **Figaro** cafés, at 185 and 186 Bleecker Street, were landmarks during the 1950s beatnik era.

Bleecker Street then crosses LaGuardia Place to Broadway, which marks the boundary between Greenwich Village and the East Village.

▬ EAST VILLAGE*

Map III, CD3.

In this rapidly changing neighbourhood, residents range from Bowery vagrants, punks at St Mark's Place, Hell's Angels on 3rd Street to young upcoming artists, young professionals and Ukrainian and Puerto Rican immigrants. The East Village is one of the rare areas in New York which is still seeking an identity among the trendy cafés, art galleries, avant-garde theaters and nightclubs.

Except for **Astor Place**, the East Village has never been a fashionable area. The elevated subway on Third Avenue, constructed in the late 19th century, disqualified it immediately as a desirable residential neighbourhood. This part of the Lower East Side was home to generations of German, Jewish, Russian and, more recently, Puerto Rican immigrants. In the 1960s, it became a hippie enclave. St Mark's Place was invaded by psychedelic shops and became a counterculture landmark. The **Fillmore East Theater** on Second Avenue presented legendary musicians of the era, including Janis Joplin, the Jefferson Airplane and Jimi Hendrix.

Over the last two decades as SoHo and Tribeca have become almost as expensive as Greenwich Village, the East Village is the last area still within economic reach for New York's struggling artistic community. Tenement housing has been taken over, restored, renovated and repainted. It has inevitably become a desirable neighbourhood with trendy nightclubs and as yet undiscovered art galleries. The East Village, with its diversity, feverish activity and spontaneity, is entering a period of respectability. The inevitable New York real-estate cycle is underway; developers have taken an interest in the neighbourhood, rents are rising and the exodus has begun. This time, however, young artists can no longer stay on Manhattan; they have been pushed to Brooklyn, Queens or New Jersey. The East Village undoubtedly will be transformed over the next 10 years. The time to visit is now, while the diverse mixtures of people who have populated this area for more than a century are still here.

Lafayette Street, III, C3, has been one of the New York's most elegant streets since it was constructed in 1826.

The **Bayard Building**, III, C3 (1898) at 65 Bleecker between Broadway and Lafayette Street is the only New York skyscraper built by Louis Sullivan, a pioneering Chicago architect. It represents a break with the Greek Revival and Renaissance styles popular at the time. The columns on the building façade reveal the relationship between function and form. The use of terracotta on the façade and the cherub-lined cornice are remarkable.

At **376-380 Lafayette Street**, III, C3, on the corner of Great Jones Street is a commercial building designed in 1888 by Henry J. Hardenbergh, architect of the Dakota Apartments and the Plaza Hotel. Constructed as a warehouse, it mixes Gothic Revival and Renaissance styles on the façade decoration. To the east the **Engine Company No. 33** at 44 Great Jones Street is so well maintained that it presents a striking contrast to the general state of disrepair in the surrounding neighbourhood. The building dates from 1898 and was designed in a flamboyant Beaux Arts style, with an elegant central arch on the façade.

The massive **De Vinne Press Building**, III, C3, a Romanesque Revival structure constructed in 1885, stands on the corner of 4th and Lafayette Streets. The powerful appearance of the dark brick building and the elegant arches and walls mask the fact that the building was originally simply a publishing house. The **Old Merchant's House** at 27 E. 4th Street, between the Bowery and Lafayette Street, was formerly a private home constructed in 1832. It was converted into a **museum** and now exhibits the original furnishings of the house *(open Sun 1-4pm; closed*

A busy shopping street in the Village.

Aug). This Federal and Greek Revival house belonged to the Tredwell family until 1930. It has a secret tunnel leading to the East River, probably used by Tredwell, a noted abolitionist, as an escape route for runaway slaves. The **Samuel Tredwell Skidmore House** at nº 37 has suffered over time, but the entrance framed with Ionic columns retains some of its former elegance.

Colonnade Row, III, C3 (1833), originally known as La Grange Terrace, extends from 428 to 434 Lafayette Street. It consisted of nine houses with Westchester marble Corinthian columns which housed such illustrious families as the Astors, the Delanos, the Vanderbilts and the Gardiners. The four remaining houses are now occupied by fashionable restaurants and bars.

The building opposite Colonnade Row, at nº 425, is the **Public Theater** (1849). Modeled after a Renaissance palace, it was originally the Astor Library, a public institution opened in 1854 by John Jacob Astor. In 1912, the Astor Library merged with several other private libraries to form the New York Public Library and left the building. In 1965, New York theater producer Joseph Papp succeeded in persuading the city to purchase and renovate the building. It has since been headquarters for the Public Theater and New York Shakespeare Festival. Seven auditoriums offer 25 new productions per year and activities include jazz, movie and literary performances. Many famous plays have been performed for the first time in these theaters, including *Hair* and *A Chorus Line.*

The **Astor Place Opera House,** III, C3 (1847), formerly stood on the west side of Lafayette Street at 13 Astor Place. It is famous for the event that occurred on May 10, 1849, when a riot broke out against the presence of British actor William Macready. The army was called in to disperse the crowd, but not before more than 30 people died and 150 were injured.

One of the city's most famous bars, **McSorley's Old Ale House,** III, C3, at 15 E. 7th Street, was founded by John McSorley in 1850. This picturesque institution remains from the era when most of the neighbourhood residents were Irish immigrants. Women have been admitted to the bar only since 1970.

This section of the East Village now has a large Ukrainian community, centered around St George's Ukrainian Catholic Church. The **Ukrainian Museum,** II, C2, is at 203 Second Avenue, near 12th Street *(open Wed-Sat 1-5pm).*

Eighth Street becomes **St Mark's Place,** III, CD3, east of Third Avenue. During the 1960s, this street was the meeting place for New York's counterculture. It is still the main commercial street in the East Village.

Second Avenue, perpendicular to St Mark's Place, was called the Jewish Rialto at the turn of the century due to the large number of Yiddish theaters lining the street. Actors Jacob Adler, Paul Muni, Stella Adler and Molly Picon began their careers in these theaters.

The charming **St Mark's-in-the-Bowery,** III, C3 (1799), on Second Avenue at 10th Street, is the second oldest church in New York after St Paul's Chapel. The church is well-known for its public campaigns in favour of the neighbourhood's disavantaged population. Former governor Peter Stuyvesant and six generations of his family are buried in the cemetery to the east of the church.

The **Renwick Triangle** west of 10th Street, between Second and Third Avenues, is a group of 16 Italianate private homes designed and built by James Renwick in 1861. The entire neighbourhood is constructed on Stuyvesant's former property *(bouwerie),* which extended from the East River to Fourth Avenue, between 5th and 17th Streets. Peter Stuyvesant's great-grandson decided to divide the land into lots, orienting the property according to the road which led from the Bowery Road to the family mansion. Modern-day Stuyvesant Street follows the route of this former local road.

42ND STREET: FROM TIMES SQUARE TO THE EAST RIVER

Map IV, BCD3. — Subway: Times Sq./42nd St. (lines 1, 2, D, N, R); Times Sq./Broadway (line 7); Grand Central/42nd St. (line 4); Grand Central/Lexington Ave. (line 7). Bus: lines 104, 106.

Forty-second Street is among Manhattan's best known and most frenzied streets. Located in Midtown, it links the piers on the Hudson River and the Lincoln Tunnel to the headquarters of the United Nations on the East River. Celebrated in innumerable songs, this street symbolizes the co-existence of Manhattan's opposing worlds, from the dilapidated housing on the West Side and the lights of Broadway to the opulence around Grand Central station and the imposing United Nations Building.

▬ TIMES SQUARE★★★

Map IV, B3.

Times Square, New York's most famous intersection at Broadway and 42nd Street, owes its name to *The New York Times*, which occupied One Times Square in 1905. The huge, imaginative billboards around the square are part of the reason for its fame and it has been nicknamed 'The Great White Way' and 'Crossroads of the World'. This is the heart of the **Theater District★★**, which extends from 40th to 53rd Streets, between Avenue of the Americas and Ninth Avenue.

As the city expanded, New York theaters followed the example set by the wealthy classes and fashionable businesses and gradually moved Uptown. The city's first theater opened its doors in the Financial District when New York was still a British colony.

In 1883, the Metropolitan Opera House was located between 39th and 40th Streets. Ten years later, the Empire Theater was opened on the corner of Broadway and 40th Street; in the next 30 years, 71 theaters, numerous hotels and restaurants followed. In the 1920s and 1930s, enormous cinemas were opened in this neighbourhood, some with seating for up to 3000 spectators.

Certain critics claim that Times Square reached its pinnacle of fame years ago. The Depression in the 1930s left many theaters empty; later, television, radio and video finished off many more. The neighbourhood is run-down today and the grand era of theater marquees is only a memory. The streets are lined with shops selling inexpensive merchandise, while drugs, pornography and prostitution are rampant on the sidewallks. Many of the 24-hour cinemas show nothing but X-rated movies.

Nevertheless, the city tried to revive the neighbourhood by driving out the dealers and undertaking a program of renovation and improvement. Neon is once again fashionable and several skyscrapers, currently under construction, have provided space for the gigantic neon signs formerly on the theaters.

Reduced-price theater tickets are available for same-day performances at the TKTS office or at SEATS (ballet, modern dance). See 'Entertainment', pp. 34.

▬ WEST OF BROADWAY

Map IV, B3 .

The legendary **Knickerbocker Hotel,** IV, B3 , formerly occupied 142 Broadway, at the corner of 42nd Street. Inaugurated in 1902, this hotel, with a mansard roof, was owned by the powerful and wealthy Astor family. Woody Allen tried to bring it back to life in his film *Radio Days* (1987).

A branch office of the **New York Convention and Visitors Bureau,** IV, B3 , provides tourist information at the corner of 42nd Street and Broadway *(open Mon-Fri 9am-6pm, Sat and Sun 10am-8pm;* ☎ 212 593 8983). To the west, the block between Broadway and Eighth Avenue typifies the recent deterioration of the neighbourhood. Drug dealers ply their trade in front of pornographic cinemas, peep-shows and erotic bookshops.

Nevertheless, some famous theaters still remain from the heady days of legitimate theater. Some have been transformed into cinemas and the original façades have been disfigured by decaying movie marquees. The old **Victory Theater** at nº 207 was constructed in 1900 by the famous impresario Oscar Hammerstein, grandfather of the dramatist. Inaugurated in 1903, the **Lyric Theater** at nº 213 featured many famous actors, including Douglas Fairbanks, Fred Astaire and the Marx Brothers. The **New Apollo Theater** at nº 229 is once again offering performances after many years of disuse.

The old **Empire Theater** across the street at nº 240 was inaugurated in 1912 and transformed into a cinema in the 1930s. In 1904, the **Liberty Theater** at nº 234 opened its doors.

The **Port Authority Bus Terminal,** IV, B3 , on the south-west corner of 42nd Street and Eighth Avenue, is one of the largest bus terminals in the world. Many of the 200,000 daily users travel to the suburbs, but buses also provide service to all parts of the United States.

The former **McGraw-Hill Building** at nº 330 stands next to the station. It is remarkable for its blue-green terracotta façade and setbacks, long windows and Art Deco lobby. In the early 1930s, publisher McGraw-Hill built this handsome building with the intention of improving a dilapidated industrial neighbourhood. The goal was never fully successful and, in 1973, the company moved to their current headquarters to Rockefeller Center.

South of 42nd Street, Ninth Avenue resembles an international food market, with products from all over the world. Every year in mid-May, it is transformed into a pedestrian street for the **Ninth Avenue Street Festival.** Thousands visit the festival, which features all types of cuisine, crafts, musicians and street performers.

In the early 20th century, the infamous Hell's Kitchen extended to the west of Ninth Avenue, between 30th and 57th Streets. Gangs virtually controlled this slum neighbourhood; police ventured into the area only in groups of three or more. Around 1910, the property owners, the New York Central Railroad, formed a militia which patroled the area, arresting gang members. Today the neighbourhood has been renamed Clinton, after the Dewitt Clinton Park, IV, A2 , on 52nd Street and Eleventh Avenue.

The Off-Off Broadway theaters and Theater Row, specializing in classical and avant-garde productions, are between Ninth and Tenth Avenues, on the southern side of 42nd Street. Opposite, Manhattan Plaza, constructed in 1977, is a housing development for performing artists.

Times Square, the heart of New York's Theater District.

▬ NORTH ON BROADWAY

Map IV, B3.

The triangular area formed by the intersection of Broadway and Seventh Avenue is the former home of *The New York Times*. The third floor of the building has an electronic billboard which provides the latest news and weather reports to pedestrians below. Opposite, on the southern side of 42nd Street, an amusing mural represents the former Times Building.

This celebrated daily newspaper left One Times Square for its current location at 229 W. 43rd Street. Since its creation in 1851, *The New York Times* has been a New York institution and is one of the most respected newspapers in the United States.

The **Paramount Building,** IV, B3 (1927), with its interesting setbacks and rooftop globe, is at 1501 Broadway, between 43rd and 44th Streets. Its sumptuous lobby formerly led to the Paramount Theater.

The enormous contemporary building between 44th and 45th Streets, **One Astor Plaza,** IV, B3, occupies the former site of the Astor Hotel. The **Theater Museum** *(open Wed-Sat noon-8pm, Sun noon-5pm)* in the gallery of the **Minskoff Theater** presents the history of New York theater.

Some 40 theaters remain in this section of Broadway; many present musical comedies which often become world famous. During the height of Broadway's fame in the 1920s, a successful musical comedy could earn up to $1 million (the construction price of a theater) during a single season. The theater season of 1927-1928 set a record with 257 shows in this neighbourhood.

The **Shubert Theater,** IV, B3, at 225 W. 44th Street, behind 1 Astor Plaza, houses the offices of the Shubert Organization, created by the Shubert brothers, the most successful impresarios in the United States. Next door, **Shubert Alley** is now used by theater-goers, but it was formerly the meeting place for actors, singers and dancers trying to get hired by the Shubert brothers. Opposite, **Sardi's*,** at n° 234, is the renowned restaurant that has long been a meeting place for actors and spectators alike.

There are many famous theaters on 44th and 45th Streets, including the **Broadhurst,** the **Saint James,** the **Booth,** the **Royale** and the **Plymouth.** The monumental, futuristic 48-floor **Marriot Marquis Hotel** (1985), on the corner of 45th Street and Broadway, has 1 800 rooms. The glass elevators in the center of the building, lit up by dozens of small lights, are visible from the hotel bar.

The **Lyceum Theater,** IV, B3 (1903) at 149 W. 45th Street is the oldest legitimate theater in the district. Duffy Square on the corner of 46th Street, between Broadway and Seventh Avenue, has a statue of George M. Cohan, the composer of such famous songs as *Give My Regards to Broadway* and *I'm a Yankee Doodle Dandy.*

From here, return to Times Square and continue eastwards on 42nd Street, passing Bryant Park and the New York Public Library (see 'Fifth Avenue' p. 106). East 42nd Street starts on the opposite side of Fifth Avenue.

▬ GRAND CENTRAL TERMINAL**

Map IV, C3.

Grand Central Terminal, constructed in 1913, straddles Park Avenue. Designed by Reed & Stem and Warren & Wetmore, it is a good example of the Beaux Arts style and one of the largest railway stations in the world. The overwhelming façade on Park Avenue includes three immense windows framed by majestic columns, reminiscent of ancient triumphal arches. A sculptural group, *Transportation,* crowns the façade, depicting Mercury, Hercules and Minerva with the American eagle. At the base of the façade stands a bronze statue of Cornelius Vanderbilt, commissioned by Vanderbilt himself.

Commodore Vanderbilt, so named because he made his fortune as a ferryboat entrepreneur, succeeded in the 1860s in obtaining a mono-poly of all the New York railway lines. In 1871, he decided to construct a station on the corner of Park Avenue and 42nd Street to centralize the tracks in Manhattan, using the Paris Gare du Nord as a model. The tracks, which extend from 42nd to 52nd Streets and from Madison to Lexington Avenues, were entirely covered and a large station was con-structed above ground.

Forty-eight underground tracks were laid on two levels with a network of interconnecting passageways. Trees were planted on the north side of the station, giving Park Avenue the elegant appearance it has today. Following the inauguration of Grand Central Station in 1913, the neighbourhood became a desirable residential and business district with prestigious offices and luxury apartment buildings.

To visit Grand Central, start at the main entrance on 42nd Street and cross the main waiting room which leads to the legendary main con-course. Finished in marble, this gigantic area is 374 ft/114 m long and 118 ft/36 m wide. The 125 ft/38 m high ceiling is decorated with the constellations. The most widely used decorative element is the oak leaf, the Vanderbilt family symbol. More than 150,000 people use this station every day. The walls are lined with immense advertisements and store-fronts. The handsome bronze ticket windows commemorate the great era of American train travel.

The staircase on the west side of the concourse leads to the lower level, the platforms and to the **Oyster Bar****. This wonderful restaurant, with a huge counter and beautiful tiled ceiling and walls, serves every kind of seafood, including more than 10,000 oysters per day. Underground passageways below this level connect 43rd Street to 49th Street, forming a labyrinth in the heart of Midtown. Hundreds of homeless people have adopted this underground world as a shelter, and it becomes increasingly crowded as winter approaches.

Grand Central Terminal occupies extremely valuable land. Over the years, many proposals have been made to transform the interior into office space or to construct a skyscraper over the station. Public opinion has always been opposed to these plans and, in 1965, the city designated the site a historical landmark. Realizing the potential commercial value of the land, the railway company appealed the judgment but, in 1978, the Supreme Court confirmed the city's decision.

▬ *FROM THE PAN AM BUILDING* TO THE UNITED NATIONS****

Map IV, CD3.

The 59-storey **Pan Am Building** rises up directly behind the station. It was constructed in 1963 by Emery Roth & Sons, Pietro Belluschi and Walter Gropius, one of the Bauhaus architects. Grand Central sold its air rights to Pan Am in 1958, leading to the construction of this building which unfortunately blocks the view from Park Avenue.

The **Grand Hyatt Hotel,** IV, C3 (1908), east on 42nd Street, has a mirrored façade which reflects the surrounding buildings. The interior of this 30-storey, 1400-room hotel includes a large atrium.

The imposing Romanesque façade of the **Bowery Savings Bank** (1923) at 110 E. 42nd Street is one of the masterpieces of bank design in New York. The immense entrance arch leads to a central room which houses all bank services. The room is 180 ft/55 m long, 82 ft/25 m wide and is framed by marble columns. The beamed ceiling rises 66 ft/20 m above a mosaic floor. Opposite at n° 122 is the admirable Art Deco **Chanin Building**, constructed in 1929 by the Sloan Robertson firm. The base of the building is handsomely decorated with ceramics and the lobby has exceptional marble-and-bronze decorative elements.

The graceful silhouette of the **Chrysler Building****, IV, C3 (1930), stands at 405 Lexington Avenue, between 42nd and 43rd Streets. For several months, this 1040 ft/317 m building was the tallest in the world.

In the 1920s, Walter Chrysler, a self-made man and founder of the automobile company, decided to construct a skyscraper dedicated to the idea of progress. He contacted architect William Van Alen, a former student of the Paris École des Beaux-Arts and the Laloux atelier. He gave free reign to this architect who had gained a reputation in New York for his simplified designs.

A fierce competition began between Van Alen and his former partner, H. Craig Severance. Severance had the commission to design the highest building in the world for the Bank of Manhattan at 40 Wall Street. When Van Alen publicly announced his intention to build 925 ft/280 m high, Severance decided to add a mast to the Bank of Manhattan, making it stand 927 ft/280 m high. Severance didn't take into consideration Van Alen's foresight — he had secretly designed a 123 ft/30.2 m spire on top of the Chrysler Building. It was hidden on the 65th floor, then raised to the top of the building through a hole in the roof. Within 90 minutes, Van Alen had won the competition by raising the height of the Chrysler Building to 1040 ft/317 m, making it the tallest building in the world. The victory was short-lived since several months later the 1250 ft/378 m Empire State Building surpassed it.

The Chrysler Building's richly decorated interior is a treasure of Art Deco style. The main entrance on Lexington Avenue leads to a triangular lobby supported by two octagonal columns. The slightly sloping floor leads the visitor to two banks of elevators. The walls and columns are covered with red Moroccan marble, the floor is made of travertine and the window frames are designed in nickel-plated steel. The lobby incorporates an impressive lighting system. Indirect light is provided by lamps placed between the onyx Mexican panels and the nickel-plated steel fixtures. At the end of the lobby, the elevator doors are inlaid with eight different types of wood representing abstract Art Deco designs. The richness of the decoration extends even to the fans placed inside the elevators. Two marble-lined staircases on the north and south sides of the lobby lead to the mezzanine and basement levels. The Chrysler Building has been recently restored to its original beauty.

The **Automat**, IV, C3, on the south-east corner of 42nd Street and Third Avenue is an interesting curiosity. This type of automatic cafeteria was widespread in the 1930s. At the time, these automats were crowded with people who dropped a few coins in the slots, then opened the glass doors to lunch on apple pie, meat pie or a warm soup. The precursor to today's fast-food establishments, the last automat in New York now serves the occasional sentimental visitor and provides a resting place for many vagrants.

The **Daily News Building**, IV, C3 (1930) on the south side of 42nd Street at n° 220 between Second and Third Avenues was designed by Raymond Hood, architect of the former McGraw-Hill Building on W. 42nd Street. The flat roof, uncommon at the time, conceals a water tower. The lobby is decorated with an immense globe of the earth.

The main entrance to the **Ford Foundation Building***, IV, D3 (1967), is at 320 E. 43rd Street, off Second Avenue. With this building, architects Kevin Roche and John Dinkeloo created one of the most successful designs of the 1960s. The interior atrium, 132 ft/40 m high, houses a popular garden. The open brick, glass and steel building is the headquarters of the Ford Foundation, a philanthropic organization which provides grants in the arts and sciences.

Farther to the east, the residential **Tudor City** dates from 1928. It extends from 40th to 43rd Streets, between First and Second Avenues. It includes more than 2500 apartments and a 500-room hotel. The 12 buildings are unified by an interior park giving it the appearance of a village. Tudor City was named after the building style which uses brick, stained-glass windows and Gothic Revival elements. The walls on the east side do not have any windows because in the 1920s, this side looked out over unsightly slaughterhouses and breweries.

▬ *THE UNITED NATIONS*★★★

Map IV, D3. — Subway: Grand Central/42nd St. (lines 4, 5, 6, 7). Bus: Lines 15, 27, 101, 102, 104, 106.
Information: *Open daily 8am-5:30pm; guided tours 9:15am-4:45pm.*

Standing on the banks of the East River and stretching from 42nd to 48th Streets, United Nations Plaza is a splendid architectural achievement. Some of the most famous architects of their time, each representing their country of origin, co-operated in the design of this institution, presided over by Wallace K. Harrison from the United States. Architects for the project included Le Corbusier (France), Oscar Niemeyer (Brazil) and Sven Markelius (Sweden).

The League of Nations, predecessor of the United Nations, was based in Geneva. John D. Rockefeller acquired the property at Turtle Bay for $8.5 million and proposed this area as the headquarters for the United Nations, founded in 1945. The proposal was accepted, but it took several years to design and construct all the necessary buildings. The first session was held in October 1952.

Several organizations function under the auspices of the United Nations, including UNESCO (United Nations Educational, Scientific and Cultural Organization), the IMF (International Monetary Fund), the WHO (World Health Organization) and UNICEF (United Nations International Children's Emergency Fund). The four buildings forming United Nations Plaza cover 20 acres/8 hectares of land. These include the 39-storey Secretariat, the first glass-and-steel skyscraper in New York, the Conference Building, the General Assembly Hall and the Dag Hammarskjöld Library.

Visitors are guided by young people from member countries, sometimes wearing traditional dress. The visit lasts about two hours and is not open to children under five. The main lobby of the General Assembly Hall has many interesting elements, including the seven bronze doors donated by Canada, a tapestry representing world peace, a Chagall stained-glass window and the 138 emblems of the member countries.

The famous United Nations post office is in the basement. Stamps issued and postmarked by the United Nations are highly valued by collectors. The library, with a selection of publications from around the world and a souvenir shop, is worth a visit.

The main point of interest is the **General Assembly Hall.** There are 350 seats reserved for delegates, 250 for the press and 800 for the public. Interpreters work in cubicles on either side of the hall, providing simultaneous translations of speeches given during meetings. The General Assembly meets once annually for a three-month working session, from September to December.

The visit continues with a tour of the Conference Hall. With the exception of the technical installations, including radio and television studios, the only real interest here lies in several works of art donated by different countries. These include Persian carpets, Tunisian mosaics, Brazilian frescos and a superb Rouault painting, *Christ Crucified*, presented by Pope Paul VI during his 1965 visit.

FIFTH AVENUE

Maps III and IV. — Subway: 59th St./Lexington Ave. (line 4); 34th St./Ave. of the Americas (lines B, D); Fifth Ave./42nd St. (line 7). Bus: lines 1, 2, 3, 4, 5.

Fifth Avenue★★★, the most famous New York avenue and the major north-south thoroughfare, is also the dividing line between the East and West sides. The most prestigious New York stores are here, side by side with luxury hotels, elite clubs and some of the most fashionable churches. Visit this area during working hours, when it is most animated. Fifth Avenue is a fairyland of lights and decorated store windows during the Christmas season. Many New Yorkers bring their children to see the window displays and stop by the giant Christmas tree and ice-skating rink at Rockefeller Center.

Around 1850, the wealthiest New York families began to leave the growing commercial ambience of lower Manhattan, and moved to Fifth Avenue near 34th Street. The Astors, Vanderbilts, Schermerhorns and Morgans built elegant homes, making it the most distinguished New York neighbourhood. Towards the end of the century, however, the district began to change. Businesses invaded the area, following their well-to-do customers. Large stores and hotels were constructed on Fifth Avenue and once again the affluent residents decided to abandon their homes to move further Uptown. The residential neighbourhood is now centered above 59th Street.

▬▬ THE EMPIRE STATE BUILDING★★★

Map III, B-C1. — Subway: 34th St./Ave. of the Americas (lines B, D).

The formidable 102-storey Empire State Building stands at 350 Fifth Avenue, between 33rd and 34th Streets. This New York landmark covers 2.5 acres/1 hectare and the tower soars to a height of 1472 ft/449 m. The gray shades of the granite, aluminum and nickel accentuate the symmetrical setbacks, the proportions of the façade and the simplicity of the Art Deco decoration. The grandiose dimensions of this skyscraper can best be seen from a distance, in contrast to the adjacent 30-storey buildings.

The Empire State Building became the tallest building in the world in 1931, overtaking the Chrysler Building. It remained so for more than 40 years until it was surpassed by the Sears and Roebuck Tower in Chicago. In 1976, the World Trade Center relegated it to third place.

The Empire State Building provides office space for 15,000 employees. The staircase has 1860 steps and the 67 elevators can carry 10,000 people per hour to the two observatories. The light at the top can been seen from 90 mi/150 km away. The upper 30 floors remain lit up at night, although the lighting changes with the season or event. The building is illuminated with green lights for St Patrick's Day, white lights at Easter and the national colours, red, white and blue, are used for public holidays and on election days. An average of 1,750,000 people visit every year.

The block occupied by the Empire State Building has been prestigious since the early 19th century. In 1827, the Astor family purchased the land. In 1859, John Astor III and William Astor constructed two mansions, which were soon replaced by the Waldorf-Astoria, one of the most select hotels in Manhattan. The hotel bar was a favourite meeting place for Guggenheim, Morgan and Frick.

As so often in New York, the neighbourhood changed and, in 1929, the hotel was sold and rebuilt on the corner of Park Avenue and 50th Street. With a limited budget of $50 million and a deadline of 18 months, developers decided to tear down the hotel and erect in its place the highest skyscraper in the world. On October 1, 1929, demolition of the Waldorf-Astoria began. Newspapers closely monitored each phase of the construction. The workers, called 'skyboys', maintained an incredible work rhythm for the era, 4.5 floors a week, with a record of 14.25 floors in two weeks. The inauguration on May 1, 1931, was a national event. From his office in the White House, President Hoover pressed a switch illuminating the entire skyscraper.

The first suicide from the Empire State Building occurred in 1933; 15 others have followed. Also in 1933, Hollywood made the tower more famous by using it in the film *King Kong*. The lovestruck gorilla takes refuge on the top of the building where he is attacked by an airplane. In 1945, fiction became reality when a plane crashed into the 79th floor of the building, killing 14 people. Despite the publicity generated around the building, it was not an immediate commercial success. The Depression had started and the offices weren't fully occupied until 1941.

The monumental lobby is 99 ft/30 m long and rises three storeys. The walls are lined with pink-and-gray European marble and silver-and-gold geometric designs decorate the ceiling. A panel depicting the seven wonders of the world plus the Empire State Building was added later.

Elevators to the two observatories are on the concourse level downstairs *(open daily 9:30am-midnight)*. Weather conditions and visibility are indicated at the ticket counters. The **Guinness World Record Exhibit Hall** is also on the concourse level *(open daily 9:30am-5:30pm)*.

The 86th-floor platform observatory has an open terrace with a protective grating; the 102nd floor is fully covered and glassed-in. Express elevators carry visitors directly to the observation floors. There is a spectacular **panoramic view*****, especially as the city lights are turned on at sunset. The building is in Midtown and offers the most complete view of the city, including the Downtown skyscrapers, City Hall, the start of the grid system north of Houston Street, the Midtown skyscrapers, Central Park and Harlem to the north.

▄▄ DEPARTMENT STORES

B. Altman, III, C1 (1906), occupies the east side of Fifth Avenue from 34th to 35th Streets. It was one of the first stores to intrude into the then residential neighbourhood. Its restrained façade was modeled after a Florentine palace so as not to spoil the appearance of the street. J. P. Morgan, a Fifth Avenue resident, is reputed to have advised Mr. Altman not to put his name on the store right away. Benjamin Altman, the son of a Lower East Side milliner, was one of the 'merchant kings' of the time. When he died in 1913, he left his collection of paintings, including several Rembrandts, to the Metropolitan Museum of Art. This department store has been overshadowed by the more glamorous establishments further Uptown but, nevertheless, the spacious and generally calm departments provide a pleasant shopping environment. An art gallery on the eighth floor shows temporary exhibitions.

Several buildings remain from the era when this part of Fifth Avenue was more affluent, including the former **Gorham Building,** III, C1, 390 Fifth Avenue (at the corner of 36th Street), and the former **Tiffany Building,** III, C1, 409 Fifth Avenue. Gorham, a silver company and jeweler, and Tiffany & Company, a jeweler, built their stores in the same year and used the same architects, McKim, Mead and White. The Tiffany Building, abandoned when its owner moved to the corner of Fifth Avenue and 57th Street, was modeled after the Palazzo Grimani in Venice. This Venetian influence can still be seen, despite several unfortunate remodelings.

Lord & Taylor, III, C1, occupies the south-west corner of Fifth Avenue and 38th Street. It is New York's oldest department store. In 1824, Samuel Lord, a 21-year-old Englishman from Yorkshire, came to America to seek his fortune. On his arrival in New York, he borrowed $900 from his wife's uncle and opened a novelty shop on the Bowery. He became partners with George Taylor, his wife's cousin, the following year, and together they created Lord & Taylor. In 1852, the cousin returned to England, while Samuel Lord remained in America to run the flourishing business. Today, it is still one of the finest stores in New York.

During World War 1, this neighbourhood was considered to be the center of fashion in the United States. The 'Fifth Avenue' label represented the pinnacle of refinement and good taste. These stores catered to an affluent clientele throughout the 1920s. Discount stores have long since invaded the area and downgraded its earlier appearance.

One of the most beautiful buildings in Manhattan, the **American Standard Building,** IV, C3 (1924) more commonly known as the American Radiator Building, was constructed at 40 W. 40th Street. Designed by Raymond Hood, one of the Rockefeller Center architects, this building is remarkable for its black bricks and gilded and sculpted terracotta tower.

▬ *BRYANT PARK*

Map IV, BC3. — Subway: Fifth Ave./42nd St. (line 7).

Bryant Park (1884) was named after William Cullen Bryant (1794-1878), a journalist and free-thinker who played an important role in the creation of Central Park and the Metropolitan Museum of Art. Located behind the public library, it was, until recently, a shady domain of drug dealers and users. It has been cleaned up and is now a safe and pleasant park.

During the 19th century, Bryant Park was called Reservoir Park because it was located next to the Croton Reservoir, the present-day site of the New York Public Library. Inaugurated in 1842, the reservoir was built to compensate for the chronic water shortages which were believed to be a factor in the cholera epidemics. Water was also needed to fight the large fires which periodically swept through the city. The Crystal Palace, a replica of the famous London building, was built in the park to house the 1853 World's Fair.

The **SEATS ticket office,** IV, BC3, on the northern edge of the park at 42nd Street offers half-price tickets for same-day ballet performances and concerts. The **Grace Building,** IV, BC3, 1114 Avenue of the Americas, on the corner of 42nd Street opposite the park, was built in 1974. The **Solow Building,** IV, C2, is a similar version of this building located on 59th Street.

Easter Parade on Fifth Avenue.

▬ THE NEW YORK PUBLIC LIBRARY***

Map IV, C3. — Subway: 42nd St./Ave. of the Americas (lines B, D); Fifth
Ave./42nd St. (line 7). Bus: Lines 1, 2, 3, 4, 5.
Information: *Open Mon-Wed 10am-9pm, Fri and Sat 10am-6pm; free
guided tours Mon-Sat 11am-2pm. Opening hours are subject to change
so call for information,* ☎ *(212) 661 7220. Temporary exhibitions from
the library collection are held regularly.*

The main branch of the New York Public Library, on Fifth Avenue between 40th and 42nd Streets, houses an exceptional collection, the second largest in the United States after the Library of Congress in Washington, D.C. It contains more than 30 million books, manuscripts and documents and administers 81 branch libraries. An average of 1.5 million people use the 800 volumes of catalogues and 87 mi/140 km of stacks every year. Its most treasured collections include a first edition of Shakespeare's works, a letter written by Christopher Columbus, a hand-written copy of the Declaration of Independence and a collection of over 100,000 photographs of New York City.

The immense New York Public Library collection results from the merger of two privately financed libraries (the Astor and Lenox libraries) and an enormous donation from politician Samuel J. Tilden. Real estate speculator John Jacob Astor gave $400,000 just before his death for the creation of a public library intended for America's working classes. James Lenox was particularly interested in Anglo-Saxon literature and history. At his death in 1880, he donated his personal library of 85,000 books plus $500,000 to the city. In 1886, Samuel J. Tilden, a one-time governor of New York State, left his collection of 15,000 volumes and $2 million to the city. The city decided to consolidate the three collections into a single central library. Andrew Carnegie donated $5.2 million towards the creation of a system of branch libraries throughout the boroughs.

Completed in 1911, the library is one of the finest examples of the Beaux Arts style in New York. Architect Thomas Hastings was never fully satisfied with the façade. At his death, he left a large sum of money intended to finance a remodeling project, but the work was never undertaken.

The immense edifice is set back from Fifth Avenue. The terrace, surrounded by a parapet, is guarded by two handsome lions, sculpted by Edward Potter. The three entrance arches are framed by Corinthian columns. In the niches behind the fountains, to the right and left of the steps, are statues representing Truth and Beauty. Six allegorical figures on the frieze above the entrance represent History, Music, Religion, Poetry, Theater and Philosophy; they were sculpted by Paul Wayland Bartlett.

In contrast to the elaborate main entrance, the west side, facing Bryant Park, is more functional in design; tall windows provide light to the seven floors of the building. The monumental entrance hall, entirely finished in white Vermont marble, is flanked by two wide staircases which frame a central arch. This arch leads to the recently renovated **Gottesman Exhibition Hall** decorated with 24 marble columns and a carved oak ceiling.

Room n° 316 on the third floor, to the east of the McGraw dome, is dedicated to Edna Barnes Salomon. It is decorated in pink French marble and houses the temporary and permanent exhibitions from the library collection. The Catalogue Room to the west of the dome leads to the showpiece of the library, the **Main Reading Room,** 98.4 yd/90 m long by 27.3 yd/25 m wide. It is one of the most beautiful reading rooms in the United States with high ceilings, good light and superb tables and lamps.

▬ PRIVATE CLUBS AND THE DIAMOND DISTRICT

The glass and steel **Manufacturers Hanover Trust Building,** IV, C3, designed by architects Skidmore, Owings and Merrill, stands at 510 Fifth Avenue, on the corner of 43rd Street. It was an innovation in 1954; up to that time, banks had always preferred Classical domed 'temples'.

Several of New York's main private clubs are centered on the nearby cross streets. The prestigious **Century Association,** IV, C3, at 7 W. 43rd Street was founded in 1889 by William Cullen Bryant as a club for intellectual debates and meetings. Its membership includes a limited number of architects, government officials, city planners and university professors who meet to discuss major contemporary issues. Architects

McKim, Mead and White, members of the club, copied a Veronese Renaissance palace in its construction, using granite, terracotta and brick. Above the main entrance is a Palladian loggia.

The **Harvard Club**, IV, C3, was founded in 1894 as the New York head-quarters for the Harvard University students association. The façade at 27 W. 44th Street is reminiscent of the Georgian style of the Cambridge, Massachusetts, university. Designed by the architects of the Century Association, this club has several large rooms which are visible from 45th Street.

In 1901, the **New York Yacht Club**, IV, C3, constructed the luxurious Beaux Arts building at 37 W. 44th Street. Poseidon, dolphins, anchors and ropes decorate the original home of the America's Cup, given to the United States in 1851 by Queen Victoria. The windows have been sculpted to resemble the sterns of ships, complete with stone waves and spray.

The renowned **Algonquin Hotel***, IV, C3 (1902) at 59 W. 44th Street has lodged innumerable famous writers, including H.L. Mencken, F. Scott Fitzgerald, William Faulkner and Tennessee Williams. The Round Table, a celebrated group of writers in the 1920s presided over by Dorothy Parker, used to gather in the Rose Room. The lobby is still a wonderful place to have a cocktail or a cup of tea in the afternoon, savouring the quiet ambience with your drink. The Mechanics' and Tradesmen's Institute nearby at n° 20 was built originally in 1891 as a free technical school. It has been converted into a library and a museum, the **John M. Mossman Collection of Locks** *(open Mon-Fri 9am-4pm)*.

The **Chase Building**, IV, C3, stands at 535 Fifth Avenue at 44th Street. When it was inaugurated in 1926, *The New Yorker* wrote that it 'had the grace of an overgrown grain silo'. Craig H. Severance, architect for the project, did not appreciate the joke and sued the magazine for libel. *The New Yorker* was ordered to print a public apology.

The **Fred F. French Building**, IV, C3 (1927), on the corner of 45th Street, is a more detailed version of the Chase Building. When con-structed, its 38 storeys dominated the Manhattan skyline and were the pride of the French real estate company. The setbacks are decorated with geometric polychrome faience. The flat roof was one of the first of its kind, designed to support the water tower. The tower is concealed behind panels on the north and south sides which depict Progress due to Integrity, Diligence and Thrift. Bronze doors open onto a lobby which is a mixture of Art Deco designs and Assyrian motifs. The decoration, designed by Sloan, was inspired by the Ishtar doors of Babylon.

West 47th Street between Fifth Avenue and Avenue of the Americas, IV, B-C3, is called 'Diamond Row' because more than $400 million worth of diamonds are traded daily on this block. Major transactions don't take place in the shops, but on the sidewalk, in back rooms or on upper floors. A simple handshake consummates a deal which may involve millions of dollars. Diamond cutting and trading were two of the rare occupa-tions open to Jews in the Middle Ages. These skills have been passed down for generations and today many of the traders are Hassidic Jews, recognizable with their beards, wide-brimmed hats and dark clothing. Two clubs on W. 47th Street, the **Diamond Trade Association** at n° 15 and the **Diamond Dealers Club**, IV, C3, at n° 30, are reserved for dia-mond traders.

Fifth Avenue north of 47th Street becomes the glamorous street of inter-national fame. At n° 597, note the glass and black iron storefront of the former bookstore **Charles Scribner's and Sons***, IV, C3. One of the most famous stores in New York, **Saks Fifth Avenue**, is on the east side of Fifth Avenue, between 49th and 50th Streets. Andrew Saks began his career as a peddler in Washington, D.C. In 1923, his son sold the modest store on 34th Street for $8 million and set up a new store the following year at the current prestigious address. Business has flourished and the Christmas window decorations at Saks are legendary.

▬ *ST PATRICK'S CATHEDRAL*★★

Map IV, C3. — Subway: 47th-50th Sts./Rockefeller Center (lines B, D). Bus: lines 1, 2, 3, 4, 5.

St Patrick's Cathedral, between 50th and 51st Streets, is the seat of the Roman Catholic Archdiocese of New York. Constructed by James Renwick and consecrated in 1879, the cathedral seems dwarfed by the surrounding skyscrapers, although the twin spires dominated the neighbourhood when it was first built. The Gothic style integrates French and English architectural elements.

In 1928, the Catholic church bought the property, at that time surrounded by open fields, as a cemetery for the Old St Patrick's Cathedral located in Little Italy. The ground proved to be too rocky for a cemetery and the bishops decided to construct a church. The work lasted from 1858 to 1888 and cost twice the original estimated cost.

The cathedral is 328 ft/100 m long by 164 ft/50 m wide. The spires rise 328 ft/100 m above the street and the nave is 108 ft/33 m high. The façade is finished in marble.The general layout is a Latin cross oriented east to west. The three bronze doors and portals were added in 1949. Inside, the main altar, the organ and the stained-glass windows are noteworthy.

There is a good view of the Rockefeller Center complex (see p. 116) from the west side of Fifth Avenue.

▬ *UP FIFTH AVENUE TO CENTRAL PARK*

Map IV, C2. — Subway: Fifth Ave./53rd St. (line E). Bus: lines 1, 2, 3, 4, 5.

The **Olympic Tower**, IV, C2 (1976) at 51st Street rises above St Patrick's and occupies most of the block. Constructed by Greek shipping magnate Aristotle Onassis, it was one of the first multi-use buildings on Fifth Avenue. It includes a passage through to 52nd Street in compliance with the new zoning laws which allowed developers to build higher in exchange for public-use areas around the base. The rarely used public passageway is an unfortunate example of the limits of this zoning program.

The main offices of **Cartier**, IV, C2, occupy 651 Fifth Avenue, north of the Olympic Tower. In the 19th century, the Vanderbilt family lived in three private homes between 51st and 52nd Streets. Alarmed by the influx of stores in a previously residential neighbourhood, William Vanderbilt sold the property to multi-millionaire Morton F. Plant, who constructed an Italian Renaissance-style residence on the site. He later resold it to the Vanderbilts in 1916, who in turn leased the building to Pierre Cartier for his New York jewelry store.

Since the building was only five storeys high, Cartier had the right, according to New York zoning laws, to sell his valuable 'air space' which represents the maximum theoretical capacity of the site. Cartier sold these air rights to his neighbour, the Olympic Tower. The façade and pilasters on 52nd Street have nevertheless been well conserved.

West 52nd Street was well known in the 1930s and 1940s as **Swing Street**. Bop music was born in night clubs which featured some of the best black musicians of the era, including Dizzy Gillespie, Thelonius Monk, Charlie Parker and Art Tatum. The **21 Club** is the only establishment remaining from this famous era, at nᵒ 21. Once a speakeasy, it became and has remained a favourite restaurant for New York celebrities.

The **Tishman Building**, IV, C2 (1957), at 666 Fifth Avenue was an innovation in its time, incorporating an embossed aluminium façade. It houses the Air France ticket offices and includes a beautiful waterfall by Isamu Noguchi. The **Top of the Sixes** restaurant on the top floor is a good place to stop for a drink— it has a terrific panoramic view.

The neo-Gothic style of St Patrick's Cathedral on Fifth Avenue provides an interesting contrast to the sleek lines of the Olympic Tower.

The neo-Gothic **St Thomas Episcopal Church,** IV, C2 , was constructed in 1914 and has been a favourite church for many New York society weddings. Located on a narrow lot, the church is asymmetrical and does not have a transept. It was designed by the group of architects who built the Cathedral of St John the Divine. At the time, the nearby buildings were only a few storeys high. The architects chose to use mediaeval building techniques, whereby the columns support the entire weight of the structure. Several years after completion of the church, however, steel beams had to be added to compensate for serious bulging in the walls. The portal represents St Thomas rising after recognizing the resurrected Christ. The 'Bride's Entrance' is located to the left. The remarkable

80 ft/24 m reredos is constructed of ivory-coloured stone from Ohio. The central section representing the Cross is a copy of a work by Augustus Saint-Gaudens.

The **Museum of Modern Art**, IV, C2 (see 'Museums and galleries' p. 153) can be seen farther north on 53rd Street.

The **Museum of Broadcasting***, IV, C2, at 1 E. 53rd Street was created in 1975 and 'collects, preserves, interprets and exhibits' radio and television programs. Visitors can request individual showings of major events, ranging from President Kennedy's funeral to the Ed Sullivan show featuring the Beatles *(open Wed-Sat noon-5pm, Tues noon-8pm)*.

The museum was founded by CBS Chairman William S. Paley. He was also responsible for the marvellous little **Paley Park** located at n° 3. The waterfall masks the noise from neighbouring streets and is an oasis of peace and tranquillity in the very heart of Manhattan. The need for additional space has led to the decision to move the museum. The new site will be at 23 W. 52nd Street.

Major American and European jewelers have glittering window displays on either side of Fifth Avenue north up to Central Park. **Tiffany's, Bugatti, Harry Winston, Van Cleef & Arpels** and **A la Vieille Russie** make this neighbourhood one of the most opulent in the city, IV, C2.

The **University Club** IV, C2 (1899), at 1 W. 54th Street, an enormous Renaissance palace, is a vestige from the 19th century. The three-storey granite façade actually masks seven floors inside. The decoration of the interior is sumptuous, but it is unfortunately not open to the public. The building front is decorated with the emblems of the most prestigious American universities. It evokes the affluent epoch when certain New York millionaires belonged to as many as 15 private clubs.

In 1936, the **Rockefeller Apartments,** IV, C2, were constructed at 17 W. 54th Street at the same time as Rockefeller Center. This is considered one of the most prestigious addresses in the neighbourhood.

The **Saint Regis Hotel,** IV, C2 (1904), is right off Fifth Avenue on E. 55th Street. The bronze guard kiosk and luxurious lobby add a nostalgic charm to the modern neighbourhood. John Jacob Astor IV, owner of the Waldorf Astoria, realized the economic potential of this area following the success of his first hotel. He took special care with the design, installing 40 Steinway pianos in the suites, providing gold-plated flatware for the restaurants and individual thermostats in each room, an unheard-of luxury at the time. The hotel is famous for the **King Cole Room,** decorated with Maxfield Parrish frescos. Woody Allen filmed the nightclub scenes for *Radio Days* (1987) in this ballroom.

Eat Street, IV, BC2, occupies the entire block of W. 56th Street between Fifth Avenue and Avenue of the Americas. As indicated by its name, it is lined with restaurants.

The 28 floors of the **Corning Glass Building,** IV, C2 (1959) stand on the south-east corner of 56th Street. The building materials reflect the vocation of the large glass fabrication company. The Steuben Glass shop windows on the ground floor are convex and practically invisible. There is a lovely fountain here which is a pleasant place to stop on a hot summer day.

The **Trump Tower,** IV, C2, rises between 56th and 57th Streets. This 61-storey building is a multi-use tower, designed around an immense six-storey-high atrium, finished with dark pink marble and a cascading waterfall.

Several elegant stores lease space in the Trump Tower, including **Bonwit Teller, Charles Jourdan** and **Ludwig Beck.** Bonwit Teller leads to a second atrium, which has flower beds, trees and benches. The top floors of the tower house the personal apartments of wealthy celebrities like Sophia Loren.

Tiffany & Company*, IV, C2, the most famous jeweler in New York, has been located at 727 Fifth Avenue at the corner of 57th Street since 1940.

In the late 17th century, Jacques Tiphaine left his native city of Sedan for Manhattan. In 1837, his descendant, Charles Tiffany (whose name was anglicized) opened a novelty store in association with John Young near City Hall. He sold costume jewelry until unexpected circumstances provided the two partners with a fortunate opportunity. In 1848, Young left for Paris which was in the throes of revolution. A shrewd businessman, he bought marvellous jewels from aristocrats anxious to flee the country. He brought them back to America where they attracted an immense amount of interest from curious New Yorkers. This episode established Tiffany's reputation as an internationally famous jeweler.

Affluent New Yorkers flocked to buy not only the magnificient jewels, but also the sumptuous Tiffany glass lampshades and vases. These were created by Louis Comfort Tiffany, son of the company's founder. Painter and artistic director for his father's firm, Louis Tiffany was also an interior decorator for many illustrious clients, including the White House. Numerous churches in the New York area still contain Tiffany stained glass. Louis Tiffany's residence on Long Island has been partly reconstructed in the American wing of the Metropolitan Museum of Art (see p. 147).

The enormous yellow 'Tiffany' diamond, found in South Africa in 1877, is displayed in the elegant Fifth Avenue store. It was also here that parts of *Breakfast at Tiffany's* were filmed.

The beautiful boutiques and art galleries on 57th Street confirm the cosmopolitan chic of this area.

Grand Army Plaza, IV, C2, located between 58th and 60th Streets, is a European-style public square that marks the beginning of Central Park. It is in front of the Plaza Hotel, famous for its beauty and history. The Pulitzer fountain and pools, an equestrian statue of General Sherman and the horse-drawn carriages (see p. 123) contribute to the picturesque aspect of this square.

The **General Motors Building,** IV, C2 (1986), stands on the site of the former Savoy Plaza Hotel. Certain New York critics condemned the 50-storey building for the impersonality of its unbroken white marble façade and columns. The building has a sunken plaza and a showroom that displays General Motors automobiles. The fantastic toy store **F.A.O. Schwarz*** occupies the first two floors of the building. This is a paradise for children and adults alike, with every imaginable kind of toy, including stuffed animals of all sizes and shapes and a wonderful assortment of miniature trains.

Bergdorf Goodman, IV, C2 (1928) is one of the most fashionable stores in the United States. The window displays and selection of men's and women's clothing have often launched new fashions throughout the country. The building stands on the former site of Cornelius Vanderbilt's mansion, a neo-Gothic structure containing 137 rooms which occupied the entire block.

The **Solow Building,** IV, C2 (1974) at 9 W. 59th Street is a twin of the Grace Building. Its swooping form and size have been much criticized as inappropriate in relation to the Plaza.

The **Plaza Hotel**,** IV, C3 (1907) is one of New York's most famous buildings. Architect Henry Hardenbergh, who also designed the Dakota Apartments, chose a French Renaissance style. The brick front provides a contrast to the rounded corners and balustrades and the magnificent slate and copper roof. Rooms on the north side of the hotel have a superb view over Central Park. Certain rooms, including the Palm Court with its admirable Tiffany glass porch, have disappeared in the wake of unfortunate renovations. Yet some beautiful rooms still exist, including the **Oak Room** — still another place well worth stopping for a drink. The Plaza was architect Frank Lloyd Wright's favourite hotel.

The elegant **Sherry Netherland Hotel** at 781 Fifth Avenue faces Central Park and overlooks Grand Army Plaza. The famous **A la Vieille Russie** on the ground floor exhibits jewelry from imperial Russia and a selection of 17th-century French furniture.

ROCKEFELLER CENTER

Map IV, BC3. — Subway: 47th-50th St./Rockefeller Center (lines B, D). Bus: lines 5, 6, 7 (Uptown); lines 1, 2, 3, 4, 5 (Downtown). Information: *Guided tours of Rockefeller Center (including Radio City Music Hall) are available Mon-Sat 9:45am-4:45pm (every 30 minutes) from the main floor of the RCA Building, 30 Rockefeller Pl. Observation Roof (RCA Building): open Oct-Mar, daily 10:30am-7pm, Apr-Sept, daily 10am-9pm.*

Rockefeller Center** is a group of 21 buildings which covers 22 acres/9 hectares and includes commercial skyscrapers, theaters, private streets and squares, shops, restaurants and miles of underground passageways. It houses offices, television studios, exhibition halls and the famous Radio City Music Hall entertainment center. Close to 250,000 employees and visitors use it daily. The buildings are magnificent and together form the largest group of skyscrapers in the world.

In the early 19th century, the site of Rockefeller Center belonged to Columbia University, which had constructed brownstones and leased them to wealthy families. By the end of the century, John D. Rockefeller became worried about the deteriorating condition of the neighbourhood near his property and purchased the surrounding land around Fifth Avenue and 54th Street. In 1928, the Metropolitan Opera, located between Broadway and Seventh Avenue and 39th and 40th Streets, decided to join the affluent New Yorkers in their exodus Uptown. The Opera became interested in Columbia's land and approached Rockefeller with the idea that he should purchase the property and give it to the Opera. The oil magnate preferred to maintain a commercial interest in the development and proposed building an opera house integrated with a business center. Before construction of the Opera could begin, 200 buildings needed to be demolished, the skyscrapers built and major firms had to be attracted to the site.

The Opera withdrew from the project following the 1929 stock market crash. Rockefeller was left with three blocks of dilapidated housing and an annual rent of $3 million to pay to Columbia. He was ultimately pleased with the cancellation of the Opera plan, as he considered it a handicap from a financial standpoint. His promoter selected a group of architects to create an overall design for a business and cultural center (radio, theater

A statue of Prometheus adorns the lower plaza of Rockefeller Center.

and cinema). Construction of the first block of 14 buildings began in 1930, in the middle of the Depression. From the beginning it was a record-breaking undertaking: from 1930 to 1938, close to 88,000 tons of concrete and 39 million bricks were used. The project had the uneasy distinction of creating the largest mortgage in the world at that time, over $44 million, raising questions as to whether this undertaking would perhaps be the last for the Rockefeller empire. Nevertheless, the work continued on schedule and the center rapidly took shape.

The Rockefeller family decided to invest heavily in the ground-floor decoration of the buildings and sent emissaries to Europe to try to convince Matisse and Picasso to participate in an international contest to include the world's best painters. Matisse explained that his paintings could not be properly appreciated in a passageway; Picasso would not even receive the American envoys. The Rockefellers then selected Frank Brangwyn, José María Sert and Diego Rivera.

Despite his communist sympathies, Rivera agreed to paint a mural for the entrance of the RCA Building. As the date for the inauguration approached, the Rockefellers were shocked to discover the fresco did not correspond to the submitted model. In a work which was supposed to illustrate *Man's Quest for a Better Future,* Rivera represented germs swarming over decadent capitalists in a nightclub, a worker's demonstration, policemen with clubs and red flags draped along the walls. Already anxious about the fresco's content, the Rockefellers moved to action when, just before the inauguration, it was discovered that Rivera had given the leader of the worker's demonstration the face of Lenin. They tried to negotiate with the painter, but he refused to change the mural. Not able to reach an amicable agreement, the project manager ordered Rivera off the scaffolding, gave him a check for $14,000 and escorted him to the door of the building. Six months later the fresco was destroyed, without ever being seen by the public.

This incident was soon forgotten in the wake of the center's success. Within the first year 80% of the space was rented. By 1954, the center had expanded to the west side of Avenue of the Americas and towards 47th and 52nd Streets, creating a concentric area around the initial core of buildings. Rockefeller, Inc., became owner of the entire property in 1985.

▬ VISIT

For an overall view of the center, start on Fifth Avenue between 49th and 50th Streets. The **Channel Gardens****, IV, C3, are in the center, so named because they lie between the **British Building** (1933) to the north and the **Maison Française** to the south. European shops line the gardens on either side. The modest size of these two buildings contrasts with the massive concrete RCA Building. The Channel Gardens, decorated with pools and flower beds whose imaginative arrangements are changed often, lead down to the lower plaza. Used as an open-air café in the summer, the plaza is transformed into an ice-skating rink in the winter. At the top of the stairs John D. Rockefeller's personal credo is engraved. The west wall of the plaza is dominated by a statue of Prometheus, who stole the gift of fire from the gods. The plaza is often crowded, especially during Christmas season when visitors come to view the giant Christmas tree installed on the plaza and the skaters on the lower plaza. Don't let the crowds keep you away — this is one of the most beautiful sights in New York.

The 70-storey **RCA Building****, IV, C3 (1933) rises 853 ft/260 m behind Rockefeller Plaza. The discrete setbacks are formed by several elevator shafts. The building is roughly rectangular, narrowest on the east and west sides with a wide, massive slab façade on the north and south. The façade successfully integrates aluminum, an original window arrangement and a mix of gray- and cream-coloured limestone. The architects paid particular attention to the landscaped areas between the buildings.

The RCA (Radio Corporation of America) headquarters have been located in the building since its inauguration.

A sculpture of the Genius of the Universe with a remarkable gilded beard welcomes visitors to 30 Rockefeller Plaza. The enormous ground-floor entrance is decorated in the Art Deco style. José María Sert replaced the Rivera frescos with murals exalting the victories of Humanity. The elevator area was decorated by Sert and Brangwyn. Elevators provide access to the Observation Roof, which offers a spectacular view over Midtown Manhattan, the Pan Am Building and Park Avenue, IV, C3.

Guided **tours of the NBC** (National Broadcasting Company) **television studios** are given daily from 10am-4pm, except Sundays and public holidays. Information is available on the ground floor. The famous **Rainbow Room** on the 65th floor has been a favourite New York restaurant since before World War II.

The concourse level can also be reached from the ground floor of the building. This is a spider's web of corridors interconnecting the buildings and subway lines. There are more than 1.9 mi/3 km of underground Art Deco or modern passageways lined with shops, restaurants and exhibition areas.

Radio City Music Hall*, IV, B2-3, between 50th and 51st Streets on Avenue of the Americas, is famous for its fabulous Art Deco decor, the 6200-seat auditorium and the Rockettes, a troupe of precision dancers. The largest theater in the world opened its doors in 1932. Until 1968, the program of movies and productions attracted up to 5 million visitors per year. With the advent of television, attendance gradually decreased as public tastes changed. By 1978, when only 2 million tickets were sold, the Music Hall was slated for demolition. Public opinion opposed this plan, the building was declared a landmark and the theater reopened in 1979 after extensive renovation. The new format featuring concerts and stage productions with the famous Rockettes has been a more popular and commercial success (for information, ☎ 212 757 3100).

The interior is one of the best examples of the Art Deco style in New York and in the United States. A visit to Radio City Music Hall is as essential as a trip to the Empire State Building or a walk in Central Park. It is possible to take a guided tour of the Music Hall, separate from the Rockefeller Center tour (information available in the main entrance of the RCA Building).

The low ceiling of the ticket lobby is a deliberate contrast to the enormous dimensions of the grand lobby, which measures 131 ft/40 m long, 49 ft/15 m wide and 59 ft/18 high. Subdued lamps illuminate the black-and-red marble walls, black ceiling and dark carpet. The three mezzanines, reached by a gigantic staircase, offer the best view over the lobby. A fresco by Ezra Winter, *The Fountain of Youth,* decorates the stairway on the north side. In the center hang two giant crystal chandeliers, each weighing 2 tons and measuring 30 ft/9 m across.

Staircases at the end of the lobby lead down to a vast room decorated with a profusion of black-and-gray glass and chrome trim. Even the Art Deco electrical elements, mirrors and plumbing fixtures in the restrooms contribute to a unity of style in this luxurious building.

Eleven double stainless steel doors decorated with bronze bas-reliefs lead from the lobby to the auditorium. The ceiling is oval-shaped, and the arch above the stage (60 ft/20 m high, 100 ft/32 m wide) is formed by a series of overlapping half-circles painted with perpendicular rays, giving the impression of a sunburst. The stage machinery was considered a great innovation in theatrical architecture at the time it was built.

Many companies were attracted to Rockefeller Center once its success had been established. To compensate for the lack of space, the center crossed Avenue of the Americas in the 1950s. A new type of architecture can be seen on the west side, reminiscent of the modern buildings in the Financial District. The 45-storey **Celanese Building**, IV, B3 (1973), with a shopping plaza, occupies the block between 47th and 48th Streets.

The 51-storey **McGraw-Hill Building**, IV, B3 (1972), was constructed at 1221 Avenue of the Americas. The architects wanted to comply with the new city zoning laws which allowed higher buildings if, in exchange, open public areas were integrated into the design. A plaza was built and a sculpture entitled *Sun Triangle,* which indicates solar movement throughout the year, was commissioned from Athelstan Spilhaus. A waterfall and a tree-lined park offer an attractive resting place on the western edge of the building.

To the north stands the **Exxon Building,** IV, B3 (1971). At 750 ft/230 m, it is the second tallest skyscraper in the center after the RCA Building. Its ultra-modern style uses a profusion of vertical columns. The lobby is decorated with a tapestry reproduction of a theater curtain designed by Picasso in 1924. There is also an abstract sculpture, *Moon and Stars*, by Mary Callery.

The aluminum and glass **Time & Life Building,** IV, B3 (1959) houses the group which publishes *Time, Life* and *Fortune*. The undulating design of the marble sidewalk contrasts with the vertical lines of the building. The immense lobby is decorated with two works, *Portals* by Joseph Albers to the west of the elevators and *Relational Painting no. 88* by Fritz Glarner to the east.

The **Associated Press Building,** IV, B3 (1938), on 50th Street, was part of the original Rockefeller Center design. An Isamu Noguchi sculpture above the entrance depicts the slightly out-dated tools of the journalist's trade, a pad and pencil, camera, telephone, teletype and wirephoto.

Return to Fifth Avenue to see the **International Building,** IV, C2 (1938). It has two low wings, similar to the neighbouring buildings on 49th and 50th Streets. A five-ton sculpture of Atlas supporting the world on his shoulders stands in front of the entrance (49 ft/15 m high). The superb lobby is 4 storeys high, 59 ft/18 m wide and 82 ft/25 m long. Four escalators have replaced the large staircases traditionally constructed in older buildings. The restrained decor, the elegant dark green-and-white marble columns and the indirect lighting contrast with the severe design of other Rockefeller Center buildings. There is an excellent view of St Patrick's Cathedral across the street.

Central Park, surrounded by skyscrapers, offers a green oasis in the heart of Manhattan.

CENTRAL PARK

Map p. 125. — Subway: Fifth Ave./59th-60th Sts. (lines N, R); 59th St./Columbus Circle (lines A, B, C, D). Bus: lines 1, 2, 3, 4.

Information: *Visitors' Information Centers at the Dairy, in the heart of Central Park at 65th St., open daily 10am-4:30pm,* ☎ (212) 397 3156, *and at the Arsenal, Fifth Ave. and 64th St., open Mon-Fri 9am-5pm.*

Central Park★★★ has been popular with New Yorkers since it was inaugurated in 1876. With an estimated 13-20 million annual visitors, the park offers a haven of open space and recreation possibilities. There is something for everyone, and during summer months, it fills up with joggers, roller skaters and young people break dancing to ghetto blasters. There is a superb view of the New York skyline, a veritable wall of skyscrapers surrounding the park on the east, south and west sides. It is a wonderful spot for a moment of calm away from the agitation and turmoil of the city streets.

The city has been renovating sections of the park since 1980. Buildings have been repaired, paths maintained, pools and ponds drained and cleaned. Thousands of new flowers and trees have been planted. This program is so popular with New Yorkers that enthusiastic groups of volunteers have been organized to help with the upkeep and conservation of the park. Following a period of slight disrepute, due to its high crime rate and deteriorating facilities, the park is now more popular than ever.

A visit to Central Park is a must for a visitor to Manhattan. The best time to go is during warm weather. This vast landscaped park is the heart of New York, where the greenery provides oxygen to the automobile-clogged city. New Yorkers use the park to relax and exercise, when they are able to find time in this hectic city!

Central Park has always been the subject of development projects which resurface periodically. At one time or another, there were proposals to construct a hippodrome, an airfield and even an underground 25,000-car parking lot. Fortunately, these projects have been vetoed, mainly due to the zealous protection of the many friends of Central Park, working to preserve this unique city park.

Central Park extends over 840 acres/340 hectares (5% of the total surface area of Manhattan) from 59th to 110th Street in the north and between Fifth Avenue and Central Park West. The highest point is 131 ft/40 m at the top of Vista Rock in Belvedere Castle. There are entrances everywhere from neighbouring streets and many playgrounds for children. Cars are not allowed in Central Park on weekends and holidays. Visitors walk and use bicycles, roller skates, skateboards and horse-drawn carriages to get around. During summer months, Central Park offers free evening concerts and theater and opera performances.

In 1884, the poet and journalist William Cullen Bryant proposed the creation of a large park. Many well-known New Yorkers were enthusiastic about the idea and in 1856 the city paid $5 million for a plot of land north of the city. Two years later, Frederick Olmsted and Calvert Vaux won a competition for their landscape design which integrated the existing topography and nature with man-made elements. One of their far-sighted provisions was to include four lowered streets crossing the park east to west to provide for traffic, without disturbing the tranquillity and calm of the park. Work began in 1857, once the squatters and grazing animals were moved out of the area, and lasted until 1870.

About 10 million truckloads of soil were brought in, 5 million plants and trees were planted and 25 mi/40 km of paths were laid before Central Park was opened to the New York public. It quickly became the parade ground for New York's high society and a favourite weekend picnic site. The neighbourhoods bordering the park became sought-after residential areas.

In 1965, Central Park was classified a historical monument, protecting it from any future development plans.

▬ VISIT

Central Park can be divided into two sections. The first, which extends from 59th to 86th Streets, up to the Reservoir, is the most popular area. To the north, from 86th to 110th Streets, the park is not as well kept up and it is not recommended to wander alone in isolated areas. Any area of the park may be dangerous at night and it is best to stay on the sidewalks bordering it to the east, south and west. Normal caution is all that is required during the summer performances, but it is not wise to stray too far from the crowd. See also 'Parks', p. 43.

From Grand Army Plaza to the Lake, B4 to AB2

Leaving Grand Army Plaza, there is an entrance to the park via East Drive. The **pond**, B4, lies to the left, surrounding a hill which houses a bird sanctuary with swans, ducks and many other species. Take one of the many paths to the pond where there is an interesting view of Manhattan's skyscrapers reflected in the water.

A bridge leads to the **Wollman Memorial Rink,** B4, which is used for concerts as well as skating. Ponies can be rented in the area south of the **Central Park Zoo.** To the north, the **Children's Zoo***, B3 *(open daily 10am-4:30pm),* is home to many baby animals and presents marionette shows. East Drive then leads to the **Information Center** (the **Dairy**). The **Mall,** B3, extends to the north, a beautiful tree-lined avenue decorated with busts of Schiller, Beethoven, Walter Scott, Shakespeare, Christopher Columbus and an unknown Indian hunter. Roller skaters and cyclists use the area to the left of the avenue to demonstrate their often spectacular talents.

Sheep Meadow**, A3, one of the most beautiful areas in Central Park, extends to the west. Until 1934, this section of the park was actually grazing land for several dozen sheep. It is now a pleasant spot for a nap or picnic in the sun. The Mall also leads to a bandshell where summer concerts are presented. There is a children's playground behind the statue of *Mother Goose*. The path then crosses 72nd Street and leads to **Bethesda Fountain,** B3, and to the lake. In the same area, the **Strawberry Fields** garden, A3, was given to the city by Yoko Ono in memory of her husband John Lennon, assassinated in 1980 in front of their apartment in the Dakota on Central Park West and 72nd Street (see p. 128).

To the right, the path leads to the docks, where boats and bicycles can be rented during spring and summer. There is also a cafeteria with a view of the lake. The silhouettes of the buildings on Central Park West rise up from behind the woods and rocks around the lake. **Conservatory Pond★,** B2, to the east of the large lake, was named after a conservatory which was originally planned for this site; the project was later abandoned. Miniature sailboats and motorboats can be rented here. A statue of *Hans Christian Andersen★* stands to the west of the pond with a small duck at his feet. Amateur storytellers gather at the base of the statue every Saturday from 11am to noon, May through September. The charming statue of *Alice in Wonderland★*, a New York favourite, is to the north.

Belvedere Castle and the Great Lawn, A2 to AB1

Return to Bethesda Fountain and follow the path along the western edge of the lake which leads to a small footbridge, the **Bow Bridge** (1859), with a beautiful view over the area. On the other side of the bridge is **The Ramble,** A2, a small wooded hill crossed by a river.

Belvedere Castle, A2, a Gothic Revival castle used as a weather station, is the meeting place for New York ornithologists. The interesting **Shakespeare Garden,** A2, to the left, contains only plants mentioned in the English dramatist's works. The castle offers a splendid panorama over the northern section of Central Park. To the left, the **Delacorte Theater** presents free performances during the summer *(tickets available from 6:15pm for a same-day performance)*.

Belvedere Lake, AB2, lies opposite, surrounded by cherry trees. On the other side of the lake is the **Great Lawn,** AB1, a favourite spot for soccer, football and baseball games. This immense grassy area is the site of operas and symphonies performed to huge picnicking crowds on summer evenings. During the Depression, the Great Lawn was one of the more infamous shantytowns in the nation, when thousands of homeless people lived in the park.

A statue of the Polish King Jagiello to the right of the lake is the summer gathering place for folk dancers on Saturdays and Sundays. **Cleopatra's Needle,** B1, stands at the end, in front of the Metropolitan Museum of Art. It is a twin of the London statue, 66 ft/20 m high, 224 tons and was sculpted from a solid piece of pink granite over 3000 years ago. Originally from Heliopolis, it was given to the city by Khedive Ismail Pasha in 1878. Transportation alone cost $100,000, paid for by William H. Vanderbilt.

The Reservoir, AB1

To the north of the lake is the Reservoir, which occupies a quarter of the total surface area of Central Park, extending from 86th to 97th Streets. Thousands of joggers use the 1.58 mi/2.54 km running track around the reservoir daily. The northern section of the park, up to 110th Street, is less interesting and best avoided, although there are several tennis and handball courts. The **Harlem Meer,** used for boating, is located at the north-east corner of the park.

Map of Central Park.

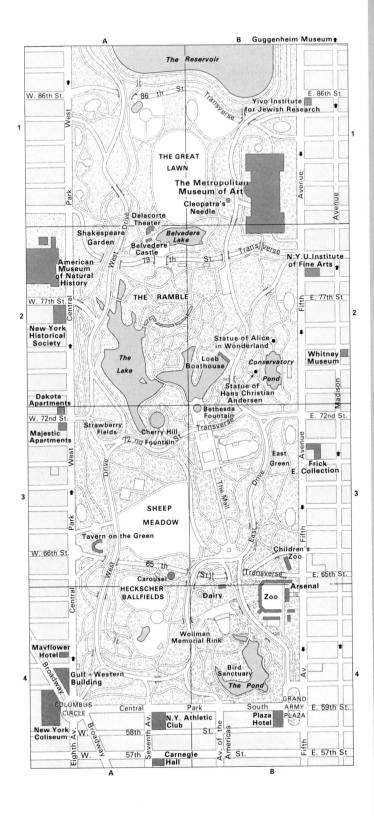

THE UPPER WEST SIDE

Maps IV, AB1-2; V AB3. — Subway: 59th St./Columbus Circle (lines A, B, C, D); 66th St./Lincoln Center (line 1); 81st St./American Museum of Natural History (lines B, E). Bus: Lines 7, 10.

U ntil recently, many affluent New Yorkers spurned the Upper West Side, preferring instead the longstanding elegance of the East Side. Artists and intellectuals were the first to appreciate this relaxed and attractive neighbourhood. Sheltered from industrial activities and major urban transformations, the Upper West Side has been able to preserve many brownstone-lined streets. The first luxury apartments in New York City were built in this area for families who could afford private homes yet preferred apartments. Prior to the construction of the Dakota Apartments in the 19th century, apartment rentals were reserved for less affluent families.

The Upper West Side is in the midst of upheaval. Sadly, major urban transformation has started. Longstanding neighbourhood shops are being converted into elegant boutiques, entire buildings are being renovated and dilapidated blocks seem to be turned overnight into respectable and sought-after housing. Young couples are attracted to the area because of the numerous facilities for children.

With the changing population and neighbourhood renova-tions, the traditional boundaries of the Upper West Side are no longer distinct. Does it begin at Lincoln Center or 52nd Street? End at 110th Street or continue to Columbia University? There is no doubt, however, that the Upper West Side is bordered by two marvelous parks: Central Park and Riverside Park, extend-ing from 72nd to 124th Streets along the Hudson River.

The itinerary starts at Columbus Circle, on the south-west corner of Central Park and roughly follows Central Park West. Lincoln Center can be visited during the same day, but a separate itinerary for it is also included (see p. 131).

Columbus Avenue, Amsterdam Avenue, Broadway and West End Avenue typify New York City's cosmopolitan char-acter. People from all over the world, with different econo-mic and cultural backgrounds, seem to integrate well with the neighbourhood's established residents. The Upper West Side is a relaxed residential neighbourhood, in contrast to its alter ego across Central Park, the more fashionable East Side.

FROM COLUMBUS CIRCLE TO THE DAKOTA

MapIV, AB1-2 .

Columbus Circle, IV, B2 , formed by the intersection of Central Park South, Eighth Avenue and Broadway, was laid out in 1867 to facilitate access to the Upper West Side and is the center of New York City. In the early 20th century, the neighbourhood of San Juan Hill stood to the west of the intersection. A statue of Christopher Columbus, for whom the circle is named, reigns over the busy streets below.

The vaguely Moorish building to the south of Columbus Circle houses the **New York City Department of Cultural Affairs** (2 Columbus Circle). The **Visitors Information Center,** IV, B2 , of the New York Convention and Visitors Bureau occupies the marble-lined ground floor *(open Mon-Fri 9am-6pm, Sat, Sun and public holidays 10am-8pm;* ☎ *212 3978222)*. This center provides extensive tourist information, including listings of hotels, restaurants and cultural events and information on transportation. A city art gallery on the first floor presents temporary exhibitions.

The **Maine Memorial,** IV, B2, at the entrance to Central Park commemorates the warship *Maine,* sunk in 1898 in Havana Bay, an event which triggered the Spanish-American War.

Eighth Avenue becomes **Central Park West**** at Columbus Circle. This large avenue corresponds to Fifth Avenue on the other side of the park and runs north to 110th Street. Every building, except for two, on Central Park West up to 96th Street was built before 1931, a remarkable fact in a city which is in a constant cycle of demolition and reconstruction. It is lined with museums and churches and the cross streets have beautiful rows of townhouses.

When constructed in 1931, the **Century Apartments,** IV, B2 , at 25 Central Park West, between 62nd and 63rd Streets, represented the pinnacle of Art Deco elegance, with two towers, handsome terraces and bay windows.

The **West Side YMCA** (1930) at 5 W. 63rd Street offers accommodation, cultural and sports activities for men only.

The two **Ethical Culture Society,** IV, B2 (1910) buildings occupy the entire block between 63rd and 64th Streets. Created in 1876, this association is dedicated to man's 'moral progress' through education and experimental teaching methods. The stone building farthest to the north is a rare example for the Art Nouveau style in New York.

Note the monumental entrance of the **Prasada Apartments,** IV, B1 (1907), on the south-east corner of 65th Street. Farther north, **55 Central Park West** was constructed in the Art Deco style in 1929. The architect used bricks which vary in colour from red to cream, from the base to the building summit, to give the impression of sunlight striking the building. This handsome building was the background for the film *Ghostbusters* (Reitman, 1985).

Neo-Gothic buildings designed as artists' studios line **67th Street,** one of the West Side's most elegant streets. The oldest studio at n° 27 dates from 1905. The most famous and most sought-after studios are in the **Hotel des Artistes** (1918) at n° 1. Famous people who rented the superb two-floor studios in this hotel include Isadora Duncan, Noël Coward, former mayor John V. Lindsay, painter Norman Rockwell and muralist Howard Chandler Christy, whose murals decorate the walls of the elegant ground-floor **Café des Artistes.**

The **Synagogue of the Congregation Shearith Israel,** IV, B1 (1897), occupies the corner of 70th Street, at 99 Central Park West. This is one of the oldest Jewish institutions in the United States, formed originally by Brazilian immigrants in 1654. Inside, an exhibition of objects and documents retraces the history of this community.

Brownstones, once private homes for affluent New York families, line **71st Street.** The building at n° 20 dates from 1889 and has been well maintained. The façade decoration of these brownstones is often highly developed; note the cupids at **n° 24** and the lions at **n° 33** and **n° 39**.

The **Majestic Apartments**, IV, B1, between 71st and 72nd Streets, were designed and constructed in 1930 by the promoter and architect of the Century Apartments. The ceramic and orange brick façade and the two sculpted towers are famous landmarks on the Central Park West sky-line.

Cross 72nd Street to reach the **Dakota Apartments***, IV, B1, one of the most famous buildings in New York.

The Dakota was designed in 1884 by Henry J. Hardenbergh, architect of the Plaza Hotel on Fifth Avenue (see p. 115). The mansard roof, turrets, multi-shaped windows and fireplaces are representative of what is called in New York the 'chateau style', a mixture of English Victorian and German Renaissance elements. The building façade incorporates beige brick, ceramic and stone.

Edward S. Clark, the building's developer and heir to the Singer sewing machine fortune, wanted to promote property he owned to the north of the city. Central Park was not yet finished and the neighbourhood consisted of shacks and open fields. His friends thought his idea extravagant and his building 'as far away as the Dakotas'. Amused at the criticism, Clark adopted the name and called his project the Dakota Apartments. He then ordered Far West motifs to be added to the building, including ears of corn, arrowheads and, above the main entrance, an Indian head.

Clark designed his apartment building for an elite clientele. The inside was lined with marble, mahogany and oak. A generator system and telephone exchange were installed in the basement. Tennis courts and stables were reserved for residents and 150 chambermaids, launderers and tailors were hired. The enormous ground-floor dining room offered a new menu every day. Despite this enormous expense, high society snubbed the building, considering it too far from Fifth Avenue. It found favour with successful artists and intellectuals, including William Steinway and music publisher Gustav Schirmer. When Tchaikovsky visited New York, he was invited to dinner by Schirmer and taken to the roof to admire the view over the city. Returning to Russia, Tchaikovsky, who did not speak English well, recounted that the American publisher owned a palace larger than the Czar's.

The Dakota is designed around a central courtyard. Instead of one main staircase, there are four entrances, each providing access to different sections of the building. Very popular among artists and entertainers, residents have included Boris Karloff, O. Ciano, S. Magowan, Leonard Bernstein, Lauren Bacall, Roberta Flack, John Lennon and Yoko Ono. Lennon was tragically assassinated on December 8, 1980, in front of the building. Roman Polanski filmed *Rosemary's Baby* in the Dakota in 1968.

The **San Remo Apartments**, IV, B1, between 74th and 75th Streets, were designed in 1930 by architect Emery Roth. This is a neo-Gothic structure with two towers, each of which has a small rotunda on the top. Between Central Park West and Columbus Avenue, **74th Street** and **76th Street** have been designated historical districts because of the handsome townhouses constructed in the late 19th century. Stone was used more often than the traditional brownstone. Several styles are represented on 76th Street: **n° 8** and **n° 1** are neo-Baroque, **n° 31 to 37** are neo-Classical and others are neo-Italian Renaissance and Romanesque Revival.

■ THE NEW-YORK HISTORICAL SOCIETY

Map V, B3.

The severe neo-Classical façade of the New-York Historical Society Building stands at 170 Central Park West. Founded in 1804, this association houses a museum and library dedicated to American art and history, primarily concerning New York State and New York City *(open Tues-Fri 11am-5pm, Sat 10am-5pm, Sun 1-5pm; ☎ 212 873 3400)*. It includes an admirable collection of American painting and furnishings from the colonial period, antique silver, toys and fire trucks.

Basement: The Fahnestock Collection includes fire trucks, vehicles and documents covering the history of New York transportation.

First floor: Silver collection including several 19th-century Tiffany pieces and work by sculptor John Rogers.

Second floor: The New York Gallery exhibits paintings depicting the city and its buildings. The Audubon Gallery presents a permanent exhibit dedicated to naturalist John James Audubon. The museum owns 432 watercolours of *Birds of America**, painted by Audubon. Antique toys are also on display. The library includes 600,000 volumes.

Third floor: Several rooms are devoted to American crafts. The Print Room has publicity posters and photographs of New York City and its celebrities.

Fourth floor: The rooms include exhibits depicting the Dutch colonial period. There is also a landscape and portrait gallery.

▬ *THE AMERICAN MUSEUM OF NATURAL HISTORY***

Map V, B3.

The large group of buildings forming the American Museum of Natural History and the Hayden Planetarium occupies the blocks between 77th and 81st Streets (*open Mon, Tues and Sun 10am-5:45pm, Wed, Fri and Sat 10am-9pm;* ☎ 212 873 4225). Several guided tours of the museum are given daily. Information is available at the main information desk on the second floor.

The Museum of Natural History, founded in 1869, attracts close to 3 million visitors every year. It includes extraordinary collections in the fields of biology, paleontology, anthropology and mineralogy with 34 million items exhibited in the 38 rooms of the four-floor museum. The dioramas are remarkably realistic. Eleven scientific departments sponsor research in various fields.

The museum is a children's paradise. The **Discovery Room** allows children to touch and smell numerous elements from natural environments. Magicians, storytellers and marionette shows are featured on Saturdays.

The museum buildings cover four full city blocks. The 22 buildings form a patchwork architectural group, illustrating the various New York styles. President Grant laid the first stone in 1874. Four wings were added to the main building between 1877 and 1935. The wing on 77th Street, faced with pink Vermont granite, is typically Romanesque. The main entrance on Central Park West includes an immense arch framed by four Ionic columns.

The museum collections, which originated from a donation by French naturalist Edouard Verreaux, today include 8 million insects, more than 8 million invertebrate fossils and almost as many birds and mammals. The library contains more than 320,000 volumes.

First floor: This floor is essentially devoted to the natural history of the North American continent, including flora, fauna and the first inhabitants. The totem poles are magnificent. The main room houses exhibitions concerning fish and oceanography. The department of human biology is to the left of the entrance. Towards the rear of the first floor is the very rich collection of minerals, including the *Star of India*, the largest sapphire in the world (563 carats).

Second floor: This floor concentrates on the natural and cultural history of Black Africa. Other rooms present exhibits on Mexico and Central America, including pottery, funerary urns, steles and other items from the pre-Columbian culture. The Aztec section includes a beautiful sun stone.

Third floor: The reptile and amphibian section includes 6.6 lb/3 kg toads and 5 ft/1.5 m salamanders. The primate room has an interesting collection of stuffed gorillas, chimpanzees and orangutans. There are also dioramas of the Blackfoot Indians hunting buffalo. The bird room is remarkably diverse and colourful.

Fourth floor: The history of the earth and New York geology is presented on this floor. The exceptional collection of prehistoric animals includes marvellous examples of fossilized skeletons: an immense brontosaurus, a mummified dinosaur and a formidable 49 ft/15 m Tyrannosaurus rex.

The **Hayden Planetarium*** is on the north side of the museum, on 81st Street *(open Mon-Fri 12:30-4:45pm, Sat and Sun noon-4:45pm,* ☎ 212 873 8828). The admission fee to the Planetarium includes free entrance to the museum. More than 22 million spectators have attended the shows since it was inaugurated in 1935. The main attraction is the **Sky Theater,** with a highly sophisticated projector which reproduces the history and future of the Universe on the inside dome of the Planetarium (82 ft/25 m diameter). Shows are given twice daily *(1:30pm and 3:30pm)* on weekdays; additional showings are available on weekends, Wednesday at 7:30pm and Saturday morning at 11am. The program is changed four times a year.

The 22 screens of the **Guggenheim Space Theater** are used for fascinating audiovisual presentations. The theater also exhibits a reproduction of the solar system and a 34-ton meteorite. The Planetarium library is open to the public by appointment.

The **Hall of the Sun** presents the relationship between the earth and the sun, and between our sun and other solar systems.

The itinerary ends here, but visitors interested in New York architecture will find other interesting buildings to the north and west of the museum.

▬ *AROUND THE MUSEUM OF NATURAL HISTORY*

The **Beresford,** V, B3 (1929), at 211 Central Park West, on the corner of 81st Street, is unique for its two enormous façades and three Baroque towers. Two interesting buildings to the north are the **Eldorado** (300 Central Park West) and especially the **Ardsley,** V, B2, constructed in 1930 by the architect of the Beresford and the San Remo (320 Central Park West, on the corner of 92nd Street). The Ardsley is considered to be one of Manhattan's most beautiful Art Deco apartment buildings. The neo-Baroque **First Church of Christ Scientist,** V, B2 (1903) at 1 W. 96th Street is reminiscent of some of the large London churches.

Many of the cross streets to the west of the museum typify the casual elegance of the Upper West Side. The **Dorilton,** IV, B1, at 171 W. 71st Street, is a remarkable example of the Beaux Arts style popular at the turn of the century. The famous **Ansonia Hotel,** IV, A1, at 2109 Broadway, between 73rd and 74th Streets, was designed by French architect Paul Duboy with a profusion of turrets, wrought-iron balconies, cornices and mansards. This 17-storey hotel was immensely successful after its inauguration in 1904, mainly because of the central heating and air conditioning systems, two swimming pools, steam baths and gymnasium. There was a veritable farm on the roof, including chickens and goats, where hotel guests could purchase fresh eggs. The excellent soundproofing in the rooms attracted well-known musicians and actors, including Stravinsky, Caruso, Chaliapin, Toscanini and Lily Pons.

Opposite, the **Apple Bank for Savings,** IV, A1 (1928) at 2100 Broadway, designed by the architects of the Federal Reserve Bank on Wall Street, was modeled after an Italian Renaissance palace. The inside decoration includes 27 different types of marble. The **Apthorp Apartments** (1908) at 2207 Broadway (or 390 West End Avenue) is one of the neighbourhood's monuments. Remarkable for its beautiful neo-Renaissance façade, it was one of the first buildings constructed around a central courtyard. The **Belnord,** V, A3, at 225 W. 86th Street, was designed according to the same plan and is another neo-Renaissance architectural treasure.

LINCOLN CENTER

Map IV, AB1-2
Information: *Guided tours are available daily 10am-5pm at Avery Fisher Hall,* ☎ *(212) 877 1800, ext. 516.*

Lincoln Center on Broadway, between 61st and 66th Streets, is a cultural center dedicated to the performing arts: opera, theater, music and dance. The six buildings house the **Metropolitan Opera**, the **New York City Opera**, the **New York City Ballet**, the **New York Philharmonic**, the famous **Juilliard School of Music**, a **museum** and a **library** specializing in the performing arts.

Several architects were selected to design Lincoln Center, following the example of Rockefeller Center. New York critics did not appreciate the results, finding the center mediocre. Yet Lincoln Center has been used as a model by other cultural centers throughout the United States.

John D. Rockefeller headed the committee of New Yorkers responsible for supervising the project. This group selected as main architect Wallace K. Harrison, who had participated in the design of the Metropolitan Opera House and in the overall design of the United Nations and Rockefeller Center. Work began in 1959 on a site which had been a notorious New York slum. *West Side Story* was filmed in the streets of this neighbourhood just before it was demolished to make way for Lincoln Center.

The total capacity of all the Lincoln Center theaters is more than 13,000 spectators. More than 5 million people attend performances every year. The Center's continuing operation is largely assured by private donors and gifts from philanthropic organizations. It is the heart of New York's cultural life and has contributed to the revival of the Upper West Side.

The plaza opposite Columbus Avenue and Broadway is surrounded by **Avery Fisher Hall** to the north, the **New York State Theater** to the south and the **Metropolitan Opera House**, IV, AB1-2, to the west. A black marble fountain in the center of the plaza is the traditional meeting place

---

A night at the opera with Jessye Norman

Jessye Norman, one of the great sopranos of our time and one of the leading stars of the Metropolitan Opera, has fully mastered the classical repertoire, but she is also very proud of her black American heritage. She has recorded gospel music, popular songs and has even appeared successfully on Broadway. When she talks about New York, a city she knows intimately, her face and deep voice reflect a trace of mischievousness.

'You have to admit, New York is certainly the most passionate city in the world. As Frank Sinatra said, "The city stays open all night long." Day or night in New York, unlike any other city in the world, there is always some kind of entertainment or activity going on. This is what draws foreigners to New York.

'I like Greenwich Village very much. It is a real village in which you feel that the people who live there are really at home. I also like the wonderful boutiques in SoHo and Tribeca and the French restaurants, **Montrachet** and **Chanterelle**.

'But I also go to simpler restaurants. The **Good Enough to Eat** on the Upper West Side is a great place! The food is very fresh and prepared simply. They have never heard of *nouvelle cuisine* there and so much the better! They serve good, straightforward food.

'I often go to see my friend Bobby Short at the **Café Carlyle** on the Upper East Side. He's a wonderful singer. The café is small, which creates an intimate atmosphere.

'My favourite season in New York? Autumn, certainly. September is the most beautiful month of the year. You can walk easily around the city. The tourists have all left and you feel as if you have New York all to yourself!'

fo theater-goers. The buildings are faced with cream-coloured travertine from Italy and all the façades incorporate Classical architectural elements.

Avery Fisher Hall, designed by Max Abramovitz, was the first building constructed. The façade includes a peristyle with 44 columns. When inaugurated in 1962, it was called Philharmonic Hall; it was renamed in 1973 following a donation by stereo manufacturer Avery Fisher. The hall houses the auditorium and practice rooms of the prestigious New York Philharmonic, directed by Zubin Mehta.

The acoustics of Avery Fisher Hall have been a favourite topic of debate in the New York art world. In 1962, the musicians complained of echoes and inaudibility and the roof, walls and seat coverings were changed several times, with no success. Over the years, major orchestras visiting New York have categorically refused to play in the hall. Finally, in 1976, architects Philip Johnson and John Burgee and acoustic specialist Cyril Harris attacked the problem. They completely remodeled the auditorium and successfully solved the acoustic problems of the 2700-seat hall. The New York Philharmonic gives four concerts a week from September to May and the Mostly Mozart Festival takes place every summer.

There are several interesting works of art inside, including *Orpheus and Apollo* by Richard Lippold, *The Archangel* by Seymour Lipton, *K458-The Hunt* by Dimitri Hadzi, a bust of Beethoven by Bourdelle and a bust of Gustav Mahler by Rodin.

The New York State Theater was designed by Philip Johnson and Richard Foster and constructed in 1964. A series of double columns in front of the glass façade support a balcony. This building is the home of the New York City Ballet and the New York City Opera, directed by Christopher Keene. The back wall of the enormous foyer is decorated with a Jasper Johns painting entitled *Numbers*. The stairway landings have works by Nadelman and Lipchitz. The ceiling of the Grand Promenade on the upper floor is covered with gold leaf. The 2700-seat auditorium was designed without a central aisle for better visibility. It includes five circular balconies and is illuminated by an immense diamond-shaped chandelier.

The centerpiece of Lincoln Center, the Metropolitan Opera House, stands on the west side of the plaza. This immense 10-storey building with five marble arches on the façade was designed by Wallace K. Harrison (1966). A monumental mural by Marc Chagall is visible to the left through the windows of the opera house, entitled *The Triumph of Music,* depicting dancers and musicians and including references to opera, jazz and New York City. Former Metropolitan Opera manager Rudolph Bing is represented in a gypsy costume. The predominantly yellow mural to the right is entitled *The Sources of Music* and refers to Orpheus, King David and major figures in musical history, including Mozart, Verdi and Wagner.

The only opera house in New York City in the 1870s was the Academy of Music on 14th Street. The 15 boxes of the theater were reserved by New York's oldest families and inaccessible to the 'new' capitalists, the Whitneys, Morgans and Vanderbilts. In reaction against this discrimination, these families joined together to construct the world's largest opera house. The Metropolitan Opera House was inaugurated in 1883 on Broadway, between 39th and 40th Streets. It included 122 boxes on three levels, designed so that it was easier to see neighbouring boxes than the stage itself. The Metropolitan Opera House finally found its present home in Lincoln Center. The premier performance was given on September 16, 1966, featuring Barber's *Antony and Cleopatra,* commissioned for the occasion. With 3790 seats, the 'Met' became the largest opera house in the world.

The **Guggenheim Bandshell** (1969) in Damrosch Park to the south of the Metropolitan Opera House presents free concerts in summer.

The **Vivian Beaumont Theater** (1965), designed by Eero Saarinen, has suffered from financial and artistic problems since its inauguration. Following a succession of resignations and remodelings, it re-opened in

The Lincoln Center Plaza, with the New York State Theater (left), the Metropolitain Opera House (center) and Avery Fisher Hall (right).

1986 with a decidedly contemporary program. The interior is decorated with a David Smith sculpture, *Zig IV.* The 1100-seat auditorium is considered one of the best in the city. The 300-seat **Mitzi E. Newhouse Theater** specializes in avant-garde productions. Note the Henry Moore sculpture, *Lincoln Center Reclining Figure,* in the middle of the pool in front of the theater.

The **Library and Museum of the Performing Arts** to the left of the theater was designed by Skidmore, Owings and Merrill. This branch of the New York Public Library houses documents concerning the history of theater, dance and music and presents free exhibitions, concerts, films and conferences *(open Mon, Tues and Thurs 10am-8pm, Wed and Fri noon-6pm, Sat 10am-6pm).* Near the library entrance is Alexander Calder's *Le Guichet.*

The illustrious Juilliard School of Music is across 65th Street. Created in 1905 as the Institute of Musical Arts, it was renamed in 1920 after a donation by philanthropist Augustus D. Juilliard. The current building, designed by Pietro Balluschi and inaugurated in 1969, is the most recent in Lincoln Center. The Juilliard School provides professional instruction in music, dance and theater. Small rehearsal rooms and theaters are available for student use. The building houses **Alice Tully Hall,** a 1100-seat concert hall specially designed for chamber music. It is also used for the **New York Film Festival,** organized every autumn by the Lincoln Center Film Society.

MORNINGSIDE HEIGHTS

Maps V, AB1; VI, AB3. — Subway: 110th St./Cathedral Parkway (line 1). Bus: line 10.

Morningside Heights, formerly known as Harlem Heights, is bordered by the Harlem plain to the east, the Hudson River to the west, 110th Street to the south and 125th Street to the north. Although small, this area is nevertheless home to some of Manhattan's most prestigious institutions.

Columbia University dominates the life of the neighbourhood. The thousands of students determine the character of the adjacent streets, filled with small restaurants, bars and 24-hour bookstores. The proximity of Harlem, a symbol of urban poverty and decay, is also a strong influence on Columbia's identity.

Until the late 19th century, this rural region was occupied only by an orphanage and insane asylum. The opening of Riverside Drive in 1880 and Morningside Drive in 1887 initiated the development of the surrounding property. In the early 20th century, Columbia University and the Cathedral of St John the Divine moved to the area, attracting some of Manhattan's affluent families.

▬ CATHEDRAL OF ST JOHN THE DIVINE★★

Map V, B1.

Information: *Open daily 7am-5pm. Guided tours are available Mon-Sat at 11am and 2pm, Sun at noon,* ☎ (212) 316 7400.

The unfinished cathedral of the Episcopal Diocese of New York stands majestically on Amsterdam Avenue at 112th Street. Although it was begun in 1892, construction is still underway. It is the largest Gothic church in the world with a surface area of 121,000 sq ft/36,000 sq m. The total length is 601 ft/182 m. The west side is 207 ft/63 m wide and the transept measures 108 ft/33 m. The height of the nave vault is 124 ft/53 m and, when finished, the towers will rise 291 ft/88 m.

In a city with a tradition for breaking construction records, the idea of building the world's largest cathedral was greeted enthusiastically. In 1872, following a proposal by Bishop Horat, the decision was made to begin the project. In 1888, architects Heins and La Farge won the architectural contest with their design for a Romanesque cathedral incorporating neo-Byzantine elements. The long axis of the cathedral was to be aligned along the ridge of Morningside Heights with a main entrance on 110th Street. The bishops eventually opted for a traditional church layout with the altar to the east and main entrance to the west.

The first stone was laid in 1892. J.P. Morgan personally financed the excavation work and, by 1911, the choir and the four supporting arches for the dome were completed. Several years later, the original plans were dropped in favour of a Gothic design and the central nave was lengthened by 80 ft/25 m. In 1916, the nave foundations were started again, but the architects encountered so many obstacles that money ran out, leaving the north transept unfinished.

Construction was interrupted during World War II. In 1967, the bishop announced that the cathedral might never be finished. A new campaign was launched in 1978 to finish the towers and the transept. Work is again underway, one century after the first stone was laid. The stone masons, carpenters and other construction workers on the site are working under master craftsmen to complete the world's largest cathedral.

Four of the five doors on the west façade are carved in Burmese teak. The only finished sculptures are on the far left portal. The 60 panels on the bronze doors of the central portal were cast in Paris by Barbedienne; they depict scenes from the Old and New Testaments. A statue of St John the Divine stands on the central post, looking toward Heaven. Directly above him on the tympanum is a majestas representing Christ in Glory. The large rose window above the main portal measures 40 ft/13 m in diameter.

The interior of the cathedral is one of the most beautiful in the city. The stained-glass windows on the north side of the narthex depict the Creation; the glass to the south is called the 'prototype window', with scenes from the Old Testament. Note the beautiful 15th- to 17th- century Greek, Russian and Byzantine icons.

The nave is divided into five aisles. Alternating massive and slender piers support the central nave. The cathedral's aim is to provide a place of worship for all people and this theme is reflected in the stained-glass windows and chapels. The floor of the nave is decorated with medallions representing important people and locations in Christian history and events in the life of Christ. Several works of art are hung in the side aisles, including Mortlake's tapestries woven from cartoons by Raphael.

Several neo-Romanesque elements from the first church design are visible in the crossing of the transept, including unfinished arches, the impressive temporary dome from 1909 and the Tennessee marble pulpit from 1916. Beautiful 17th-century Italian tapestries decorate this part of the church.

The Romanesque choir is enclosed by eight granite 55 ft/17 m columns, each weighing 130 tons. The sculpted oak choir stalls were modeled after those in the Taormina cathedral in Sicily. Note the two menorahs (seven-branched candlesticks).

From here, admire the large rose window which is directly above the central portal on the west side. The ambulatory leads to the **Chapel of Tongues,** so named because each one is dedicated to a different nationality. The beautiful glazed terracotta *Annunciation* in the south ambulatory is attributed to Luca della Robbia (15th century). Construction of the baptistery to the north of the choir was financed by the Stuyvesants, one of New York's oldest families. The 13 ft/4 m baptismal font was modeled after the font in the Italian cathedral of Sienna.

There is a **museum** in the northern section of the transept devoted to the history of the cathedral's construction. It includes a model of the finished monument. The entrance to the Religious Art Museum is to the south of the transept.

The 12 acres/5 hectares surrounding the cathedral are occupied by the diocese's administrative buildings, the bishop's residence and a co-educational school. The **Biblical Garden** contains only plants which are mentioned in the Bible.

St Luke's Hospital on 113th Street to the north of St John the Divine was founded in 1846 by the Episcopal Church. The Roman Catholic **Eglise de Notre Dame** occupies the corner of Morningside Drive and

114th Street. Construction of the still-unfinished Napoleonic-style church began in 1914 for a French-speaking congregation. A replica of the grotto at Lourdes is visible behind the altar.

The official residence of the president of Columbia University, an office held by President Eisenhower from 1948 to 1953, stands on the corner of Morningside Drive and 116th Street. This street then leads to the Columbia University campus.

■■■*COLUMBIA UNIVERSITY*★★★

Map VI, AB3
Information: *For free guided tours of the campus, visit 201 Dodge Hall (116th St. and Broadway),* ☎ (212) 280 2796.

Columbia University, originally called King's College, was founded in 1754 during the reign of King George II as an alternative to Harvard and Yale. It was initially located along the Hudson River near the current site of the World Trade Center. Anglican pastor Dr. Samuel Johnson was the first president of the class which included no more than eight students from New York society families. Renamed Columbia University after the revolution, it added a women's university, the prestigious **Barnard College,** in 1889. After the move to Morningside Heights in 1897, Columbia became one of the country's most prestigious universities. Some of the more famous graduates include: Alexander Hamilton, first Secretary of the Treasury; John Jay, first Chief Justice of the Supreme Court, and Gouverneur Morris, United States Ambassador to France during the revolution. In the 20th century, the young Franklin D. Roosevelt spent several years studying law at Columbia before entering politics. Several Columbia professors have received the Nobel Prize.

Columbia University is bordered by 114th Street to the south, 121st Street to the north, Morningside Drive to the east and Claremont Avenue to the west. Close to 18,000 students are enrolled. The Columbia Schools of Law, Business, Journalism, Arts and Sciences and Architecture are considered to be among the best in the United States.

A Lipchitz sculpture, *Bellerophon Taming Pegasus,* symbolizing the control over the forces of disorder by law, stands in front of the famous **law school,** VI, B3 (1961), on the corner of 116th Street and Amsterdam Avenue.

Cross the avenue to reach **College Walk,** VI, B3 the pedestrian continuation of 116th Street. The campus was designed in 1893 by architects McKim, Mead and White. The original buildings were constructed on a terrace to the north of College Walk according to the neo-Classical style popular at the time. The initial project called for buildings organized around several small courtyards, with a large lawn in the middle. The university ultimately preferred open space to this plan.

Butler Library (1934), the large university library to the south of the quadrangle, houses 4,800,000 books, making it one of the largest in the country. **Ferris Booth Hall** next door is the student center. The monumental **Low Memorial Library★** (1897) to the north dominates the campus. This enormous building, designed by McKim, originally served as the library; it currently houses the administrative offices. The colonnade and 135 ft/41 m dome were modeled after the Pantheon in Rome. A statue of *Alma Mater* (1903) by Daniel Chester French sits on the steps of the library. It is often the object of affectionate practical jokes by students.

St Paul's Chapel (1904) to the east of the Low Library combines neo-Classical and neo-Byzantine elements. The woodwork is modeled after the Santa Croce cathedral in Florence. **Buell Center** to the south is the oldest building on the campus, dating from 1878.

Avery Hall north of the chapel houses the famous **School of Architecture.** The library is the largest in its field in America.

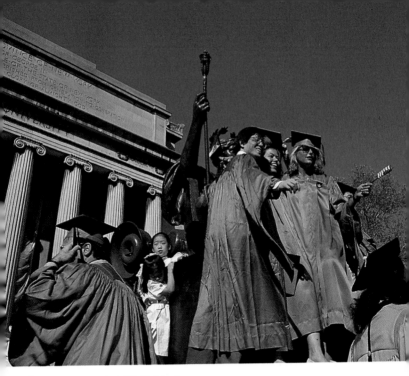
Commencement ceremonies at Columbia University.

In the 1930s, the **Pupin Physics Laboratories** on the corner of 120th Street and Broadway was the center of nuclear fission experiments conducted by Urey, Fermi and Rabi, who received the Nobel Prize for their efforts. **Dodge Hall** to the south is the departure point for guided tours and home of the highly reputed **School of Journalism,** founded by Joseph Pulitzer in 1912. Every spring, a jury awards the prestigious Pulitzer prizes from here.

Barnard College, VI, A3, is on the other side of Broadway, between 116th and 120th Streets. A plaque on the mathematics building at 117th Street commemorates the battle of Harlem Heights won by General Washington against British troops on September 16, 1776.

Leaving Columbia, the **Union Theological Seminary,** VI, A3 (1910) on the corner of Broadway and 120th Street is another famous New York institution. The neo-Gothic architecture and the building layout are reminiscent of Oxford and Cambridge universities in England.

The large neo-Georgian **Jewish Theological Seminary** (1886) on the corner of 122nd Street and Broadway is a major center for Jewish scholars in America. The library houses an exceptional collection of documents concerning Jewish history. In 1966, a fire devastated the building, destroying more than 65,000 books.

The beautiful neo-Gothic silhouette of **Riverside Church,** VI, A3 (1930), stands to the west, on 122nd Street. Affiliated with the Baptist congregation, this church is an interdenominational place of worship known for its progressive ideas and community service. The Rockefeller family was one of the more generous benefactors of the church. The carillon tower contains 74 bells, including the 20-ton Bourdon bell, the largest ever cast.

New Yorkers have never been fully satisfied with the proportions of the 410 ft/125 m tower and the 213 ft/65 m long nave. Nevertheless, the building is noteworthy for its stonework, woodwork and stained glass. Many elements recall the Chartres cathedral in France, particularly the Christ in Glory on the tympanum. Note the admirable 16th-century Flemish stained-glass windows and, south of the narthex, a chapel modeled after the Romanesque church of St Nazaire in Carcassonne. The church includes 50 stained-glass windows made in Boston, Chartres and Reims. The labyrinth formed by the flooring evokes the one in the Chartres cathedral. The chancel screen depicts seven aspects of the life of Christ, surrounded by people who have embodied the Christian ideal: Luther, Savonarola, Milton, Florence Nightingale, Pasteur and Bach. A Jacob Epstein sculpture, *Christ in Majesty*, hangs on the nave wall. Another work by Epstein, *The Virgin With Child*, can be seen outside the church on Claremont Avenue. The narthex leads to the tower which offers a splendid view over the northern section of Manhattan and the Hudson River. Concerts are held Saturdays at noon, Sundays before and after services and at 3pm.

▬ GENERAL GRANT NATIONAL MEMORIAL

Map VI, A3.

The General Grant National Memorial, more commonly known as Grant's Tomb, is situated to the north on 122nd Street *(open Wed-Sun 9am-5pm)*. Modeled after the Halicarnassus mausoleum, this granite-and-marble tomb contains the remains of Ulysses S Grant, commander-in-chief of the Union Armies during the Civil War, later President of the United States from 1868 to 1876. More than 90,000 subscribers participated in the construction of this monument. Once a popular site with New Yorkers, it is now rarely visited.

A wide staircase flanked by two eagles leads to the entrance of the tomb. The words pronounced by Grant during his investiture in 1868, 'Let us have peace', are engraved above the cornice. The alabaster windows which illuminate the austere interior recall Napoleon's tomb at Les Invalides in Paris. Grant's main victories and the surrender of General Lee are represented above the windows.

The sarcophagi of Grant and his wife lie in the crypt, surrounded by the busts of Generals Sherman, Sheridan, Thomas, Ord and McPherson. Several exhibition rooms are devoted to the life of General Grant.

HARLEM

Maps V, BCD1; VI, BCD2-3. — Subway: 110th St./Central Park North (line 2); 125th St./Broadway (line 1); 125th St./St Nicholas Ave. (lines A, B, C, D). Bus: lines 4, 5, 7, 10, 104.

For a visitor to New York, Harlem evokes both the golden age of jazz clubs and contemporary urban poverty linked to racial conflict. Neither of these two clichés holds true today: the 1920s are long gone, the original jazz stars of the era are dead and much of the slum housing of the 1960s and 1970s has disappeared. Although poverty and social tension still exist, Harlem is made up of close to 1 million Blacks representing every economic level. Some of the most extreme contrasts in New York clash visibly in this neighbourhood: middle-class families in the beautiful Sugar Hill buildings live next to drug dealers and vagrants in decaying buildings; elegant boulevards intersect sordid streets filled with potholes.

After many years of neglect, Harlem is currently undergoing profound transformation. Instead of moving to more affluent neighbourhoods, many successful Blacks have chosen to move back to the area they grew up in. Buildings are being restored and neighbourhoods cleaned up. The famous Apollo Theater has re-opened with ambitious projects and the Schomburg Center for Research in Black Culture has acquired an international reputation for its research into Black civilizations. Museums, cultural centers and theaters offer interesting programs. The transformation is slow, yet Harlem has changed more in the 1980s than in the two preceding decades.

Harlem comprises three distinct areas: **Central Harlem,** which is Black Harlem; **Spanish Harlem** or **El Barrio,** largely populated by Puerto Ricans, situated to the east of Park Avenue and north of E. 96th Street, and what was formerly **Italian Harlem** on the east side of 116th Street, a vestige from an earlier era.

This itinerary covers Black Harlem, which starts at 110th Street along Central Park and extends to 168th Street. Morningside Park and Columbia University mark the western edge of Harlem. See 'La Marqueta' p. 176 for a description of Spanish Harlem.

Certain areas of Harlem should be avoided. In contrast to the other itineraries, many of the sites are relatively distant from one another, even though they are close to 125th Street, the main commercial street. Several sightseeing companies offer guided tours, including **Harlem Spirituals, Inc.** (see p. 48), so that a visitor can discover the neighbourhood in complete safety, taste the local cooking and, on Sundays, attend a religious service, complete with gospel singing.

In the 17th century, the Dutch founded a village which they named after a city in the Netherlands — Haarlem. This hilly region was linked to the city 10 mi/16 km to the south by a

Dizzy Gillespie

Dizzy Gillespie is a jazz legend. A talented trumpet player, he was saxophonist Charlie Parker's partner. Together they broke away from traditional jazz and created bebop, with its complex and tight rhythms.

Dizzy was born in 1917 in South Carolina. He moved to New York in 1937 and first played in the Harlem nightclubs, only later moving Downtown. He created his bebop look: goatee, black beret, tortoiseshell glasses and extravagant suits. It is impossible not to recognize him on stage with his distant, quizzical look and grimaces. A vigorous person, his appetite for life is as great as his talent.

'When I got to New York, it was the capital of black music. That's where you had to go if you wanted to make it. It was the era of swing and the Count Basie, Duke Ellington and Fletcher Henderson big bands. People like Parker, Thelonius Monk, Kenny Clarke and myself wanted to react against the easy, fabricated rhythm of swing. Bebop created a real scandal when it was born in Harlem in the 1940s. New York critics murdered us! But we didn't care whether they wanted to listen to our music or not.

'At the time, Manhattan was incredibly safe. When the show was over, we walked home in the early morning. Nobody bothered us. Not possible today.

'Anyway, now I live in the suburbs, but I still love Manhattan. My favourite restaurants? The **Brazilian Pavilion** or **Victor's**, a Cuban restaurant. I always order a plate of rice and black beans; it reminds me of Southern cooking.'

former Indian path (Broadway). The fertile soil attracted wealthy landowners who established large estates; several of these remain, including the Morris-Jumel Mansion and the Hamilton Grange. The region remained essentially rural until the late 19th century, except for an area to the east, north of 86th Street, which was a working-class neighbourhood. Harlem was then a center for bicyclists, picnics, weekend strollers and boaters.

Encouraged by the extension of the subway, real-estate promoters began to develop the area for wealthy New Yorkers seeking space and leisure activities. Beautiful buildings were constructed, lining the newly paved avenues and streets. Sports clubs were formed; restaurants and theaters opened soon after to cater to the affluent clientele. The Harlem Opera House was inaugurated in 1889, followed by a symphony orchestra, a casino, hotels, department stores and even a yacht club. By the turn of the century, Harlem had become one of New York's elegant neighbourhoods. Real-estate speculation was a lucrative business for promoters until the stock market crash resulted in a collapse of the housing market. The arrival of Philip A. Payton, a Black real-estate agent, changed the future of Harlem. He offered high rents to building owners provided they would rent to Blacks. Thousands of Blacks moved to Harlem in the years following this agreement.

When slavery was abolished in 1860, New York's Black population numbered 20,000, mainly concentrated in ghettos in Greenwich Village. In the late 19th century, this population moved north to the Tenderloin district (between 30 and 40th Streets, along Broadway) and to Hell's Kitchen (near 45th Street and Seventh Avenue). Meanwhile, a developing Black middle class was denied access to affluent neighbourhoods. Harlem offered this minority the opportunity for decent and comfortable hous-

Friendly faces on Harlem's 125th Street.

ing for the first time. Blacks arriving from the South and other parts of the United States also found apartments here and, by 1918, Harlem had become a Black neighbourhood with a population of 100,000 people.

At the time, Harlem was the only 'elegant' Black neighbourhood in America. Many apartments offered at least a minimum of comfort and the spacious avenues contrasted with the sordid alleyways of other Black districts throughout the country. When Duke Ellington arrived in Harlem from Washington, D.C., he is said to have cried, 'It's like a Thousand and One Nights!' Jazz exploded in the neighbourhood after World War I, attracting people from all over the city. Black music, Black theater and Black literature flourished in New York in the 1920s. The most glorious days of the legendary Cotton Club and Connie's in Harlem lasted through this decade, ending with the Depression in the 1930s.

▄▄ VISIT

Martin Luther King Jr. Boulevard (or 125th Street) and Lenox Avenue are Harlem's two main streets. The ambience on Saturday, a busy shopping day, is always very animated. There are many discount stores, fast-food establishments and small grocery stores.

The celebrated Apollo Theater*, VI, B3 (1913), is at 253 W. 125th Street, between Seventh and Eighth Avenues (Adam Clayton Powell Jr. Boulevard and Frederick Douglass Boulevard, respectively). This music-hall was once off-limits to Blacks. Starting in 1934, Black revues and orchestras were produced in the theater. An impressive list of artists who performed in the theater over the following four decades includes Bessie Smith, Billie Holliday, Duke Ellington, Count Basie, Dizzy Gillespie, Charlie Parker, Thelonius Monk, Aretha Franklin and many others. The Apollo closed in 1976, but recently re-opened after extensive renovation. Interesting talent shows are held every Wednesday night.

The Theresa Towers, VI, B3 (1910), at 2090 Seventh Avenue on the corner of 125th Street, became famous overnight during Fidel Castro's visit to the United Nations in 1960 when the young revolutionary chose to stay in this hotel in the heart of Harlem.

The Studio Museum of Harlem, VI, B3 (144 W. 125th Street), has devoted exhibitions to contemporary Black artists since its creation in 1970 *(open Wed and Fri 10am-5pm, Sat and Sun 1-6pm, ☎ 212 864 4500)*. It is also used as a cultural center for the Black community. The museum has a rich collection of photographs and presents films and concerts.

St Martin's Episcopal Church, VI, C3, stands nearby, on the south-east corner of Lenox Avenue and 122nd Street. This Romanesque church was constructed in 1888 when promoters were trying to attract wealthy white New Yorkers to the neighbourhood.

The celebrated Schomburg Center for Research in Black Culture*, VI, B2 (1978), stands at 515 Lenox Avenue, between 135th and 136th Streets. The collection of 80,000 volumes and 50,000 photographs concerning Black history and civilization is based on the donation of Arthur Schomburg's personal library.

The most famous nightclub of the jazz era was the legendary Cotton Club, VI, C1, on Lenox Avenue at 143rd Street. The white owners employed Black orchestras and dancers, but refused entrance to Black spectators. Duke Ellington's orchestra played at the Cotton Club from 1927 to 1931.

The curious blue-grey Tudor-style façade of the Abyssinian Baptist Church, VI, B2, stands at 132 W. 138th Street. The congregation owes its fame to two preachers, Adam Clayton Powell and his son, Adam

Clayton Powell Jr., a Congressman who fought against racial discrimination in America. Following Powell's death in 1972, the city renamed the part of Seventh Avenue which crosses Harlem after him.

The **Saint Nicholas Historic District**, VI, B2, includes a section of row houses which extends between Seventh and Eighth Avenues and 138th and 139th Streets. The restrained elegance of these houses contrasts with the general appearance of the rest of Harlem. The houses were built in 1891 for affluent white families. Long interior courtyards provided access to horse-drawn carriages. Harlem residents call this privileged area 'Striver's Row', apparently for the ambitious Black families who worked here in the hope of one day living here.

Sugar Hill, VI, AB1, the traditional middle-class area of Harlem, includes the area from Saint Nicholas to Edgecombe Avenues and from 143rd to 155th Streets. Its name comes from the 'sweet life' enjoyed by the more affluent Black residents, including Count Basie, Duke Ellington, boxer Sugar Ray Robinson and Supreme Court Judge Thurgood Marshall.

The **Morris-Jumel Mansion*** (1765), a former colonial estate on the north-west corner of 160th Street and Edgecombe Avenue, is a mixture of Federal and Georgian architectural styles. This hilltop mansion overlooking the Harlem River was the country home of British Colonel Roger Morris. Morris, a personal friend of George Washington, decided to return to England when the American Revolution broke out. Because of the mansion's strategic position, it served as Washington's headquarters during the battle of Harlem Heights in 1776. Following many years of neglect, wine merchant Etienne Jumel purchased and restored the house. In 1832, his widow married Aaron Burr, once Vice-President of the United States.

The interior of the mansion is now a **museum** which houses the reconstructed private apartments of the former owners *(open Tues-Sun 10am-4pm)*. Mr. Burr's room on the second floor is furnished in the Federal style, while Mrs. Jumel preferred the Empire style. Note General Washington's desk and the furniture which belonged to Napoleon.

Sylvan Terrace, opposite Jumel Terrace, between 160th and 162nd Streets, is a charming alley which was originally the access road to the Morris-Jumel Mansion. It is lined with fine wood houses constructed in 1882.

Hamilton Grange, VI, B2 (1802), in the center of Hamilton Heights, is jammed between two buildings at 287 Convent Avenue, between 141st and 142nd Streets. This two-floor house was Alexander Hamilton's country home. Originally located a bit to the north, it was moved to its present location in 1889. Hamilton spent the last years of his life in this house, before he was fatally wounded in a duel with one of his political enemies, Aaron Burr, future husband of Mrs. Jumel.

Aunt Len's Doll and Toy Museum, VI, B1, at 6 Hamilton Terrace, exhibits more than 3000 dolls and toys *(open Tues-Sun by appointment only, ☎ 212 9264172)*.

The **City University of New York**, VI, B2, on Convent Avenue, was founded in 1849 as a free institution providing university education for any student who could pass the entrance examinations. The first students were almost all immigrants. No longer free, but subsidized by the city and still not very expensive, enrollment now exceeds 50,000 students. The beautiful neo-Gothic buildings of the North Campus (on Convent Avenue, between 138th and 140th Streets) were constructed in 1905 from schist dug out from the first subway excavations. The South Campus, between 130th and 135th Streets, houses the Finley Student Center and Goldmark Hall, a former chapel built in 1847.

The steep slope of **Morningside Park**, VI, B3 ; V, B1, juts upward at 123rd Street. Designed in the 19th century by Olmsted and Vaux, the Central Park landscape architects, the park is today the dividing line between Columbia University and Harlem. The wooded hills provide a pleasant view, but visitors are warned to avoid this park.

MUSEUMS AND GALLERIES

The 150 museums, which house exceptional art collections, and innumerable art galleries make New York City one of the world's most important international art centers.

This guide provides a selective list of museums, including the five major art museums, followed by a number of other museums devoted to various subjects, classified in decreasing order of interest.

The art galleries (p. 160) are organized according to neighbourhood. A short description of the work exhibited by each gallery is included.

▬ *FRICK COLLECTION*★★★

1 E. 70th St., ☎ (212) 288 0700.
Map IV, C1. — Subway: 68th St./Hunter College (line 6). Bus: lines 1, 2, 3, 4.
Information: *Open Tues-Sat 10am-6pm, Sun 1-6pm, closed Tues during July and Aug.*

The elegant and refined Frick Collection is housed in the French neo-Classical former mansion of steel baron Henry Clay Frick (1849-1919), designed by architect Thomas Hastings. It includes paintings by 14th- to 18th-century masters, antique silver, French furniture and Limoges china, all arranged to resemble a luxurious private home rather than an anonymous museum.

The **Anteroom** is reserved for temporary exhibits.

The **Boucher Room** is a replica of an 18th-century French *boudoir*. The panels on the walls representing *The Arts and Sciences*★★ were painted by Boucher for Mme de Pompadour's boudoir in the château de Crécy.

The **Dining Room** includes a series of works by English painters: Hogarth, *Miss Mary Edwards;* Reynolds, *General John Burgoyne* and Gainsborough, *The Mall at St James's Park*★★.

In the **West Vestibule** are the *Four Seasons*★★, painted by Boucher in 1755, and a Boulle desk.

The **Fragonard Room** contains *The Progress of Love*★★, a famous series by Fragonard painted for Mme Du Barry, Louis XV's mistress. It also has 18th-century French furniture by Riesener, Sèvres porcelain and a **bust**★ by Houdon.

The unique spiral design of the Guggenheim Museum on Fifth Avenue.

Frick Collection

New York

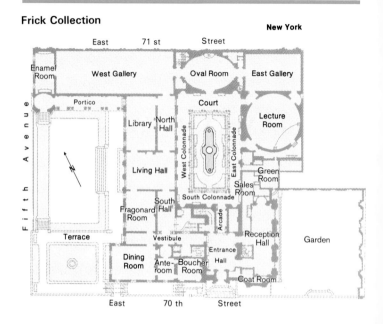

Next door, the **South Hall** has two superb Vermeer paintings, *The Officer and Laughing Girl* and *The Music Lesson*, a Boucher and a Renoir. The furniture includes a secrétaire and chest of drawers constructed by Riesener for Marie-Antoinette.

The **Living Hall** is one of the most beautiful rooms of the museum. The Venetian, Spanish and German schools are represented by Bellini, *St Francis in Ecstasy***; Titian, *Man in a Red Cap*** and *Portrait of Pietro Aretino***; El Greco, *Saint Jerome** and Holbein, *Sir Thomas More*** and *Thomas Cromwell**. Note the handsome Boulle furniture and Chinese porcelain.

The **Library** contains Italian Renaissance sculptures, portraits of Henry Frick and the famous Gilbert Stuart portrait of George Washington (another version exists in the Metropolitan Museum of Art). English painters exhibited here include Gainsborough, Reynolds, Constable and Turner.

The **North Hall** exhibits drawings and engravings, a Houdon bust and *The Portrait of the Comtesse d'Haussonville**** by Ingres.

The **West Gallery** includes magnificent European paintings: three Rembrandts, including the admirable *Self-Portrait**** (1658) and *The Polish Rider***; *Wisdom and Strength** by Veronese; the *Portrait of Vincentio Anastagi*** by El Greco; portraits by Frans Hals and Velázquez *(Philip IV of Spain)*; several works by Van Dyck; Constable and Turner landscapes**; *The Education of the Virgin*** by Georges de la Tour and Goya's *The Forge*.

The **Enamel Room** contains a beautiful collection of Limoges enamel and *Saint Simon*** by Piero della Francesca. Paintings include Van Eyck's *Virgin and Child With Saints and Donors* and Memling's *Portrait of a Man*.

The **Oval Room** includes a statue of *Diane* by Houdon and several Whistler portraits.

The **East Gallery** exhibits paintings by Goya, Van Dyck, *Portrait** by David and an admirable *Sermon on the Mount* by Claude Lorrain.

The beautifully colonnaded **Court** is a marvelous place to stop and rest, with its lovely fountain, sculptures and greenery.

SOLOMON R. GUGGENHEIM MUSEUM***

1071 Fifth Ave., between 88th-89th Sts., ☎ (212) 860 1313.
Map V, C3. — Subway: 86th St./Lexington Ave. (lines 4, 5, 6). Bus: lines 1, 2, 3, 4.
Information: *Open Tues 11am-8pm, Wed-Sun 11am-5pm.*

The Guggenheim Museum (1959) is the only New York museum for which the architecture is as famous as the collection. Architect Frank Lloyd Wright's design has been compared to a roll, a washing machine, an extravagant hat or a space ship which has landed on Fifth Avenue. In fact, the museum is a hollow cylinder surrounded by a 1417 ft/432 m spiral ramp.

Start on the top floor (take the elevators from the ground floor) and walk down the spiral ramp to view the paintings. An enormous skylight illuminates the interior.

Founded in 1939 by copper magnate Solomon R. Guggenheim, the Museum for Non-Objective Art was devoted to non-figurative European art. The collection was later renamed after its founder and enlarged to include all currents of modern art.

The museum owns more than 4000 paintings, sculptures and drawings, including one of the world's largest Kandinsky*** collections and paintings by Klee, Chagall, Léger, Rousseau, Picasso, Braque, Dubuffet, Miró and Delauney (Eiffel Tower series). Sculptors Brancusi and Calder are well represented, along with the New York School (Kline, Rothko, Newman, Pollock and Gottlieb).

A separate room houses the admirable **Thannhauser Collection** of Impressionist and post-Impressionist painters, including Manet, Degas, Renoir *(Woman With a Parrot***), Gauguin, Van Gogh, Cézanne, Vuillard, Toulouse-Lautrec *(Moulin de la Galette*)* and several early works by Picasso.

The museum organizes excellent temporary exhibits. A major addition is currently under way, which will enable the museum to exhibit most of the collection.

METROPOLITAN MUSEUM OF ART***

82nd St. and Fifth Ave., ☎ (212) 879 5500.
Map V, C3. — Subway: 86th St./Lexington Ave. (lines 4, 5, 6). Bus: lines 1, 2, 3, 4.
Information: *Open Tues 10am-8:45pm, Wed-Sat 10am-4:45 pm, Sun 11am-4:45pm.*

The fabulous collections of the Metropolitan Museum of Art include more than 3 million paintings, sculptures and art objects from every continent in the world, dating from prehistoric times to the present. Despite constant renovations and additions, the 270 rooms of the 'Met', covering 111 acres/45 hectares, can exhibit only one quarter of the total collection at a time. Nevertheless, it would take weeks to thoroughly visit the Egyptian, Greek, Roman and Mediaeval sections, the European and American painting collections, the Primitive Arts galleries, the Arms and Armour, the musical instruments, the drawing collection and the costume exhibits. The **Cloisters** in Fort Tryon Park in northern Manhattan is a branch of the 'Met' (see p. 177).

The idea of creating a major art museum in New York first surfaced in Paris in 1866. During a dinner in the Bois de Boulogne, a group of affluent Americans decided to found an institution comparable to the great European museums. In 1870, the Metropolitan Museum of Art was opened on the corner of Fifth Avenue and 54th Street. It was later transferred to 14th Street, finally moving to its current site in 1880.

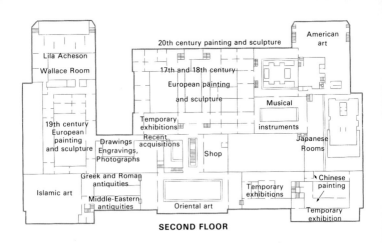

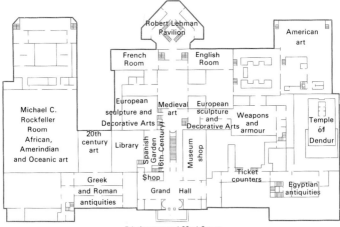

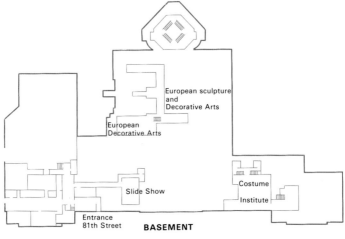

The Metropolitan Museum of Art

The Metropolitan Museum of Art on Central Park is one of the largest museums in the world.

Calvert Vaux, one of the Central Park landscape architects, selected a neo-Gothic style for the museum's first building. The west side of this original structure is still visible from Central Park. The imposing main building was constructed by Richard Morris in 1902, who adopted a monumental scale reminiscent of ancient Roman baths. Corinthian-capped columns frame three enormous arches on the neo-Classical Renaissance façade. Curious stone blocks directly above the columns were probably intended for sculptures which were never completed. During warm weather, museum-goers meet on the wide staircase at the Fifth Avenue entrance, where entertainment is often provided by street musicians.

The Met — Recommendations

Philippe de Montebello, Director of the Metropolitan Museum of Art since 1978, recommends short but frequent visits to avoid exhaustion and to concentrate on a section or a specific period.

It is better to visit the museum early in the morning on weekdays. Avoid weekends.

His favourites from the vast number of European paintings on the second floor include: Tiepolo, *The Triumph of Marius* and *The Fall of Carthage;* Andrea Mantegna, *Adoration of the Shepherds;* the famous *Harvesters* by Brueghel the Elder and the marvelous Van Eyck diptych of the *Crucifixion* and the *Last Judgment.* He particularly likes the self-portrait of *Rubens, his wife Héléna Fourment and their son Peter Paul.* Mr. de Montebello considers Velázquez's *Juan de Pareja* 'one of the greatest paintings' by the Spanish master. He also selected the famous Rembrandt *Self-Portrait* from what is one of the largest Rembrandt collections in the world. He completed his list of favourites with: Watteau, *Mezzetin;* David, *The Death of Socrates;* Manet, *The Spanish Singer;* Van Gogh, *The Cypresses* and Seurat, *Sunday Afternoon on the Island of the Grande Jatte.*

The Metropolitan Museum of Art, like all New York museums, is well organized and provides numerous visitor services. Free guided tours are available daily (ask at the Information Desk in the Great Hall). The Uris Center for Education in the basement offers comprehensive visitor information, including maps and material concerning the collections and temporary exhibits.

The Metropolitan Museum collections, divided into 18 main departments, are regularly enlarged through museum purchases and private donations of works or money. The exhibits are so vast that only one or two departments can be comfortably visited in one day.

The Great Hall on the first floor, which includes the Information Desk, a checkroom and the museum gift shops, leads to the cafeteria and restaurant in the south wing and to the Thomas J. Watson Library and Grace Rainey Rogers Auditorium.

First floor

Egyptian art***

The Egyptian collection to the north of the Great Hall is one of the largest in the world. Architectural digs sponsored by the museum have considerably enlarged the collection, which includes more than 10,000 objects from the predynastic period (before 3100 BC) to the Byzantine era (8th century). The collection contains sculptures and reliefs from the 1st to the 10th dynasty (3100-2040 BC). Objects recovered from Thebes include a granite bust of *Queen Hatshepsut* from the 18th dynasty (1503-1482 BC), with the distinctive royal *nemes* headdress.

Admirable sarcophaghi and funerary items from the 19th to the 26th dynasty (1300 BC-AD 500) and works executed during the Ptolemaic and Roman periods depict the later years of Egyptian culture.

The **Temple of Dendur**** in the Sackler Wing was given to the United States by the Egyptian government. To save the temple from submersion following the construction of the Aswan Dam, it was dismantled piece by piece and reassembled in this vast wing. It was built by Emperor Augustus in the 1st century BC, but the design is similar to the traditional Egyptian layout used in earlier centuries.

Greek and Roman art***

The Greek and Roman collections include beautiful sculptures, vases, jewelry and wall paintings.

Among the remarkable Cycladic statuettes, note the *Harp Player*** (3000 BC). Represented in an unusual sitting position, the musician plays with his head bowed. The care taken with detail is admirable, particularly given the primitive tools available at the time.

The archaic Greek sculpture collection includes a magnificent pink marble *Kouros*** (statue of a young man) from the 7th century BC. It is one of the museum's oldest Greek statues. The rigid position of the toes with the extended left foot and the hands clenched into fists reveal the Egyptian influence on this pre-Classical work.

Greek pottery reached its peak of technical refinement with the *Euphronios Krater* (500 BC), a red figure Krater representing a mythical scene. Note the different tones in the colour of the hair and beards.

Do not miss the bedroom *(cubuculum)* from a villa at Boscoreale near Pompeii, buried by the Vesuvius eruption in AD 79. The scenes painted on the walls evoke theater decoration.

The Michael C. Rockefeller wing**

The artistic treasures of Africa, the Pacific Islands and pre-Columbian America are housed in this wing. More than 2000 works of art are exhibited, including bronze sculptures from Benin, sculpted wood from the Dogons, ritual sculptures by the formidable New Guinea Asmats, American Indian pottery and Eskimo objects.

This impressive collection and the rooms were donated to the museum by Nelson Rockefeller in memory of his son Michael, who died during an expedition to West New Guinea in 1961.

The Lila Acheson Wallace wing (20th-century art)***

The museum's most recent room, inaugurated in February 1987, houses 9000 contemporary and modern art sculptures, drawings and paintings.

Assembled by Bill Lieberman, the collection includes work by: Klee (close to 90 paintings); Picasso, the famous *Gertrude Stein;* de Kooning; Daniel Smith and Max Beckmann, the *Debut Triptych.* Other painters included here are Edward Hopper, Georgia O'Keeffe and Jackson Pollock (*Autumn Rhythm***). Finally, there are an exceptional number of Abstract Expressionist paintings.

Mediaeval art***

The Mediaeval Art Collection is exhibited in five rooms in the Met and also in the Cloisters in northern Manhattan (see p. 177). More than 4000 works can be viewed, including the best of Byzantine art, ivories, Roman and Gothic jewelry, stained-glass windows, tapestries and French enamels.

A **Romanesque Chapel***** has been reconstructed behind the main staircase, at the entrance to the tapestry room. Most of the tapestries were woven in French and Flemish workshops during the 14th to 16th centuries. The *Annunciation* dates from the early 15th century, but its origins are uncertain. Discovered in Spain, it was probably woven in Arras.

A beautiful 17th-century Baroque choir screen in the **Mediaeval Sculpture Gallery** was originally used in the Cathedral of Valladolid. The sculpture collection includes a *Virgin and Child*** from Burgundy (15th century), discovered in the Clarissa convent in Poligny (France). Note the sense of intimacy between the mother and child.

Arms and armour**

Handsome equestrian armour, swords, daggers, halberds, lances and shields are exhibited alongside superb muskets, pistols, arquebuses and flintlocks. The collection includes more than 15,000 items from around the world.

The American wing***

This wing houses the world's largest collection of American art. It covers three floors and spans more than three centuries, from the colonial period to the 20th century. To follow the exhibit in chronological order, start on the third floor and go down. American painting and sculpture are on the second floor (except for contemporary and modern art).

The **Garden Court** exhibits the neo-Classical façade of the United States Bank (1824), Tiffany windows and the loggia from Louis Comfort Tiffany's home. The paintings in the court are by some of America's most famous painters: Stuart, portrait of *George Washington***; Hathaway, *Woman With Her Dogs****; Leutze, the epic *Washington Crossing the Delaware**** and Sargent, *Madame X***. Do not miss the paintings from the **Hudson River School,** including those by its most famous artist, Thomas Cole. Remarkable Tiffany glass pieces inspired by the Art Nouveau style are exhibited. Among the many replicas, note the living room from the Little House (1915), designed in Minnesota by architect Frank Lloyd Wright.

European sculpture and decorative arts***

This department contains 60,000 works from the 15th to the 20th centuries, with a particularly extensive French section. In addition to an admirable *Virgin and Child* by Andrea Della Robbia and works by Bernini and Canova *(Perseus With the Head of Medusa),* note the numerous French sculptors represented, including Houdon, Monnot, Lemoyne, Carpeaux, Degas, Rodin and Maillol.

The most successful reconstructions are the Spanish Renaissance patio from the castle of Lélez Blanco and the 18th-century storefront from 3, quai Boudon in Paris. Do not miss the admirable porcelain and metal-work sections.

Lehman Pavilion**

New York banker Robert Lehman donated his fabulous collection to the Met, provided the museum reconstruct his 54th Street home to house it. This collection of masterpieces, valued at $100 million in 1975, includes more than 300 paintings and 1000 drawings by 14th- to 20th-century European artists.

Various schools of painting are represented: Siennese, *Expulsion From Paradise*** by Giovanni di Paolo; Florentine, *Annunciation*** by Botticelli and Flemish Renaissance, with paintings by Memling and Petrus Christus. The Sitting Room contains a Rembrandt, two El Grecos *(Christ Carrying the Cross** and Saint Jerome**)* and a Goya. French 18th- and 19th-century art is represented by Ingres' magnificent *Portrait of the Princesse de Broglie** and paintings by Degas, Corot, Renoir, Cézanne, Van Gogh, Matisse, Vlaminck and Derrain.

The lower level exhibits superb drawings by Dürer *(Self-Portrait of the 22-year Old Artist),* Rembrandt, Botticelli, Leonardo da Vinci, Ingres, Degas and Cézanne.

Second floor

The central staircase leads to the second floor, which houses more than 3000 European paintings, exhibited in chronological order and according to country.

Italian school. Giotto's *Epiphany*** belongs to a series of seven panels depicting the life of Christ. This painting brings together the *Angel Appearing to the Shepherds* (background) and the *Adoration of the Magi* in a single composition. 15th-century painters include: Fra Filippo Lippi, *Man and Woman at the Window*; Sandro Botticelli, *The Last Communion of Saint Jerome*** and Sassetta, *The Voyage of the Magi**.* A selection of 16th-century paintings includes work by: Titian, *Venus and Adonis*** and *Venus and the Lute Player***; Veronese, *Mars and Venus United by Love** and Correggio. Note the remarkable spatial definition in Raphael's *Agony in the Garden*.

Spanish school. The powerful *View of Toledo*** is a marvellous example of El Greco's mystical, stormy style. Other El Greco paintings include *The Vision of Saint Jerome* and *Portrait of the Cardinal of Guevara.* Velázquez' *Portrait of Juan de Pareja*** is remarkable in its precision and wealth of detail.

Flemish school. Masterpieces include work by: Van Eyck; Memling; Bosch; Brueghel the Elder, *The Harvesters**;* Rubens, *Venus and Adonis** and Van Dyck.

Dutch school. Rembrandt's *Aristotle Contemplating a Bust of Homer*** depicts the solemn presence of the Greek philosopher through his mastery of the chiaroscuro technique. The celebrated *Self-Portrait* reveals his simplicity and psychological insight. Vermeer's *Young Girl With a Water Jug* is a masterpiece of light and painterly technique.

German school. The influence of Italian painting on the German School can be measured by Dürer's *The Virgin and Child With Saint Anne**.* Other paintings include *The Judgment of Paris* by Lucas Cranach the Elder and *A Member of the Wedigh Family** by portraitist Holbein.

English school. This section contains paintings by Hogarth, Reynolds and Gainsborough.

French school. 17th-century France is well represented by Georges de la Tour, *The Storyteller. The Rape of the Sabines* by Poussin and paintings by Claude Lorrain are exhibited along with 18th-century works by Watteau, Boucher and Fragonard.

19th-century paintings and sculptures (André Meyer galleries)

Inaugurated in 1980, these galleries are the pride of the Metropolitan Museum. Major neo-Classic and Romantic works are by: David, *The Death of Socrates*★★; Delacroix, *The Abduction of Rebecca*★★ and Ingres. Works by other artists include *Majas on a Balcony*★★ and *Portrait of Manuel Osorio* by Goya and *The Grand Canal in Venice* by Turner.

The 22 Courbet paintings include the voluptuous *Woman With a Parrot*, which created a scandal when first exhibited.

Corot, Daumier and Millet represent the Barbizon School. One room is devoted to sculptures by Rodin, Bourdelle and Maillol while another contains works by Symbolist painters Puvis de Chavannes and Moreau.

Impressionist and post-Impressionist painting highlights this collection, represented by: Manet (18 paintings); Monet (29 paintings, including *The Poplars*★★★); Degas (100 paintings); Renoir, Seurat and Pissarro. Included in the 17 Cézannes are the *Mont-Saint Victoire* and the *Card Players*★★. Works by Van Gogh include *The Arlesienne, Self-Portrait With a Straw Hat, The Irises, The Sunflowers*★★★ and *The Cypresses*★★★. The strength of Gauguin's work with colour is evident in the magnificent *La Orana Maria*★★.

Islamic art★

This is one of the world's best collections of Islamic art, famous for its metal and glass pieces, 16th- and 17th-century tapestries and illuminated manuscripts. A beautiful 18th-century house from Damascus has been carefully reconstructed in this section.

Ancient Near Eastern art

This department covers the period from 6000 BC to the Arab conquest (AD 626) and includes Sumerian stone sculptures and numerous metal objetcs. A group of Assyrian bas-reliefs and statues★★ from the Assurnasirpal palace in Nimrud depict two enormous human-headed winged bulls guarding the entrance.

Far Eastern art★

This section includes sculptures of Buddha, Chinese painting, jade pieces, porcelain and South-East Asian and Indian sculptures. Note the superb replica of a garden court★★★ from the Ming dynasty (14th to 17th centuries).

The **Japanese rooms** were inaugurated recently. An Isamu Noguchi granite sculpture adorns a small garden. The admirable Japanese screens by Ogota Korin recall the brushwork of several Western painters, particularly Van Gogh.

Musical instruments★★

Among the most remarkable pieces in this 4000-instrument collection are the first piano★★, several Stradivarius violins and exceptional mediaeval and Renaissance pieces.

Ground floor

The **Costume Institute** offers temporary exhibits devoted to haute couture or traditional and regional costumes.

▬ *MUSEUM OF MODERN ART*★★★

11 W. 53rd St., ☎ (212) 708 9480.

Map IV, BCE. — Subway: Fifth Ave./53rd St. (line E). Bus: 1, 2, 3, 4, 5 (Uptown); lines 6, 7 (Downtown).

Information: *Open Fri-Tues 11am-6pm, Thurs 11am-9pm.*

When inaugurated in 1929, the Museum of Modern Art immediately became a leading focal point of culture in New York. It houses the world's foremost collection of modern art, with 4000 paintings and

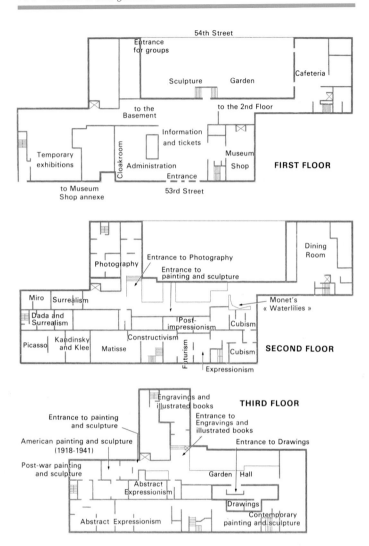

The Museum of Modern Art (MOMA)

sculptures and 50,000 drawings and engravings. It has also contributed to a renewed interest in movies and photography as significant art forms: it owns more than 20,000 photographs and a film library with 8000 films.

Art historian Alfred Barr and several members of the Rockefeller family, reacting against the conservative outlook of the Metropolitan Museum of Art, decided to create an institution devoted entirely to art created after 1880. In 1929, the museum's first task was to organize an exhibition of French Impressionists and post-Impressionists.

In 1939, the museum moved to its present site on 53rd Street, between Fifth Avenue and Avenue of the Americas. By 1984, remodeling and new construction had doubled the exhibition space, which nevertheless can accommodate only one quarter of the collection at a time.

A detailed description of the painting, sculpture, photography, architecture and decorative arts sections would resemble a complete history of modern art. Our description is limited to the most important works.

The main entrance leads to the glassed-in area, the **Garden Hall**; the **Abby Aldrich Rockefeller Sculpture Garden** extends beyond the hall. This pleasant garden in the heart of Midtown contains works by Rodin, *Balzac*★ and *The Burghers of Calais;* Maillol; Lipchitz; Picasso, *The Goat*★; Moore; Nevelson and David Smith.

Escalators to the left of the Garden Hall lead to the lower level which houses temporary exhibits in the **René d'Harnoncourt Galleries** and two theaters (films shown daily). For show times, visit the Information Desk or ☎ (212) 708 9490.

Second floor

Most of the rooms have low ceilings and carpeted floors to preserve a sense of intimacy. Escalators to the right of the first-floor landing lead to galleries devoted to the history of photography since the 19th century. There is a good collection of French and American photographers, including Lange, Berenice Abbott, Steichen, Weston and Alfred Stieglitz.

The painting and sculpture collections begin with the galleries devoted to the post-Impressionists. Note *The Sleeping Gypsy*★★ and *The Dream*★★ (1897) by Rousseau, a customs officer and friend of Picasso, Jarry and Apollinaire. The celebrated *Starry Night*★★★ is one of the few Van Gogh paintings in the collection. *Moon and Earth*★★ by Gauguin reveals the important role of colour in post-Impressionist work. Cézanne, precursor of the Cubists, is represented by a *Still Life With Apples*★★ and *The Bather*★★.

Paintings by Picasso, Braque, Gris and Léger dominate the Cubist gallery. Picasso's *Les Demoiselles d'Avignon*★★★ (1907) has been cited as one of the movement's most important works. An adjacent room is devoted to a series of *Water Lilies*★★ by Monet, in which colour predominates over line. Other admirable works in this section are by: Matisse, Derain *(The Bathers)* and Vlaminck.

The MOMA owns 17 paintings by Piet Mondrian, including *Composition in Black, White and Red*★★, a fine example of Geometric Abstract Art. Mondrian's *Broadway Boogie Woogie*★★ (1943) is a striking painting inspired by New York street life. Expressionist painters include Rouault and German artists Kirchner and Nolde. The Futurists' interest in movement and speed is represented by Giacomo Balla, Umberto Boccioni and Gino Severini. Kasimir Malevitch is undoubtedly the most important of the Russian Constructivists and Supremacists, with his works *White on White*★★ and *Red Square, Black Square*★★.

The **Matisse room** exhibits virtually all 40 works owned by the museum, including *The Dance*★★★. It provides an overview of the painter's development, which was always dominated by colour. The famous collage *The Pool*★★ is exhibited on the third floor, revealing his influence on Abstract Expressionist painters.

Klee and Kandinsky are exhibited in the same room, as they worked and taught together at the Bauhaus school. Russian artist Kandinsky was one of Abstract art's theoreticians.

Works by Picasso occupy an entire room, revealing the multiple sources of inspiration of the Spanish painter.

The museum also exhibits numerous works from the Dada and Surrealist movements: Picabia, *I Remember My Dear Udnie;* Marcel Duchamp, *The Passage From Virgin to Bride;* Dalí, *The Persistence of Memory;* Magritte; Max Ernst, *Nostalgia of the Infinite*. Note the admirable work by Spanish Surrealist Joan Miró, *Dutch Interior* (1928), inspired by the school of 17th-century Dutch painting.

Third floor

Most of this floor is devoted to 20th-century American painting and sculpture. Don't miss the paintings by Edwin Dickinson, Ben Shahn and Andrew Wyeth, particularly *Christina's World*.

Painting

The main representatives of European Abstract art are Mathieu, Bazaine, Hans Hartung, Soulage and de Staël. The prolific American school includes works by Kline; Gottlieb; de Kooning, *Woman I* and *Woman II;* Mark Rothko, *Red, Brown and Black* and Motherwell, *Elegy for the Spanish Republic*. One of the most important painters, Jackson Pollock, a central figure in the Action Painting movement, is represented by the superb *One Number 31* and *Full Fathom Five*, inspired by a Shakespearean sonnet. The essentially American Pop art movement is represented by Rauschenberg; Andy Warhol, *Ten Marilyns;* James Rosenquist; George Segal and Roy Lichtenstein, *Drowning Girl*.

Sculpture

The museum exhibits sculpture by numerous artists: Bourdelle; Brancusi, *The Bird;* Giacometti; Calder, stabiles and mobiles; Julio Gonzalez; César; Noguchi and Barbara Hepworth.

Engravings and illustrated books

This section houses several thousand works from Degas to contemporary pieces. Temporary exhibits are organized regularly. Do not miss the engravings by Austrian expressionist Egon Schiele.

Drawings

The museum collections include thousands of drawings by modern and contemporary artists (Russes, Klee, Dubuffet, etc.).

Fourth floor

Architecture, industrial design and decorative arts occupy the top floor. Works exhibited include drawings by Le Corbusier, Mies van der Rohe and Frank Lloyd Wright, furniture (Rietveld wooden chair), projects by architect Hector Guimard, automobiles and even a helicopter.

▬ *WHITNEY MUSEUM OF AMERICAN ART****

954 Madison Ave. at 75th St., ☎ (212) 570 3676.
Map IV, C1. — Subway: 77th St./Lexington Ave. (line 6). Bus: lines 1, 2, 3, 4.
Information: *Open Tues 1-8pm, Wed-Sat 11am-5pm, Sun noon-6pm.*

The Whitney Museum, devoted exclusively to 20th-century American art, is unique among museums. In 1918, heiress Gertrude Vanderbilt Whitney, a sculptor herself, set up an art gallery in her Greenwich Village studio to exhibit the works of painters and sculptors who had been refused shows elsewhere. Her personal collection grew along with public interest in contemporary art and, in 1930, she decided to create a museum for the 600 works in her collection.

Today, the Whitney Museum collection comprises more than 10,000 works (paintings, drawings, sculptures and films) by the most famous 20th-century American artists. An audacious purchasing policy and unique temporary exhibits make this one of New York's best museums. The Biennial organized by the Whitney has become a national event. Many contemporary artists regularly exhibit their most recent work during this show.

The four branches of the museum, in Manhattan and suburban locations, present exhibits to the general public. Avant-garde films and videos occupy a prominent position in the programs. This innovative trend has been highly successful, as confirmed by the 500,000 annual visitors to the museum.

The Whitney Museum Building (1966), a truncated and inverted pyramid, was designed by Marcel Breuer and constructed using rough concrete and granite. A mere seven windows on the building façade and sides illuminate the interior. A garden lies below the concrete bridge entrance.

The exhibits and organization of paintings in the Whitney are regularly changed. This guide will therefore only mention major works in the collection. All the major American movements in the plastic arts are represented, starting with **The Eight,** a group which initiated urban realism in the early 20th century. The collection includes works by two of the group's main artists, Maurice Prendergast and John Sloan.

The major school of realism in the 1930s is also represented by Ben Shahn, *The Passion of Sacco and Vanzetti;* 2500 works from the Edward Hopper bequest, including *Early Sunday Morning** and *Railroad Sunset**, Thomas Hart Benton and 900 Reginald Marsh paintings and drawings.

The influence of early 20th-century European painters can be appreciated in the work of several Americans, including Georgia O'Keeffe, *Flower Abstractions, White Calico Flower* and *It Was Blue and Green;* Stuart Davis, *Coin de Paris* and *Rue Lippe* and David Demuth, *My Egypt.* Sculptors exhibited include Isamu Noguchi, Louise Nevelson and Gaston Lachaise. The amusing *Circus* by Alexander Calder recreates miniature people and animals using wire and fabric.

The museum collection naturally includes many examples from the New York School, notably several works by Abstract Expressionist Jackson Pollock, including *Number 27.* Other major painters in this movement are Arshile Gorky, Franz Kline, Willem de Kooning, Barnett Newman, Mark Rothko and sculptor David Smith.

Pop art is also well represented with works by Andy Warhol, *Green Bottles of Coca Cola;* Jasper Johns, *Three Flags;* Roy Lichtenstein, *Little Big Painting* and hyper-realist Richard Estes, *The Candy Store.*

The Whitney Museum also owns an excellent collection of contemporary drawings and engravings and avant-garde films and videos.

▬ OTHER MUSEUMS

Abigail Adams Smith Museum**

421 E. 61st St. ☎ (212) 838 6878.

Map IV, D2. — Subway: 59th St./Lexington Ave. (lines 4, 5, 6); Lexington Ave./60th St. (lines N, R). Bus: lines 31, 103.

Information: *Open Mon-Fri 10am-4pm.*

A haven of peace in the heart of Midtown, this charming former stable (1799) was part of a 25 acre/10 hectare property which belonged to John Adams, second president of the United States. The interior has been reconstructed in the Federal style of the period, with furniture and objects from the Adams family.

Asia Society Gallery**

725 Park Ave. at 70th St., ☎ (212) 288 6400.

Map IV, C1. — Subway: 68th St./Hunter College (line 6). Bus: lines 1, 2, 3, 4.

Information: *Open Tues-Sat 10am-5pm, Thurs 10am-8:30pm, Sun noon-5pm.*

This is one of the many gifts that have been offered to New York City over the years by the Rockefeller family. The collection of Asian painting, sculpture and porcelain (from China, Japan, India and Indochina) housed in this beautiful granite building is one of the largest in the world. Temporary exhibits present various aspects of Asian cultures and civilizations.

Cooper-Hewitt Museum (Smithsonian Institution's National Museum of Design)**

2 E 91st St., ☎ (212) 860 6868.

Map V, C2. — Subway: 86th St./Lexington Ave. (lines 4, 5, 6). Bus: lines 1, 2, 3, 4.

Information: *Open Tues 10am-9pm, Wed-Sat 10am-5pm, Sun noon-5pm.*

The largest decorative arts collection in the United States occupies Andrew Carnegie's former mansion. Fabric, wallpaper, furniture, glass objects, clothing, drawings and engravings are exhibited in the 64 rooms of this elegant neo-Renaissance mansion.

Hispanic Society of America**

Broadway at 155th St., ☎ (212) 690 0743.

Map VI, A1. — Subway: 157th St./Broadway (line 1); 155th St./St Nicholas Ave. (line B). Bus: lines 4, 5.

Information: *Open Tues-Sat 10am-4:30pm, Sun 1-4pm.*

Located in the heart of the Audubon Terrace group, this museum is devoted to Hispanic art and civilization, from the prehistoric period to the present. Painting, sculpture and decorative arts are well represented. Notable works of art include paintings by El Greco, Velázquez and Goya.

International Center of Photography**

1130 Fifth Ave. at 94th St., ☎ (212) 860 1777.

Map V, C2. — Subway: 96th St./Lexington Ave. (line 6).

Information: *Open Tues-Thurs noon-8pm, Fri-Sun noon-6pm.*

This excellent museum organizes popular photography exhibits.

Pierpont Morgan Library**

29 E. 36th St., ☎ (212) 685 0610.

Map III, C1. — Subway: 33rd St./Park Ave. (line 6). Bus: lines 1, 2, 3, 4.

Information: *Open Tues-Sat 10:30am-5pm, Sun 1-5pm; closed Sun July and Aug.*

Banker J. Pierpont Morgan was an enthusiastic collector of manuscripts, engravings, books and paintings. On his death, his mansion was transformed into a library. Admirable works in the collection include: a Gutenberg Bible; a *Book of Hours*** commissioned by the Princess of Clèves; Shakespeare, Byron and Dickens manuscripts; Egyptian papyrus; cuneiform tablets from the Middle East and a portrait of *Luther and his Wife** by Lucas Cranach the Elder.

Museum of the American Indian**

Broadway and 155th St., ☎ (212) 283 2420.

Map VI, A1. — Subway: 157th St./Broadway (line 1); 155th St./St Nicholas Ave. (lines B, K). Bus: lines 4, 5.

Information: *Open Tues-Sat 10am-5pm, Sun 1-5pm.*

This museum, which is part of Audubon Terrace, is devoted exclusively to American Indian cultures, from the Arctic Circle to Tierra del Fuego. The collection includes pre-Columbian works of art and objects uncovered during archaeological digs. Alternative premises are currently being sought for the museum.

Museum of the City of New York**

1220 Fifth Ave. at 103rd St., ☎ (212) 534 1672.

Map V, C1. — Subway: 103rd St./Lexington Ave. (line 6). Bus: lines 1, 2, 3, 4.

Information: *Open Tues-Sat 10am-5pm, Sun 1-5pm.*

The museum, devoted to New York City, exhibits replicas of interiors (including John D. Rockefeller's bedroom), period costumes, photographs, a charming collection of toys and dolls and an excellent audiovisual presentation about the city's history. The museum organizes guided tours of various New York neighbourhoods every Sunday, from April through October.

American Craft Museum*

40 W. 53rd St., ☎ (212) 956 6047.

Map IV, C2. — Subway: Fifth Ave./53rd St. (line E).

Information: *Open Tues-Sat 10am-6pm, Sun 11am-5pm.*

Recently installed in this handsome brick building, this museum organizes temporary exhibits and houses an excellent collection of American crafts (wood, ceramic, glass, metal, paper).

American Numismatic Society*

Broadway at 155th St., ☎ (212) 234 3130.

Map VI, A1. — Subway: 157th St./Broadway (line 1); 155th St./St Nicholas Ave. (line B). Bus: lines 4, 5.

Information: *Open Tues-Sat 1-5pm; ring bell to enter.*

This museum, also part of the Audubon Terrace group, draws from its collection to organize temporary exhibits on the history of coins.

Bible House (American Bible Society)*

1865 Broadway at 61st St., ☎ (212) 581 7400.

Map IV, B2. — Subway: 59th St./Columbus Circle (lines 1, A, B, C, D).

Information: *Open Mon-Fri 9am-4:30pm.*

The collection includes all types of Bibles, from fragments of the Dead Sea Scrolls to the Gutenberg Bible and a braille Bible. Temporary exhibits are often organized. The specialized library contains 39,000 volumes in 1600 different languages.

Jewish Museum*

1109 Fifth Ave. at 92nd St., ☎ (212) 860 1889.

Map V, C2. — Subway: 96th St./Lexington Ave. (line 6). Bus: lines 1, 2, 3, 4.

Information: *Open Mon-Thurs noon-5pm, Tues noon-9pm, Sun 11am-6pm.*

The world's largest collection of Jewish art is housed in the former mansion of banker Felix M. Warburg. Works include menorahs, fabric, pottery, silver pieces and religious objects. The Benguiat collection includes objects from the Middle Ages to the present.

El Museo del Barrio*

1230 Fifth Ave. at 104th St., ☎ (212) 831 7272.

Map V, C1. — Subway: 103rd St./Lexington Ave. (line 6). Bus: lines 1, 2, 3, 4.

Information: *Open Tues-Fri 10:30am-4:30pm, Sat and Sun 11am-4pm.*

This institution presents work by Puerto Rican and Latin American artists. Temporary exhibits are devoted to underprivileged artists. The museum has an interesting collection of antique and contemporary Latin American handcarved figurines.

Museum of American Folk Art*

49 W. 53rd St., ☎ (212) 581 2474.

Map IV, BC2. — Subway: Fifth Ave./53rd St. (line E).

Information: *Open Tues 10:30am-8pm, Wed-Sun 10:30am-5:30pm.*

This museum was founded in 1963 to promote an appreciation of American folk art. The collection includes carved figures from the American Southwest, weather vanes, patchwork quilts, ceramics, Shaker furniture and magnificent polychrome Indian statues. The museum's gift and book shop is at 62 W. 50th St. ☎ (212) 247 5611.

Museum of American Illustration (Society of Illustrators)*

128 E. 63rd St., ☎ (212) 838 2560.

Map IV, C2. — Subway: 59th St./Lexington Ave. (line 4); Lexington Ave./60th St. (lines N, R).

Information: *Open Mon-Fri 10am-5pm.*

The immense collection of the Society of Illustrators is presented in the form of temporary exhibits organized around a theme, an author or within an historical framework. Works by Andy Warhol, Norman Rockwell and many other major artists are included in this collection.

Museum of Holography*

11 Mercer St., ☎ (212) 925 0526.

Map II, B1. — Subway: Canal St./Broadway (lines D, N, R). Bus: lines 1, 6.

Information: *Open Wed-Sun noon-6pm.*

The holographic process uses lasers to create fascinating three-dimensional images from photographs.

New Museum of Contemporary Art*

583 Broadway at Houston St., ☎ (212) 219 1222.

Map II, B1. — Subway: Spring St./Lafayette St. (line 6). Prince St./Broadway (lines D, N, R). Bus: lines 1, 5, 6.

Information: *Open Wed, Thurs and Sun noon-6pm, Fri noon-10pm, Sat noon-8pm.*

Founded in 1977, the New Museum is dedicated to art produced in the last 10 years. Under the direction of Marcia Tucker, it has taken a stand against the commercialization of art and attempts to promote serious research in creativity. The museum's policy is to auction off the entire collection every 10 years to avoid becoming entrenched in the past.

Police Academy Museum*

235 E. 20th St. at Second Ave., ☎ (212) 477 9753.

Map III, C2. — Subway: 23rd St./Park Ave. South (line 6).

Information: *Open Mon-Fri 1-5pm.*

Handcuffs, billy clubs and firearms are the main exhibits in America's most famous police museum.

Theodore Roosevelt Birthplace*

28 E. 20th St., ☎ (212) 260 1616.

Map III, C2. - Subway: 23rd St./Broadway (lines N, R). Bus: lines 1, 2, 3, 5, 6, 7.

Information: *Open Wed-Sun 9am-5pm.*

Theodore Roosevelt, a member of an old New York family, was a hunter, explorer, Nobel Peace Prize winner, adventurer and President of the United States (1901-1909). His birthplace in Gramercy Park was demolished and later reconstructed by family members. The living room, office and bedroom contain Roosevelt memorabilia.

Songwriters' Hall of Fame Museum*

875 Third Ave., ☎ (212) 319 1444.

Map IV, C2-3. — Subway: 51st St./Lexington Ave. (line 6); Lexington Ave./Third Ave. (line E).

Information: *Open Mon-Sat 11am-3pm.*

This small museum, opened in 1977, exhibits manuscripts, photographs, instruments and objects tracing the history of American music. The collection includes Gershwin's desk, Fats Waller and Elvis Presley memorabilia, pianos, guitars and synthesizers.

▬ *NEW YORK GALLERIES BY NEIGHBOURHOOD*

Uptown, IV, C1.

Uptown, particularly Madison Avenue between 57th and 79th Streets, is the most elegant section of New York City. The fashionable haute couture houses, antique shops and numerous art galleries cater to a wealthy clientele. These galleries are favourably situated near the Uptown museums.

Claude Bernard

33 E. 74th St., ☎ (212) 988 2050.

Subway: 77th St./Lexington Ave. (line 6).

Information: *Open Tues-Sat 9:30am-5:30pm.*

This branch of the Parisian gallery exhibits 19th- and 20th-century American and European artists (Cardenas, Cremonini, Morales, Ségui, Szafran, Bravo).

Carus Gallery

872 Madison Ave. at 71st St., ☎ (212) 879 4660.

Subway: 69th St./Hunter College (line 6).

Information: *Open Tues-Sat 11am-5pm.*

This gallery specializes in early 20th-century artists, particularly the Italian Futurists, Russian Constructivists, German Expressionists and the Bauhaus artists. Feininger, Kirchner, Kupka, Malevitch, Moholy-Nagy, Nolde, Schwitters.

Castelli Graphics

4 E. 77th St., ☎ (212) 288 3202.

Subway: 77th St./Lexington Ave. (line 6).

Information: *Open Tues-Sat 10am-6pm.*

Castelli exhibits limited-edition lithographs and engravings by contemporary American painters: Jasper Johns, Ellsworth Kelly, Roy Lichtenstein, Julian Schnabel, Andy Warhol. Also photographs and drawings.

David Findlay Gallery

984 Madison Ave. at 77th St., ☎ (212) 249 2909.

Subway: 77th St./Lexington Ave. (line 6).

Information: *Open Tues-Sat 10am-5pm.*

19th- and 20th-century American and European artists, particularly French painters: Boudin, Brianchon, Guillaumin, Segonzac.

Xavier Fourcade

35 E. 75th St., ☎ (212) 535 3980.

Subway: 77th St./Lexington Ave. (line 6).

Information: *Open Tues-Sat 10am-5pm.*

Contemporary American painters: John Chamberlain, Arshile Gorky, Joan Mitchell, Malcolm Morley, Barnett Newman, Tony Smith, William de Kooning. Also early 20th-century European masters: Duchamp, Bram Van Velde.

Hirsch and Adler — Hirsch and Adler Modern

21 E. 60th St., ☎ (212) 535 8810.

Subway: 59th St./ Hunter College (line 6).

Information: *Open Tues-Fri 9:30am-5:15pm, Sat 9:30am-4:45pm.*

851 Madison Ave., ☎ (212) 744 6700.

Subway: 59th St./Hunter College (line 6).

Information: *Open Mon-Fri 9:30am-5:30pm, Sat 9:30am-5pm.*

The first gallery has an impressive collection of Edward Hopper drawings, watercolours and paintings. The second exhibits modern artists such as Joan Snyder, John Lee and English artist Graham Nickson.

Knoedler Gallery

19 E. 70th St., ☎ (212) 794 0550.

Subway: 68th St./Hunter College (line 6).

Information: *Open Tues-Fri 9:30am-5:30pm, Sat 10am-5:30pm.*

Contemporary American painters, with an emphasis on Abstract

Expressionists: Richard Diebenkorn, Adolph Gottlieb, Howard Hodgkin, Robert Motherwell, Jules Olitski, David Smith, Frank Stella. Also German, Flemish and Italian masters and Impressionist painters (by appointment).

Prakapas Gallery

19 E. 71st St. ☎ (212) 737 6066.

Subway: 68th St./Hunter College (line 6).

Information: *Open Tues-Sat noon-5pm.*

This is one of the most famous photo galleries in America (photos from the 1920s and 1930s). Original prints by Laszlo Moholy-Nagy, Man Ray and others.

57th Street, IV, BC2.

This is the hub of New York's galleries Several often occupy different floors of the same building, exhibiting internationally known artists.

Blum Helman Gallery

20 W. 57th St., ☎ (212) 245 2888.

Subway: 57th St./ Ave. of the Americas (line S).

Information: *Open Tues-Sat 10am-6pm.*

Irving Blum and Joseph Helman, the gallery's two co-directors, exhibit famous contemporary painters (Diebenkorn, Ellsworth Kelly, Richard Serra) and relatively unknown artists (Bryan Hunt or Donald Sultan).

Blum Helman recently opened another gallery in SoHo (see p. 166)

André Emmerich Gallery

41 E. 57th St., ☎ (212) 752 0124. Subway: Fifth Ave./59th-60th Sts. (lines N, R).

Information: *Open Tues-Sat 10am-5:30pm.*

Contemporary American artists (Sam Francis, Helen Frankenthaler, Kenneth Noland, David Hockney) with a section devoted to pre-Columbian art and Classical paintings.

David Findlay Jr.

41 E. 57th St., ☎ (212) 486 7660.

Subway: Fifth Ave./59th-60th Sts. (lines N, R).

Information: *Open Mon-Sat 10am-5pm.*

19th- and early 20th-century American painting, particularly American Impressionists: Hassan, Homer, Inness, Kensett, Metcalf, Stuart.

Gallery of Applied Arts

24 W. 57th St., ☎ (212) 765 3560.

Subway: 57th St./Ave. of the Americas (line S).

Information: *Open Mon-Fri 9:30am-5:30pm.*

This gallery specializes in decorative arts, with an excellent permanent collection of furniture and objects designed by internationally famous architects and sculptors.

Marian Goodman Gallery/Multiples Inc.

24 W. 57th St., ☎ (212) 977 7160.

Subway: 57th St./Ave. of the Americas (line S).

Information: *Open Mon-Sat 10am-6pm.*

Contemporary American and European artists (Tong Cragg, Anselm Kiefer, Sigmar Polke, Robert Wilson) and drawings and prints by John Chamberlain, Claes Oldenburg, Susan Rothenberg, Sol le Witt.

Sidney Janis Gallery

110 W. 57th St., ☎ (212) 586 0110.

Subway: 57th St./Seventh Ave. (lines D, R, N).

Information: *Open Mon-Sat 10am-5:30pm.*

Recognized as one of New York's most famous galleries, Sidney Janis has been situated on 57th Street for more than 40 years. Exhibits include works by the leading names in modern American and European art: Albers, Duchamp, Gorky, Kandinsky, Kline, de Kooning, Léger, Mondrian, Pollock, Rothko, George Segal, Tom Wesselmann. Janis' personal collection is now in the Museum of Modern Art.

Galerie Maeght Lelong

20 W. 57th St., ☎ (212) 3150470.
Subway: 57th St./Ave. of the Americas (line S).
Information: *Open Tues-Sat 10am-5:30pm.*
This gallery, with branches in Paris and Zurich, specializes in 20th-century American and European art. Internationally famous artists exhibited include: Alechinsky, Chagall, Giacometti, de Kooning, Miró, Riopelle, Serra, Tapies.

Marlborough Gallery

40 W. 57th St., ☎ (212) 5414900.
Subway: 57th St./Ave. of the Americas (line S).
Information: *Open Mon-Fri 10am-5:30pm, Sat 10am-5pm.*
Well-known American and European sculptors and painters: Francis Bacon, Oskar Kokoschka, Henry Moore, Kurt Schwitters. Contemporary artists include: Fernando Botero, Red Grooms, Alex Katz. Photographs by Eugène Atget, Brassaï and H. Newton.

Robert Miller Gallery

41 E. 57th., ☎ (212) 9805454.
Subway: Fifth Ave./59th-60th Sts. (lines N, R).
Information: *Open Tues-Sat 10am-5:30pm.*
Contemporary and modern art, with an emphasis on Figurative paintings. Many American and European painters: Louise Bourgeois, Jedd Garet, Jean Hélion, Lee Krasner, Robert Mapplethorpe. The gallery also exhibits photographs and more classical paintings.

Pace Gallery

32 E. 57th St., ☎ (212) 4213292.
Subway: Fifth Ave./59th-60th Sts. (lines N, R).
Information: *Open Mon-Fri 9:30am-5:30pm, Sat 10am-5:30pm.*
This is one of the most prestigious New York galleries, devoted to internationally known modern and contemporary artists: Chuck Close, Jim Dine, Jean Dubuffet, Agnes Martin, Picasso, Lucas Samaras, Julian Schnabel. It has a Primitive and African arts section and also publishes art books.

Galerie Saint-Etienne

24 W. 57th St., ☎ (212) 2456734.
Subway: 57th St./ Ave. of the Americas (line S).
Information: *Open Tues-Sat 11am-5pm.*
Originally located in Vienna, this gallery has been exhibiting Austrian and German Expressionists (Gustav Klimt, Oskar Kokoschka, Egon Schiele) and American painters (John Kane, Grandma Moses) since 1939.

East Village, III, CD3.

The first gallery to move to the East Village in 1982, Fun Gallery, closed several years ago, but it attracted a multitude of small galleries in its wake. For various reasons, these galleries preferred this mixed neighbourhood of Puerto Rican and Ukrainian immigrants.

Taking advantage of low rents, galleries were set up in abandoned shops and they have created their own art market. Certain gallery owners are themselves artists who have not been able to show their work in the prominent SoHo or 57th Street galleries.

Art collectors soon became interested in this phenomenon and started investing in these relatively unknown and inexpensive artists. With a renewed interest in the neighbourhood, fashionable restaurants and clothing shops have pushed some of the older residents out, but the future of these small galleries remains precarious.

Avenue B Gallery

167 Ave. B between 10th-11th Sts., ☎ (212) 473 4600.

Subway: First Ave./14th St. (line L).

Information: *Open Wed-Sun noon-6pm.*

Gallery director Martin Hason looks for artists who resist the fashionable art trends in the East Village. Artists exhibited include: sculptors Tim Rietenbach and Lee Stoliar; painters Chris Costan and Kevin Larmée, well-known for his wall paintings throughout New York, and Bonnie Lucas, who creates fabric assemblages.

Gracie Mansion

167 Ave. A between 10th-11th Sts., ☎ (212) 477 7331.

Subway: First Ave./14th St. (line L).

Information: *Open Wed-Sun 1-6pm.*

Gracie Mansion is one of the artistic pioneers in the East Village. Before opening a gallery on 10th Street, later moving to Avenue A, Gracie Mansion was already well known in 1982 for organizing exhibits in bathrooms.

Primarily figurative post-contemporary painters and sculptors exhibited include: Guy Augerie, Mike Bidlo, Claudia Demonte, Jonathan Ellis, Rodney Greenblat, David Sandlin, David Wojnarowicz, Rhonda Zwillinger. The Gracie Mansion Store at 115 Avenue A sells objects and jewelry created by the artists.

La Mama-la Galleria second classe

6 E. 1st St., ☎ (212) 505 2476.

Subway: Second Ave./Houston St. (line F).

Information: *Open Wed-Sun 1-6pm.*

This gallery, associated with the La Mama theater, occupies a beautiful space which is particularly well suited for exhibiting sculptures (the 1988 exhibits were devoted exclusively to sculpture). Sculptures by Marcia Kaplan and Robert Taplin, paintings by Ken Burgess, Chico, Hena Evyatar and Eric Sparre.

Nature Morte

204 E. 10th St., ☎ (212) 420 9544.

Subway: First Ave./14th St. (line L).

Information: *Open Wed-Sun noon-6pm.*

Opened in 1982, this gallery is one of the oldest in the neighbourhood. Peter Nagy, himself an artist, exhibits post-punk generation painters and sculptors: Dennis Adams, Gretchen Bender, Silvia Kolbowsky, Kevin Larmon, Joel Otterson, Julie Watchel.

PPOW

337 E. 8th St., ☎ (212) 529 1313.

Subway: First Ave./14th St. (line L).

Information: *Open Wed-Sun noon-6pm.*

Contemporary work, mostly Figurative, with socio-political overtones. Artists include Pail Benney, Roxanne Blanchard, Joe Houston, Jed Jackson, Paul Marcus, Erika Rothenberg, Todd Watts.

Many SoHo galleries occupy vast loft spaces in 19th-century cast-iron buildings.

CONDESO
LAWLER
GALLERY

Sharpe

175 Ave. B at 11th St., ☎ (212) 777 4622.
Subway: First Ave./14th St. (line L).
Information: *Open Tues-Sun 1-6pm.*
Deborah Sharpe was one of the first gallery owners to venture onto Avenue B. Her gallery is today internationally known, with shows of works by architectural painters Mark Dean and Jane Irish; drawings by Peter Draken; Symbolist paintings by Sheryl Laemnle; plus works by Italian Lorenzo Bonechi and Berliner Thomas Schindler.

Zeus-Trabia

437 E. 9th St., ☎ (212) 505 6330.
Subway: First Ave./14th St. (line L).
Information: *Open Wed-Sun 1-6pm.*
Bianca Lanza exhibits works which incorporate spiritual, religious or surrealist imagery. The artists are primarily European and still unknown in the New York art world: Italians Sergio Calatroni, Pietro Finelli, Paolo Polli, Russian sculptor Leonid Sokov, American painter Elizabeth Smitt. Sculptures are exhibited in the rear courtyard.

SoHo, II, B1.

SoHo's artistic fame began in the 1960s. Artists looking for space and reasonable rents moved into abandoned commercial buildings. Galleries, restaurants and fashionable shops soon followed. Rents rose as the neighbourhood became fashionable and many artists were forced to move to Tribeca, Brooklyn or Queens. The art galleries remained, however, and provide a good overview of contemporary art.

Brooke Alexander

59 Wooster St., ☎ (212) 925 4338.
Subway: Spring St./Ave. of the Americas (lines C, E).
Information: *Open Tues-Sat 10am-6pm.*
This gallery offers an interesting selection of contemporary artists situated between Expressionism and Conceptualism. Brooke Alexander also promotes new artists.

Blum Helman Warehouse

80 Greene St., ☎ (212) 226 8770.
Subway: Prince St./Broadway (Lines N, R).
Information: *Open Tues-Sat 10am-6pm.*
This contemporary gallery was recently opened by the famous 57th Street gallery (see p. 162).

Mary Boone

417 West Broadway, ☎ (212) 431 1818.
Subway: Spring St./Ave. of the Americas (lines C, E).
Information: *Open Tues-Sat 10am-6pm; closed in July and Aug.*
Mary Boone established her reputation by exhibiting David Salle and Julian Schnabel. She shows some of the most interesting contemporary American and European artists: Jean-Michel Basquiat, Francesco Clemente, Barbara Kruger, Sigmar Polke.

Leo Castelli

420 West Broadway, ☎ (212) 431 5160.
Subway: Spring St./Ave. of the Americas (lines C, E).
Information: *Open Tues-Sat 10am-6pm.*
142 Greene St., ☎ (212) 431 6279.
Subway: Broadway/Lafayette St. (lines S, F).
Information: *Open Tues-Sat 10am-6pm.*

Leo Castelli was located Uptown from 1947 to 1968, when it moved to SoHo. Castelli gained fame by exhibiting American artists who later became famous. Artists from every movement are represented here, from Abstract Expressionism to the New Figuration, including Pop art and Minimalism: Jaspar Johns, Roy Lichtenstein, Robert Morris, Robert Rauschenberg, David Salle, Cy Twombly, Andy Warhol.

Paula Cooper Gallery

155 Wooster St., ☎ (212) 674 0766.

Subway: Broadway/Lafayette St. (lines S, F).

Information: *Open Tues-Sat 10am-6pm.*

Paula Cooper was one of the first gallery owners to move to SoHo in the 1960s. She exhibits contemporary American and European painters, sculptors and photographers, from the Figurative to the Abstract movements: Carl Andre, Jennifer Bartlett, Lynda Benglis, Robert Mangold, Elizabeth Murray, Joel Shapiro.

Crown Point Press

568 Broadway (room 105), ☎ (212) 226 5476.

Subway: Prince St./Broadway (lines N, R).

Information: *Open Tues-Fri 9:30am-5:30pm Sat 11am-5:30pm.*

This gallery specializes in engravings, with a large selection of artists: John Cage, Alex Catz, Richard Diebenkorn, Judy Pfaff, Brian Hunt, Pat Stier, Francesco Clemente.

Rosa Esman Gallery

70 Greene St., ☎ (212) 219 3044.

Subway: Spring St./Ave. of the Americas (lines C, E).

Information: *Open Tues-Sat 10am-6pm.*

Avant-garde artists from the 1920s and 1930s are exhibited here, including Ilya Chasnik, Laszlo Moholy-Nagy, Man Ray. Contemporary painters and sculptors: Peter Ambrose, John Bellamy, Don Hazlitt, Lizbett Mitty, Richard Mock, Joan Witek.

Ronald Feldman

31 Mercer St. ☎ (212) 226 3232.

Subway: Canal St./Varick St. (line 3).

Information: *Open Tues-Sat 10am-6pm.*

This is an interesting gallery devoted to contemporary and avant-garde art, with works by Joseph Beuys, Buckminster Fuller and Andy Warhol.

Richard Green Gallery

152 Wooster St., ☎ (212) 982 3993.

Subway: Broadway/Lafayette St. (lines S, F).

Information: *Open Tues-Sat 10am-6pm.*

This is one of SoHo's most recent galleries, which reflects various contemporary movements: Expressionism, Pop art, Figurative work, Constructivism, Abstraction (Donna Dennis, Robert Murray).

Metro Pictures

150 Greene St. ☎ (212) 925 8335.

Subway Broadway/Lafayette St. (lines S, F).

Information: *Open Tues-Sat 10am-6pm.*

This gallery exhibits contemporary artists who use imagery from current cultural and media sources: Werner Büttler, Jack Goldstein, Robert Longo, Laurie Simmons.

O.K. Harris

383 West Broadway. ☎ (212) 431 3600.

Subway: Spring St./Ave. of the Americas (lines C, E).

Information: *Open Tues-Sat 10am-6pm.*

This immense gallery exhibits unknown artists and organizes one-man shows for recognized artists such as Duane Hanson, Richard McLean and Eric Stoller.

Phyllis Kind

136 Greene St., ☎ (212) 925 1200.
Subway: Broadway/Lafayette St. (lines S, F).
Information: *Open Tues-Sat 10am-6pm.*

The gallery exhibits American and Naive painters (Doug Anderson, Roger Braun, Mark Greenwold, Ed Paschke). It has also organized exhibits of contemporary painters from the Soviet Union.

Tony Shafrazi

163 Mercer St., ☎ (212) 925 8732.
Subway: Broadway/Lafayette St. (lines S, F).
Information: *Open Tues-Sat 10am-6pm.*

An audacious selection of young artists awaiting discovery (graffiti, pop and primitive artists).

Sonnabend Gallery

420 West Broadway, ☎ (212) 966 6160.
Subway: Spring St./Ave. of the Americas (lines C, E).
Information: *Open Tues-Sat 10am-6pm.*

This is an important gallery which favours Pop art, Conceptualism and Minimalism. Artists exhibiting in this gallery include Alain Kirili, Dennis Oppenheim, Anne and Patrick Poirier, Robert Morris, Robert Rauschenberg.

Sperone Westwater

142 Greene St., ☎ (212) 431 3685.
Subway: Broadway/Lafayette St. (lines S, F).
Information: *Open Tues-Sat 10am-6pm.*

Contemporary American and European sculptors and painters, including Sandro Chia, Enzo Cucchi, Richard Long, Carlo Mariani.

Tribeca, II, AB1

The number of galleries in Tribeca is increasing as artists, celebrities and fashionable restaurants are attracted to the neighbourhood. The reconverted commercial buildings offer immense spaces particularly well suited for group shows.

Alternative Museum

17 White St., ☎ (212) 966 4444.
Subway: Franklin St./Varick St. (line 1).
Information: *Open Wed-Sat 11am-6pm.*

The Alternative Museum has existed since 1975, but it has only been in Tribeca since 1980. It was created by several artists to offer gallery space to unknown artists (Andrev Veljkovic organized a project called 'Collaborations' which included more than 200 artists). In addition to the permanent collection, it organizes thematic shows, jazz and folk music concerts and performances of traditional American music.

Artists Space

223 West Broadway, between Franklin and White Sts., ☎ (212) 226 3970.
Subway: Franklin St./Varick St. (line 1).
Information: *Open Tues-Sat 11am-6pm.*

This non-profit gallery, which concentrates on Abstract art, is subsidized by several organizations, including the New York State Council on the Arts and the National Endowment for the Arts.

Some of the artists exhibited are internationally famous: R.M. Fisher, Robert Longo, Laurie Simmons. It also presents public lectures and music and video programs produced by artists.

SoHo Photo Gallery

15 White St., ☎ (212) 226 8571.

Subway: Franklin St./Varick St. (line 1).

This gallery is financially supported by its members, most of whom are professional photographers. Opened 10 years ago, it exhibits works by both established and unknown photographers, including Tim Barnwell, Ross Elmi, Nina Glaser, Diane Kornberg, Len Speier.

White Columns

325 Spring St., ☎ (212) 924 4212.

Subway: Canal St./Varick St. (line 1).

Information: *Open Tues-Sat noon-6pm.*

Located at the west end of Spring Street near the Hudson River, White Columns is not exactly in Tribeca, but the spirit of director Bill Aming links it to the other Tribeca galleries. Aming organizes first-time shows for artists who have never exhibited elsewhere. Several have become well known since: Ashley Bickerton, Jon Bowman, Fab Five Freddy, Jon Kessler.

▬ *AUCTION HOUSES*

Auctions in New York are a popular pastime. It can be a risky undertaking for an amateur, so it is best to understand the ground rules before attempting a purchase. Look the objects over carefully before offering a price. Once you have made up your mind, do not get caught up in the trap of 'one more bid' and remember your budget. Don't forget that most of the people at the auction are specialists.

The Friday or Sunday *New York Times* publishes the auction schedules. Also check *The New Yorker* and *New York* magazine.

Christie's and **Sotheby's** are the two major rivals in the auction world. Their sales may be spectacular, the clientele generally fashionable and wealthy and prices can soar to unbelievable heights. In 1987, Van Gogh's *Sunflowers* sold for $39.9 million (by a telephone bid). The bidding is an impressive sight: Van Gogh's painting sold in 4.5 minutes, which translates into an increase of $147,700 per second.

Christie's

Map IV, C2.

502 Park Ave. at 59th St., ☎ (212) 546 1000.

Subway: Lexington Ave./60th St. (lines N, R); 59th St./Lexington Ave. (line 4).

Information: *Open Mon-Fri 10am-5pm.*

Christie's specializes in Far Eastern art and traditional American furniture and objects.

Christie's East

Map IV, C2.

219 E. 67th St., ☎ (212) 606 0400.

Subway: 68th St./Hunter College (line 6).

Information: *Open Mon-Sat 10am-5pm, Sun 1-5pm.*

Christie's East is smaller than the main auction house and specializes mainly in sales of furniture, glass objects, crystal and porcelain.

William Doyle Galleries

Map V, C3.

175 E. 87th St., ☎ (212) 427 2730.

Subway: 86th St./Lexington Ave. (line 4).

This is the third largest auction house in New York, which specializes primarily in American objects.

Phillips Fine Art Auctioneers

Map V, D3.

406 E. 79th St., ☎ (212) 570 4830.

Subway: 77th St./Lexington Ave. (line 6).

Information: *Open Tues-Sat 10am-5pm, Mon 10am-7:30pm, Sun noon-5pm.*

This auction house specializes in decorative arts (painting and furniture).

Sotheby Parke Bernet

Map IV, D1.

1334 York Ave. at 72nd St., ☎ (212) 606 7000.

Subway: 68th St./Lexington Ave. (line 6).

Information: *Open daily 10am-5pm..*

The largest and most important auction house in the world, it holds every record for the highest sales prices reached for paintings, jewelry, furniture and sculpture.

WALKS IN AND AROUND MANHATTAN

▬ *THE STATUE OF LIBERTY* ★★★

Map I, A2. — Regular ferry departures from Battery Park (Circle Line, ☎ 212 269 5759).
Information: *Open daily 9am-5pm;* ☎ *(212) 732 1236.*

The ferry linking Battery Park on Manhattan to Staten Island passes in front of the Statue of Liberty every trip. At just 25¢, it is the least expensive and most beautiful trip in New York.

Volumes have been written about the Statue of Liberty. Millions of tourists travel every year from all corners of the globe to visit this monumental work. As a symbol of liberty illuminating the world with her torch, it was and remains the essence of the 'New World', standing proudly on Liberty Island in New York Harbor.

French sculptor F.A. Bartholdi designed this gigantic work which measures 151 ft/46 m. Mounted on the pedestal, the flames of the torch rise close to 300 ft/100 m above the water. Commissioned in 1870, the statue was a gift to the United States from France. For Bartholdi, it also represented his tribute to the American ideals of freedom and liberty. In 1871, he left France for America, returning to Paris in 1874 to begin work on the statue. Using his mother as a model, Bartholdi crafted the image of 'The Lady', and he asked Gustave Eiffel to design a metal structure to support the 80-ton statue. The Statue of Liberty was inaugurated on October 28, 1886. Major restoration work before the celebration of the statue's centennial in 1986 strengthened its weak points.

Ferry boats transport visitors from Battery Park on the southern tip of Manhattan to Liberty Island. The trip takes about 15 minutes and offers a superb view of the southern part of Manhattan. From the docks, take the paths leading to the pedestal.

Two museums occupy the ground floor of the pedestal, the **Museum of Immigration** and the **Statue Story Room.** Visitors who wish to avoid the first 167 steps may take an elevator to the first level. From here, however, the trip is on foot. Another 168 steps lead to the crown. The view over New York Harbor from this platform is well worth the effort.

▬ *LOWER EAST SIDE*

Map II, BCD1. — Subway: Canal St./Broadway (lines D, N, R); Canal St./Centre St. (line J); Delancey St./Essex St. (line F); Essex St./Delancey St. (line J). Bus: lines 14, 21.

While the Financial District is the business district, the Lower East Side is the neighbourhood for bargains. It is bordered to the east by the East River, to the west by Mulberry Street, to the south by Canal Street and to the north by Houston Street. Anything and everything are available at unbeatable prices. This makes the Lower East Side a kind of vast, bustling market overflowing with everything from antiques to household

appliances. The neighbourhood is especially lively on Sundays when bargain-hunters descend on the area in search of great deals.

The Lower East Side, from Broadway to the banks of the East River, originally belonged to Peter Stuyvesant, the last governor of New Amsterdam. Millions of European immigrants first settled in this district, creating an interplay of nationalities which continues to this day, as new arrivals replace older ones. Artists, escaping the high rents in SoHo, have recently begun to move to this neighbourhood, which nevertheless remains as poor and dilapidated as ever.

This area still crops up in contemporary New York literature as the setting for gangster stories; in fact traces of the 1930s era are still visible. The Bowery was then called the 'Boulevard of Crime'. Today, it's a good place to buy kitchen supplies and electric lighting.

Orchard Street and **Canal Street,** II, BC1, are paradise for bargain-hunters. All kinds of merchandise are available at unbeatable prices in the dark and cluttered stores; even the sidewalks are covered with objects for sale. Orchard Street is the center for clothes (military surplus, turn-of-the-century, 1920s and 1930s clothes). Try Canal Street for more fashionable clothing and for any type of electronic spare part. The Manhattan Bridge (1903), at Canal Street, straddles the East River from Manhattan to Brooklyn.

Follow Canal Street to the west to reach **Mulberry Street,** II, BC1, often called 'Via San Gennaro' by Americans of Italian descent. This is the boundary between the Lower East Side and Little Italy; it is a good place to stop, as there are plenty of restaurants and bars serving every type of Italian speciality.

▬ *CHELSEA***

Map III, AB1-2. — Subway: 23rd St./Eighth Ave. (lines C,E); 14th St./Eighth Ave. (lines A, C, E, L); 18th St./Seventh Ave. (line 1); 23rd St./Seventh Ave. (line 1).

Chelsea is a multi-faceted, changing, unpredictable and, therefore, undefinable neighbourhood. It is in the midst of a Renaissance, after many years of neglect. This renewed interest is in part due to the antique dealers who have moved to Ninth Avenue, the many popular restaurants, the florists who have set up trees and exotic plants on the sidewalks, fashionable clothes shops and, finally, avant-garde theaters of varying success. Perhaps even more important to its new popularity is the thoroughly New York concept of a city in a perpetual state of change.

Chelsea is named after property owned by Captain Thomas Clarke which extended from the Hudson River to Eighth Avenue and from 14th Street north to 25th Street. In 1851, when the Hudson River Railroad built tracks on Eleventh Avenue, the area was mainly inhabited by working-class families. It was a popular theater district for a short period in the 1870s, until the plays and actors moved to Broadway. In 1905, the abandoned theaters were used by the budding film industry as film studios. Mary Pickford and John Barrymore produced several films here. Later, the newer Astoria Studios in Queens attracted more producers. Ultimately, the moviemaking industry left the East Coast for Hollywood.

In 1930, when the railway on Eleventh Avenue was closed, Chelsea slipped into a period of neglect, forgotten by fashion-conscious New Yorkers. Yet some of the greatest artists and writers of this century lived in the neighbourhood: Mark Twain, O. Henry, Tennessee Williams, Sarah Bernhardt, Jackson Pollock, Henry Miller, Thomas Wolfe, Dylan Thomas and Vladimir Nabokov.

The **Marxist Leninist Bookstore,** III, B2, on 15th Street between Seventh

The Statue of Liberty, recently restored, stands proudly at the entrance to New York Harbor.

and Eighth Avenues, is the only bookstore of its kind in New York City. The residential section of Chelsea lies towards 21st Street, between Seventh and Tenth Avenues, and includes some of New York's most beautiful brownstones. The legendary **Chelsea Hotel***, III, B2, at 22 W. 23rd Street, has been home to generations of American writers, actors and playwrights. It is a handsome pink building with superb wrought-iron balconies running the full length of the façade. The Chelsea Hotel may have lost some of its former distinction, but not its notoriety. It was in one of the Chelsea rooms that Sid Vicious, member of the English punk group 'The Sex Pistols', stabbed his girlfriend to death.

Do not miss the **Joyce Theater,** III, B2, on Eighth Avenue, between 18th and 19th Streets. Formerly called the 'Elgin Theater', it was a favourite spot for New York's movie-going audience. It was also the first movie theater in New York to offer midnight showings. The theater has been transformed to accommodate avant-garde dance companies.

This walk ends on **Sixth Avenue,** between 26 and 29th Streets, at the **flower market,** III, B1. Virtually all Manhattan florists purchase their flowers here. There is a wonderful smell of freshly cut flowers and the sight of the sidewalks overflowing with the colourful plants is well worth the trip.

▬ GRAMERCY PARK*** — STUYVESANT SQUARE**

Map III, C2. — Subway: 23rd St./Park Ave. South (line 6).

Gramercy Park, III, C2

Constructed on a former swamp by Samuel Ruggles in 1831, Gramercy Park, between 20th and 21st Streets on Lexington Avenue, is an exact replica of a 19th-century London park. The comfortable homes surrounding the park attracted intellectuals, artists and several famous politicians. In 1844, New York City Mayor James Harper founded what would become one of the largest American publishing firms, Harper & Row. The **Mayor's Lamps** at n° 4 mark the former city leader's home.

Gramercy Park is private and is not open to visitors. It is reserved for residents surrounding the park who have the only keys to the gates. Gramercy Park is off-limits to all but the elite residents every day but one: Christmas Eve, when it is open to everyone.

Stuyvesant Square, III, C2

In 1837, Peter Stuyvesant offered Stuyvesant Square to the city. Situated between 15th and 17th Streets on Second Avenue, the land was originally part of his farm. Yet this generous act was not totally selfless; assured that the site would be designated a landmark, the value of his property surrounding the park increased considerably.

Stuyvesant Square, like Gramercy Park, was modeled after 19th-century London parks. Yet Stuyvesant Square, crossed by Second Avenue, has lost its protected, residential character. Surrounded by hospitals, schools and churches, it has retained only a fraction of its former elegance. A statue of Peter Stuyvesant, recognizable with his peg leg, stands in the square.

Rutherford Place, forms the west boundary of Stuyvesant Square. A white marble stone on the base of the **Friends Meeting House** on 16th Street, between Second and Third Avenues, marks a stopover spot on the underground railway which sheltered runaway slaves seeking refuge in Canada.

▬ MADISON SQUARE PARK***

Map III, C2. — Subway: 23rd St./Park Ave. South (line 6).

Madison Square Park, tucked in between 23rd and 26th Streets and Fifth and Madison Avenues and surrounded by unceasing traffic, nevertheless retains an aura of old New York. From here, visitors can admire some of

New York's most interesting buildings, including the Renaissance-style Flatiron Building.

In 1847, Madison Square Park was laid out on the site of a former hunting ground. It was a popular spot for holiday outings and base-ball games. In 1853, a 10,000-seat hippodrome was constructed in the primarily residential neighbourhood. From 1877 to 1884, the arm and torch of the Statue of Liberty were exhibited in this park.

The theater which stood on the north-east corner of the square in the late 19th century was replaced by the original Madison Square Garden, the immense sports arena now located on Eighth Avenue.

The Renaissance-style **Flatiron Building**, III, C2, (1902), at the south-ern edge of the park, was one of New York's first skyscrapers. Architect D.H. Burnham designed this 20-storey, 285 ft/87 m building. The owners adopted the popular nickname, 'the flatiron', as the official build-ing name.

Continue around the park, to the impressive **New York State Supreme Court Building**, III, C2, (1900) on the corner of 25th Street and Madison Avenue. In 1954, a remodeling project enlarged the structure. Note the handsome, although somewhat extravagant, statuary at the entrance, including an allegorical *Wisdom and Strength* by Frederick Ruckstahl. Karl Bitter created the sculptural work *Peace* for the center of the building, while *Justice,* by sculptor Daniel Chester French, occupies the corner of 25th Street and Madison Avenue.

The curious **New York Life Insurance Building**, III, C1, stands on the opposite side of Madison Avenue between 26th and 27th Streets. Designed in 1928 by architect Cass Gilbert, the style appears to be modeled after the time of Louis XII. The gargoyles perched on the roof add a mediaeval character to the building design.

Since most of the buildings surrounding Madison Square Park house offices, the eating facilities are mainly limited to coffee shops. The long counters lined with stools evoke a certain nostalgic charm and meals are always reasonably priced.

▬ *PARK AVENUE*★★★

Maps IV, C1-2-3; V, C2-3. — All commercial traffic, including buses and subways, is prohibited on Park Avenue from 96th to 42nd Streets. Park Avenue can be reached from parallel streets, Lexington Avenue (running Downtown) and Madison Avenue (Uptown).

This stretch of Park Avenue is a sort of private, privileged garden extend-ing from 96th to 42nd Streets. The median strip is planted with seasonal flowers, and lighted Christmas trees in December, while both sides of the avenue are lined with opulent and austere buildings. Very few shops or businesses interrupt the calm of the residential buildings.

At the turn of the century, Park Avenue was just an open field crossed by a railway line. In 1907, when the system was electrified and covered, the newly created area above ground was used to construct fashionable residential buildings for New York's high society.

The **Helmsley Building**, IV, C3 (1929) on Park Avenue at 46th Street is one of the most familiar sights in New York City. Since 1963, the pyramidal roof has been dwarfed by the 59-storey **Pan Am Building**, constructed directly behind the Helmsley.

The **Union Carbide Building**, IV, C3 (1960) at 270 Park Avenue, between 47th-48th Streets, formerly housed the multi-national chemical firm. Note the interesting design, incorporating gray glass and black-and-white metal structures. The silver-gray **Chemical Bank Building** opposite rises 50 storeys above Park Avenue. The ground-floor lobby which rises to the third floor forms an interior garden, complete with fountains.

The 1800-room, 47-storey **Waldorf Astoria Hotel**, IV, C3, at Park Avenue between 49th-50th Streets is a New York landmark. Many of the world's celebrities have stayed here at one time or another over

The Flatiron Building, a New York landmark and one of the city's first skyscrapers.

the last 60 years. Private apartments are reserved for heads of state. It represents an obligatory rite of passage for many presidential candidates — Hoover, Nixon and Reagan have all given speeches here intended to convince the New York public, reputed to be one of the most difficult yet decisive electorates in the United States. Note the Art Deco lobby, the silver corridor and the barrel vault from the former Astor Hotel on Fifth Avenue. The interesting murals by E. Emmerson Simmons (1890) represent the 12 months of the year.

▬ *LA MARQUETA* ★

Map V, C1. — Subway: 110th St./Lexington Ave. (line 6).

Manhattan's most exotic market, La Marqueta, extends under the railway tracks at 110th Street and Park Avenue. La Marqueta ('market' in Spanish) is the meeting place for the Hispanic communities in New York. This teeming market attracts a noisy, dense crowd in search of hard-to-find tropical fruits and vegetables, making for a chaos of colours, smells and sounds.

After exploring the exotic products for sale in the market, walk east on 110th Street. This is **El Barrio,** which means 'the neighbourhood' in Spanish. It is also called Spanish Harlem, and extends from Fifth Avenue to the East River and from 125th Street south to 96th Street, VI, CD3; V, CD1-2.

Since World War I, many Puerto Ricans have moved to this area which has been home to successive waves of Italian, Jewish and Scandinavian immigrants. The South American population only started to increase in the 1960s.

This 'latinization' of a formerly black section of Harlem has added another dimension to New York's ethnic diversity. The **Aguilar Branch,** III, C1, of the New York Public Library on 110th Street, between Lexington and Third Avenues, easily identifiable by its monumental entrance, specializes in Spanish books.

Try one of the *bodegas* along the way for a sandwich or drink. They all have an unmistakable ambience, with tables set up in the middle of a narrow, crowded shop, always filled with people playing games of dominos, chess and cards.

El Barrio also has several unique shops, called *botanicas,* which sell religious, spiritual objects, including all kinds of paraphernalia needed for the practice of magic, from miraculous ointments to wax voodoo dolls. Religious figurines *(santos)* in all shapes and sizes, particularly reproductions of the Madonna, occupy a prominent place on the counters.

The picturesque atmosphere of El Barrio does not conceal the profound poverty which reigns throughout most of the neighbourhood. Visitors are advised not to be overly ostentatious when walking near 110th Street.

Do not miss the **Museo del Barrio,** V, C1, 1230 Fifth Avenue, the only museum in the United States dedicated exclusively to Puerto Rican and Latin American culture (see p. 159).

▬ THE CLOISTERS ★★★

Map I, B1-2. — Subway: 190th St./Fort Washington Ave. (line A). Bus: line 4.
Information: *Open Tues-Sat 10am-4:45pm, Sun and public holidays noon-4:45pm.*

No matter how many trips a visitor makes to the Cloisters, it is always striking to confront the strange vision of an imposing monastery perched on top of a hill in Fort Tryon Park, high above the Hudson.

The Rockefeller family acquired their reputation not only because of their immense wealth but also because they have generously supported a large number of artistic and cultural projects. The Cloisters is one example of this generosity.

John D. Rockefeller Jr. was the guiding force in the construction of the Cloisters. In 1930, he decided to give the vast property surrounding Fort Tryon to New York City. In 1935, he commissioned Charles Collens to construct the buildings which today occupy the site.

This was the fulfillment of a project begun by his father several years before. In 1925, his father donated a considerable sum of money to expand the mediaeval sculpture collection assembled by sculptor George Grey Barnard. He also wanted a worthy site to house and exhibit the collection. The brick building constructed on Fort Washington Avenue already incorporated elements from several French monasteries: Saint-Guilhem-le-Désert, Saint-Michel-de-Cuxa, Bonnefont and Trie, all located in southern France.

In 1926, with Rockefeller's financial backing, the museum was constructed and named the Barnard Cloister. It is administered as a branch

The Cloisters   New York

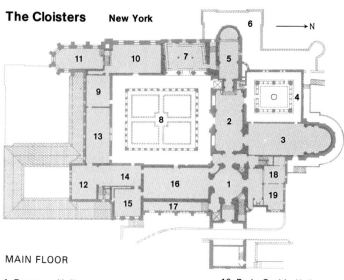

MAIN FLOOR

1 Entrance Hall
2 Romanesque Hall
3 Fuentiduena Chapel
4 Saint-Guilhem Cloister
5 Langon Chapel
6 West Terrace
7 Pontaut Chapter House
8 Saint-Michel
  de Cuxa Cloister
9 Heroes Tapestry Room

10 Early Gothic Hall
11 Gothic Chapel
12 Boppard Room
13 Unicorn Tapestries Hall
14 Burgos Tapestry Hall
15 Spanish Room
16 Late Gothic Hall
17 Froville Arcade
18 Cloakroom
19 Information

Kart. Inst. G. Schiffner, Lahr/Schwarzwald

The Cloisters   New York

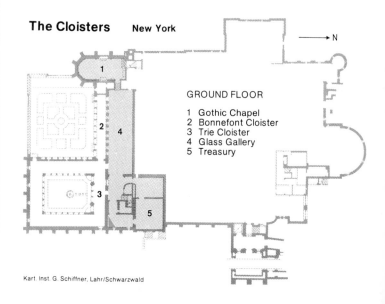

GROUND FLOOR

1 Gothic Chapel
2 Bonnefont Cloister
3 Trie Cloister
4 Glass Gallery
5 Treasury

Kart. Inst. G. Schiffner, Lahr/Schwarzwald

of the Metropolitan Museum of Art (see p. 147). The finishing touches to the museum were added by John D. Rockefeller in 1930. The museum collection has since been enlarged through major gifts and new acquisitions.

Main floor

The **Romanesque Hall** (*Torso of Christ** in painted wood) and the **Fuentiduena Chapel**, from north of Madrid, lead to the small **Saint-Guilhem Cloister**, from a Benedictine abbey founded in 804. The **Langon Chapel*** contains a *Virgin and Child** from Burgundy and exceptional 12th-century capitals.

The **Cuxa Cloister****, from a Benedictine monastery founded in 878, was reconstructed according to plans drawn up by Viollet-Le-Duc and completed with Languedoc marble. The austere and powerful **capitals**** (1125-1150) create an interesting play of light and shadow in the cloisters. Cross through the **Early Gothic Hall** (*Virgin** from the choir screen of the Strasbourg cathedral, Florentine and Siennese paintings) to reach the tapestries in the **Nine Heroes Room****. Note the two Hebrew heroes on the north wall in mediaeval dress: Joshua wearing a crown and David with a golden harp. On the opposite wall hang tapestries of Alexander with his coat of arms and Julius Caesar with a two-headed eagle.

Ground floor

Stairs lead down to the **Gothic Chapel** (tombs and funerary sculpture) and the **Glass Gallery** on the ground floor. This room houses 75 panels and roundels of early 16th-century German stained glass and a collection of sculptures from Burgundy.

Two cloisters have been reconstructed side by side, **Bonnefont**, with a mediaeval garden, and **Trie***, with superb late 15th-century capitals*. The **Treasury** contains exceptional objects: an altar piece* from Segovia (around 1445); 37 finely carved oak panels from the Jumièges Abbey in Normandy; the Antioch chalice* (6th-century); the Bertinus chalice (1222); the reliquaries; and the Book of Hours executed for the Duke de Berry by the Limbourg brothers (early 15th century).

The staircase in the Glass Gallery leads up to the **Hall of the Unicorn Tapestries*****, executed for the marriage of Anne de Bretagne and Louis XII in 1499. The visit ends with the **Boppard Room** (stained glass, Spanish alabaster altar piece), the **Burgos Tapestry Hall***, the **Campin Room** (Annunciation altar piece** painted by Robert Campin in 1425) and the **Late Gothic Hall**.

▬ *FORT TRYON PARK AND INWOOD HILL PARK*

Map I, B1-2. — Subway: 190th St./Fort Washington Ave. (line A). Bus: line 4.

Fort Tryon Park

Historically, this 66 acre/25 hectare park surrounding the Cloisters was an important lookout post high above the Hudson. Indian camps occupied the site until they were displaced by colonists.

Fort Tryon is named after the last English governor of New York. Perched 250 ft/76 m above the Hudson, Fort Tryon was the highest observation post in Manhattan and the northern outpost of Fort Washington. New Yorkers claim there have been so many battles in these hills that it is still possible to find canon balls, uniform buttons and belt buckles.

Today, this former military post offers the most **spectacular view*** of the Hudson and the George Washington Bridge, I, B2, linking New York and New Jersey. Don't miss the attractive **botanical garden** situated halfway between the Cloisters and the subway station at the South Plaza.

There is a cafeteria close to the botanical garden and the parking area. Music concerts are held Sunday afternoons in the Cloisters.

Inwood Hill Park

Situated in the far north-west corner of Manhattan, Inwood Hill Park is usually included in a visit to Fort Tryon. Several residential buildings separate the two large wooded parks. The terrain, called 'Shora-Kapkok' by the Indians because of the many caves, was used to quarter English Troops during the Revolution. It was later renamed Cox Hill.

Although the park is crowded on weekends with picnicking families, it is isolated and empty during the week. Visitors are advised to avoid the area on weekdays.

THE OTHER BOROUGHS

THE BRONX

Map I, B1-2. — Subway: lines C, D, 1, 2, 4, 5, 6.

In the film *Fort Apache: The Bronx,* Paul Newman played the role of a policeman, disillusioned by the poverty around him and the rampant corruption among his colleagues. Although certain characters in the film were certainly caricatures, it is nevertheless true that for most New Yorkers, the Bronx seems to have the worst reputation of the five New York boroughs.

The Bronx, the only New York borough on the mainland, has a population of close to 1.4 million inhabitants, consisting largely of Black and Hispanic working-class families. Yet New York's largest park, Pelham Bay Park to the north-east on Long Island Sound, and the Bronx Zoo, a large and impressive zoo, are situated in this borough.

The Bronx owes its name to the former owner of the entire region, Johannes Bronck, a Danish immigrant who moved north of the Harlem River in 1639. Until the 20th century, the Bronx remained virtually deserted, with several isolated farms and vast, unused tracts of land.

In 1840, the construction of the Harlem Railroad brought the South Bronx out of its isolation, encouraging a certain amount of industrial development. A major building boom occurred around the turn of the century. In 1909, the Grand Concourse was constructed, a gigantic avenue which crosses the entire western section of the Bronx. Builders modeled it after the Champs Elysées in Paris, including in the project a vast program to construct attractive residential buildings along the avenue.

Today, the Bronx is linked to Manhattan by a major transportation system which includes 12 bridges (two for railway lines) and six subway tunnels.

Van Cortlandt Mansion

Map I, B1-2. — Subway: 242nd St./Van Cortlandt Park/Manhattan College (line 1).

Information: *Open Tues-Sat 10am-4:45pm, Sun noon-4:45pm.*

This Georgian-style stone house, built in 1748, stands majestically in the southern section of Van Cortlandt Park. Tours are given of its restored interior by guides dressed in period costumes.

Poe Cottage

Map I, B2. — Subway: Kingsbridge Rd./Jerome Ave. (line 4).

Information: *Open Tues-Fri 9am-5pm, Sat 10am-4pm, Sun 1-5pm.*

Edgar Allan Poe (1809-1849) lived the last three years of his life in this wooden house (1812) on the corner of Jerome Avenue and Fordham Road. It has been converted into a museum and includes memorabilia from the writer's life.

Bronx Zoo**

Map I, B1-2. — Subway: E. Tremont Ave./W. Farm Sq./Boston Rd. (lines 2, 5).

Information: *Open Mon-Sat 10am-5pm, Sun and public holidays 10am-5:30pm; free admission Tues, Wed and Thurs.*

The Bronx Zoo was laid out in the late 19th century. Situated in the southern part of the Bronx Park, it covers 252 acres/100 hectares and houses 3600 animals belonging to 700 different species.

Free guided tours are available, although they are conducted on foot. To avoid walking the long distances separating exhibits, take one of the various means of transportation provided within the zoo: the **tractor train;** the **Bengali express** which crosses the section called Wild Asia; or the **Skyfari aerial tramway** which provides a stunning view of the African Plains and the remarkable Great Apes House.

Do not miss the **World of Darkness** which artificially recreates a night-time world where visitors can observe nocturnal animals at their most active. It is a spectacular, although sometimes disconcerting sight.

The **Children's Zoo** is a paradise for kids, who can easily spend the entire day feeding animals, exploring tunnels dug by moles, following rabbits and participating in the many organized activities.

Many cafeterias in the zoo offer meals and snacks at reasonable prices.

New York Botanical Garden**

Map I, B1. — Subway: Bedford Park Blvd./Grand Concourse (line D).

Information: *Open Tues-Sun 10am-4pm.*

This vast area is about the same size as the Bronx Zoo. Designed and laid out in 1891, the Botanical Garden, with several thousand varieties of plants and flowers, is a fascinating site for even the most demanding horticulturist and a marvellous spot for an afternoon outing. The Museum Building houses several exhibits concerning ecology, botany and horticulture. The library also has a herbarium which includes three million species of plants.

Yankee Stadium

Map I, B2. — Subway: 161st St., Yankee Stadium (line 4).

Yankee Stadium is home to the Yankees, one of New York's baseball teams. It is an ultra-modern 54,000-seat stadium.

If you are in New York during baseball season and enjoy boisterous and grandiose spectacles, don't hesitate to attend a game (see p. 49).

▬▬ *BROOKLYN*

Map I, AB2-3. — Subway: all lines except H, K, S, 1, 6 and 7.

With three centuries of history, 77 sq mi/200 sq km in surface area and 2.4 million residents, Brooklyn has always been able to preserve its sense of identity. It was setted by the Dutch in the 17th century and became part of New York City in 1898.

Easy connections to Manhattan were not forged until the 19th century. In 1883, the **Brooklyn Bridge**, II, CD2, linked Manhattan to Brooklyn. The **Williamsburg Bridge**, II, D1, was constructed in 1903, followed by the **Manhattan Bridge**, II, CD2, in 1909. The first subway dates from 1905 and the **Brooklyn Battery Tunnel**, II, B3, was finished in the 1950s. Finally, the **Verrazano-Narrows Bridge**, I, A3, designed by Othmar Ammann, was constructed in 1964. It is one of the longest bridges in the world. Rising 741 f/226 m above the water, it spans 2.8 mi/4.5 km linking Staten Island and Brooklyn. The Verrazano-Narrows Bridge is now the starting point for New York's celebrated Marathon.

Brooklyn Heights**

Map II, D3. — Subway: Clark St./Brooklyn Heights (line 2).

Brooklyn Heights offers one of the most stunning views of Manhattan and yet has the character of a small country town. **Montague Street** is the main commercial street in Brooklyn Heights. The **Long Island Historical Society** on the corner of Clinton and Pierrepont Streets presents films and documents tracing the history of Brooklyn and Long Island. There are many lovely homes in this area.

Prospect Park*

Map I, B3. — Subway: Grand Army Pl./Prospect Park (line 2).

The wooded hills and meadows of this large natural park (526 acres/213 hectares) were designed in 1866 by Olmsted and Vaux, the architects of Central Park. The **Brooklyn Botanic Garden**, the **Brooklyn Museum** and a public library occupy the north-east triangle bordered by Eastern Parkway, Flatbush Avenue and Washington Avenue.

Brooklyn Botanic Garden*, I, B3

1000 Washington Ave., ☎ (718) 622 4433.

Map I, B3. — Subway: Botanic Garden/Eastern Parkway (line S).

Information: *Open Tues-Fri 8am-6pm, Sat and Sun 10am-6pm; Oct-Mar, daily 8am-4:30pm.*

The 50 acre/20 hectare Botanic Garden houses a rose garden, an herb garden, a fragrance garden, a new conservatory, cherry trees, a beautiful collection of bonsai trees and a Japanese garden, which is a replica of the celebrated Ryoan-ji stone garden in Kyoto.

Brooklyn Museum**

200 Eastern Parkway, ☎ (718) 638 5000.

Map I, B3. — Subway: Eastern Parkway/Brooklyn Museum (line 2).

Information: *Open Mon and Wed-Sat 10am-5pm, Sun 1-5pm;* ☎ (718) 622 4433.

This museum houses remarkable collections of Dutch, English and American paintings, including works by Winslow Homer. It contains a section devoted to contemporary art and a superb Egyptian department.

Coney Island*

Map I, AB3. — Subway: lines B, F, N.

Coney Island's glory is a thing of the past. Little remains of its once-celebrated amusement park.

Coney Island, which means 'Rabbit Island' in Dutch, sits on the farthermost southern tip of Brooklyn on a peninsula jutting into the Atlantic Ocean. It reached its pinnacle of fame in the 1830s, when it was the favoured meeting place for New York high society. Casinos, hotels and hippodromes were constructed for their entertainment.

Fifty years later, public taste turned toward sensationalism. The clientele changed in 1884; the first roller coasters were built and Coney Island became a popular site for middle- and working-class families. Soon the entire site was covered by an amusement park.

By the end of the 1940s, Coney Island's popularity had declined. The public no longer came in large numbers to enjoy the rides, but the 5 mi/7 km boardwalk on the Atlantic still attracts considerable crowds in the summer.

New York Aquarium*

W. 8th St. and Surf Ave., ☎ (718) 266 8711.

Map I, B3. — Subway: W. Eighth St./New York Aquarium (lines D, F).

The Aquarium presents aquatic shows featuring dolphins, whales and sea lions and houses numerous exhibits.

▬▬ QUEENS

Map I, B2-3. — Subway: lines 1, B, C, F, N, R, 7.

With a total area of 112 sq mi/290 sq km, Queens is the largest of the five New York boroughs. Situated to the north-east of Brooklyn on Long Island, Queens seems to sprawl endlessly, encompassing a diverse mixture of populations, ethnic backgrounds and social and economic levels. While Long Island City is a working-class area, geographically close to Manhattan, Forest Hills, in the very heart of Queens, is an exclusive residential area.

New York's two main airports are in Queens. **John F. Kennedy International Airport,** I, B3, known as JFK, primarily serves international traffic (subway: Howard Beach/JFK Airport/159th St., line C; JFK Passenger Terminal, line H). The second, **LaGuardia,** I, B2, is primarily reserved for domestic flights (bus Q33 from the 74th St./Broadway station, line 7). JFK is one of the world's busiest airports.

The prestigious **US Open Tennis Championships** are held every year for two weeks starting at the end of August in Flushing Meadows Park north of Forest Hills. The stadium seats 20,000 people with an additional 6,500 folding seats and has 23 outdoor courts and 9 indoor courts. The courts are open to the public. For information, ☎ (718) 592 8000.

Shea Stadium, home of the New York Mets baseball team, is situated north of Flushing Meadows. It can accommodate up to 60,000 spectators.

Queens is large enough to provide space for a natural reserve, the **Jamaica Bay Wildlife Refuge** (subway: Broad Channel, line C). Situated in Jamaica Bay, this natural reserve abounds with numerous varieties of aquatic birds. The best time to visit is during spring and fall — the migratory seasons. It is administered by the National Park Service and rangers provide special demonstrations and walks through the refuge.

Don't miss the legendary **QP's Market Place,** I, B2 (subway: Queens Pl./Queens Blvd., lines E, G, R). These former warehouses are situated at Queens Plaza in Long Island City, on the corner of Queens and Northern Boulevards. They house an immense flea market where almost 500 antique dealers offer every imaginable object. Many unique items come up for sale: gas pumps from the 1920s, double doors from a former hotel, city street lamps and even traffic lights. For more information, ☎ (718) 786 4500.

▬▬ STATEN ISLAND

Map I, A3. — Take the ferry from Battery Park on the southern tip of Manhattan to Saint George on Staten Island. It is the only means of public transportation to the island. Staten Island can be reached by the Verrazano-Narrows Bridge, but by car only.

Until 1964 when the bridge was opened, the ferry provided the only access to Staten Island. The Staten Island ferry crossing takes about 25 minutes and passes directly in front of the Statue of Liberty (see p. 171).

Predictably, this isolation has meant that Staten Island developed more slowly than the other boroughs. New Yorkers like to say that Staten Island resembles New Jersey more than New York. In light of the New York snobbism towards New Jersey, this is hardly a compliment. Furthermore, Staten Island has the reputation of being a public dump; it is true that a large sanitation treatment plant here treats garbage from Manhattan.

Founded in the 17th century by the Dutch, Staten Island has never attracted the interest of politicians or even real-estate developers in the three centuries since it was colonized. In fact, the island was never even sold, merely granted to the city of New York as a trophy for winning a sailboat race organized by the Duke of York in 1687.

The **Bayonne Bridge** links Bayonne (New Jersey) to Port Richmond (Staten Island), while the **Goethals Bridge** links Elizabeth (New Jersey)

The unique Brooklyn Botanic Garden houses fascinating collections of herbs, trees and landscaped gardens.

to Howland Hook (Staten Island) and, finally, the **Outerbridge Crossing** spans the distance between Perth Amboy (New Jersey) and Tottenville (Staten Island).

The main point of interest on the island is the **Richmondtown Restoration*** at 441 Clarke Avenue *(open Wed-Sun 10am-5pm; ☎ 718 351 1617)*, an open-air museum of 30 restored buildings which were part of the former Staten Island administrative centre. Buildings in the complex include: **Voorlezer's House** (1695 school); the **Historical Society Museum** in the former County Building (1848); the **Third County Courthouse** (1837, Greek Revival style); **St Andrew's Church** (1708); **Dunne's Saw Mill** (1800); the **Carriage House** and **Stephen's Store** (1837).

The **Jacques Marchais Center of Tibetan Art** at 338 Lighthouse Avenue *(open Apr-Oct, Sat and Sun 1-5pm; ☎ 718 987 3478)* lies 0.6 mi/1 km north-east of Richmondtown. It houses a beautiful collection of Tibetan and Buddhist art and sculptures arranged in the terraced gardens.

The **Staten Island Zoo** *(open daily 10am-4:45pm; ☎ 718 442 3101)* in Barrett Park deserves a visit for its excellent reptile collection.

ENVIRONS

▬ LONG ISLAND

Regular bus service provides transportation to the Long Island region (information: Port Authority Bus Terminal, 39th St. and Eighth Ave.). The Long Island Rail Road also provides service from Penn Station.

Long Island is a narrow strip of land (118 mi/190 km × 25 mi/40 km) separated from the American continent by Long Island Sound. Many New Yorkers own summer residences on the island. In the north, the Gold Coast boasts sumptuous mansions. Their proprietors also own rights to the seafront, preventing beach access to the public for long stretches.

The southern section of Long Island is a more popular site, especially around Jones Beach. This area becomes more exclusive towards the Hamptons in the east.

North coast

Stony Brook★ is a picturesque rural town with 19th-century homes. The **Stony Brook Museum** exhibits traditional historical objects.

Sunken Meadow State Park is a vast protected beach with numerous recreational facilities for visitors.

Sands Point Park is a 207 acre/83 hectare natural reserve at Port Washington. It includes the mansion constructed by aviator H.F. Guggenheim in 1923. The house contains an admirable collection of 16th- to 17th-century French and Spanish furniture.

Cold Spring Harbor used to be a major whaling port. All that is left of this whaling era is several carefully maintained homes. The **Whaling Museum** presents detailed exhibits of this activity, including harpoons and navigational instruments.

South coast

Jones Beach State Park is a 7 mi/11 km beach which attracts large crowds as soon as the weather warms up. The wide range of facilities includes a stadium, a theater, heated pools and sports fields.

The **Hamptons** are a series of villages which extend approximately 37 mi/500 km to the east. **Westhampton, Southampton** and **East Hampton** are the main towns along the island's south shore. It is a fashionable vacation site for affluent New Yorkers.

Cars are prohibited on the 32 mi/50 km long **Fire Island**. It is particularly lively during the Independence Day holiday celebrations (July 4). It also contains a natural reserve, **National Seashore** (☎ 516 289 4810).

Montauk, on the easternmost point of Long Island, is a paradise for deep-sea fishermen. Formerly a small whaling village, it is today a favourite spot for sports fishermen.

PRINCETON UNIVERSITY

The Port Authority Bus Terminal (39th St. and Eighth Ave.) provides regular bus service to Princeton; the trip takes about two hours. The quickest way to reach Princeton is by train from Penn Station (31st St. and Eighth Ave., ☎ [212] 452 3603).

Situated 60 mi/100 km to the west of Manhattan in the state of New Jersey, Princeton has been one of America's most prestigious universities since the 18th century. It is part of the Ivy League, along with Yale, Harvard and Dartmouth, to mention several of the top schools.

Founded in 1746 by a group of Presbyterian ministers, the College of New Jersey was established first in Elizabeth and then in Newark before moving to its present site in the city of Princeton in 1756. On January 3, 1777, Washington, leading the Revolutionary Army, won the battle of Princeton against the British. In 1783, the Continental Congress was in Princeton when the peace treaty with the British was signed, ending the War of Independence. During the 150th anniversary of the College of New Jersey in 1896, it became a university and was renamed Princeton.

Princeton is a highly competitive school. Many prominent politicians and scientific researchers have received Princeton educations. With close to 6000 students and 700 professors, some of whom are Nobel Prize winners or candidates, Princeton is a training ground for some of America's most successful men and women.

Guided tours of the 2570 acre/1040 hectare campus are given by students.

The campus is organized around the superb **Nassau Hall** which houses the university administrative services. This Classical building is named after the Nassau dynasty of Orange, the reigning dynasty in England at the time the college was founded.

The **Harvey S. Firestone Library** contains 3 million books and 10 conference rooms. The **chapel,** which can hold up to 2000 people, has a remarkable 16th-century wooden pulpit from northern France. The **Art Museum** exhibits a good collection of mediaeval and Renaissance paintings.

The **Woodrow Wilson School Building,** named after the former president of the United States who was also the president of Princeton from 1902 to 1910, specializes in international affairs and public administration. The **James Forrestal Research Campus** was inaugurated in 1951. Its specialities include nuclear physics, chemistry and aeronautics.

THE HUDSON RIVER VALLEY

Boat tours of the Hudson River Valley are available starting Memorial Day (first Monday in May) to mid-September (information available from the Hudson River Day Line, Pier 81, ☎ 212 279 5151).

If traveling by car, leave Manhattan to the north by the Henry Hudson Parkway and take US route 9.

Railway service is available from Grand Central Terminal to cities and towns in the Hudson River Valley.

The Hudson River is situated entirely within New York State and has its source in the Adirondack Mountains, from whence it flows south into New York Bay. The 310 mi/500 km long river has always been an important factor in the transportation and communication links of New York State.

The Hudson River Valley is surprising for several reasons. It is spectacularly beautiful, especially during Indian summer from the end of September to the end of October. The fall colours are an unforgettable sight.

The winding, rural roads along the Hudson are a far cry from the gridded street patterns of Manhattan, Queens, Brooklyn or New Jersey. Even the town names along the route recall the days of the Indians before European settlers moved to the valley: Tuckahoe, Oscawana, and Mahansic.

The **Van Cortlandt Manor** belonged to Pierre Van Cortlandt, the first lieutenant governor of the State of New York. It is a typical example of 19th-century American architecture. Benjamin Franklin, General Lafayette and Rochambeau were all guests at this manor.

Vassar College, formerly an all-women's school, has been co-educational since 1968. It is one of the most prestigious private colleges in America.

President Franklin Delano Roosevelt was born at **Hyde Park** in 1882. The house remained in the family until it was transformed into a national historical site, the Home of Franklin Delano Roosevelt. It houses many documents and memorabilia concerning Roosevelt's career.

The sumptuous **Vanderbilt Mansion** is of interest primarily for its excellent collection of 16th- to 19th-century furniture.

West Point was created in 1794 by General Knox, then Secretary of War. The American Congress officially designated it as the United States Military Academy in 1802. Some of America's most prominent military men have graduated from West Point: General MacArthur (class of 1903), General Patton (class of 1909), General Eisenhower (class of 1915) and astronauts Borman (1950), Aldrin (1951) and Scott (1954).

The 4400 men and women cadets spend four years training at the academy.

Guided tours are available with documentary film showings (visitors information center, ☎ 914 938 2638). The **academy museum** contains surprising items, including a sword which belonged to Napoleon, Goring's baton and an impressive collection of firearms. The famous West Point cadet review is held in the autumn and in May.

The **Storm King Art Center** (10 mi/16 km from West Point) exhibits contemporary sculptures on the 73 acre/29 hectare property. The quality of the art in this open-air museum and its location make it a worthwhile visit.

▬ *ATLANTIC CITY*

New Jersey, 107 mi/170 km from Manhattan. Several buses leave daily from the Port Authority Bus Terminal (Greyhound or New Jersey Transit Companies).

Information: *Atlantic City Convention and Visitors Bureau,* ☎ *(609) 345 7536.*

This New Jersey beach town, with its celebrated 5 mi/8 km long boardwalk, was founded in 1854. Known as the Las Vegas of the East Coast, it hosts millions of visitors every year who crowd into the gambling establishments to play the slot machines, card games and roulette. The popular board game 'Monopoly' originated here, and the Miss America pageant is held here every year in September.

NEW YORK ADDRESSES

This section includes a list of hotels and restaurants, classified by neighbourhood, a selection of jazz clubs and bars and a list of the best stores and shops (see p. 208).

(see p. 208)

SYMBOLS USED

Hotels

American hotels are usually equipped with air-conditioning, telephones and bathrooms.

▲▲▲▲	Luxury hotel $200 and up
▲▲▲	First-class hotel $150 to $200
▲▲	Moderately priced hotel $80 to $150
▲	Inexpensive hotel under $80

① Restaurant
② Parking
③ Tennis
④ Pool
⑤ Garden

★ : Special weekend rates, depending on room availability. Call hotel or consult the Sunday *New York Times*.

Restaurants

Dial & Dine, ☎ (212) 226 3388. Call this number for restaurant information: opening hours, price, type of cuisine, address, whether credit cards or checks are accepted. Be forewarned, as in any city, the most popular restaurants do not necessarily always serve the best food.

Most restaurants open at 11:30am for lunch and 6pm for dinner, but check up-to-date times in advance.

Price per meal, per person:

$$$$	: over $60	AE	: American Express
$$$	: $45 to $60	CB	: Carte Blanche
$$	: $30 to $45	DC	: Diners Club
$	: $15 to $30	MC	: MasterCard
		V	: Visa

Whenever possible, credit cards accepted by the establishment are indicated.

CONTENTS

DOWNTOWN

Hotels

▲▲▲▲ **Vista International,** 3 World Trade Center, II, B2, ☎ (212) 9389100. 829 rooms. ① ② ③ ④ AE, CB, DC, MC, V. Situated between the two towers of the World Trade Center, this is the best hotel in the Financial District. Jogging track and sauna. Excellent restaurant: **American Harvest.**

▲ **Washington Square Hotel,** 103 Waverly Pl. at Washington Sq., III, B3, ☎ (212) 7779515. 200 rooms. MC, V. Located in the heart of Greenwich Village. No restaurant facilities, but the neighbourhood has many reasonably priced coffee shops.

Restaurants

Financial District, World Trade Center, Tribeca, Chinatown, Little Italy

$$$$ **American Harvest,** 3 World Trade Center, II, B2, ☎ (212) 9389100. Located in the **Vista International Hotel.** Very fine American cuisine. Closed Sun. AE, CB, DC, MC, V.

$$$$ **Montrachet,** 239 West Broadway near White St., II, B1, ☎ (212) 2192777. Elegant French decor and interesting clientele. Try the *foie gras* from upstate New York. Reservations recommended. Open Mon-Sat 6-10:45pm. AE.

$$$$ **Windows on the World,** 1 World Trade Center, II, B2, ☎ (212) 938 1111. There are three restaurants on the 107th floor (Cellar in the Sky, The Hors-d'Oeuvrerie, The Restaurant), with stunning views of New York City. Brunch on Sat and Sun. AE, CB, DC, MC, V.

$$$ **Barocco,** 301 Church St. at Walker St., II, B1, ☎ (212) 4311445. An elegant trattoria. Open Fri and Sat until midnight. Closed Sun. AE, CB, DC, MC, V.

$$$ **Ecco,** 124 Chambers St. near Broadway, II, B2, ☎ (212) 2277074. This northern Italian restaurant is a popular place for business lunches. Reservations recommended. AE.

$$$ **Flutie's,** Pier 17, South Street Seaport, II, C2-3, ☎ (212) 6930777. The seafood and steaks make this trip worthwhile. Reservations recommended. Open daily 11am-11pm. AE, DC, MC, V.

$$$ **Morgan Williams,** 55 Broadway south of Wall St., II, B3, ☎ (212) 8093150. A calm and spacious restaurant serving American and European cuisine. Closed weekends. AE, CB, DC, MC, V.

$$$ **Odéon,** 145 West Broadway at Thomas St., II, B2, ☎ (212) 2330507. Nouvelle cuisine in an Art Deco room. Open Fri and Sat until 3am. Closed Mon. AE, MC, V.

$$$ **Sweets,** 2 Fulton St., South Street Seaport, II, C2-3, ☎ (212) 8259786. This is one of New York's oldest fish restaurants, which caters to a neighbourhood clientele. Open Mon-Fri 11:30am-8:30pm. AE, DC, MC, V.

$$$ **Le Zinc,** 139 Duane St., II, B2, ☎ (212) 7321226. This is a very good and fashionable brasserie in Tribeca. Open Mon-Fri noon-3pm, 7pm-midnight, Sat 7pm-midnight. AE.

$$ **Angelo's,** 146 Mulberry St., II, BC2, ☎ (212) 9661277. Good southern Italian cuisine. Open Tues-Thurs noon-11:30pm, Fri and Sat to 1am. AE, DC, MC, V.

$$ **Bon Temps Rouler,** 59 Reade St. between Broadway-Church Sts., II, B2, ☎ (212) 5131333. Cajun cuisine and popular bar. Closed Sun.

$$ **Bridge Café,** 279 Water St. at Dover St., II, C2, ☎ (212) 2273344. Once a sailors' tavern, it is now popular with political figures. The menu is changed daily.

$$ **Costa Azzurra,** 134 Mulberry St., II, BC2, ☎ (212) 9665634. Northern Italian cuisine. Friendly service in an unpretentious setting. Reservations recommended. Open Mon, Wed-Fri noon-11pm, Sat and Sun to midnight. AE, DC, MC, V.

$$ **Fraunces' Tavern Restaurant,** 54 Pearl St. at Broad St., II, B3, ☎ (212) 2690144. This is one of New York's historic sites: Washington bade farewell to his troops in this tavern in 1783. Closed Sun.

$$ **Gianni's,** 15 Fulton St., South Street Seaport, II, C2-3, ☎ (212) 6087300. Northern Italian cuisine. Excellent pasta and a pleasant outdoor dining area. Reservations recommended. AE, CB, DC, MC, V.

$$ **Harry's at Hanover Square,** 1 Hanover Sq. between Pearl-Stone Sts., II, B3, ☎ (212) 4253412. Steaks and chops. This is a pleasant singles spot where you can enjoy a beer in a relaxed and noisy atmosphere.

$$ **H.S.F.,** 46 Bowery south of Canal St., II, C2, ☎ (212) 3741319. A very friendly Chinese restaurant, with dim sum specialities.

$$ **Phoenix Garden,** 46 Bowery, II, C2, ☎ (212) 9628934. Excellent Cantonese cuisine. Open daily 11:30am-10:30pm.

$$ **Siu Lam Kung,** 18 Elizabeth St. south of Canal St., II, C1, ☎ (212) 7320974. Popular Cantonese restaurant with a Chinese clientele. Pleasant decor and fast service. Reservations recommended.

$$ **Vincent's Clam Bar,** 119 Mott St. at Hector St., II, C1-2, ☎ (212) 2268133. Seafood specialities in a neighbourhood institution.

$ **Dai Sai Kai Restaurant,** 155 Grand St. at Lafayette St., II, BC1, ☎ (212) 9253865 or 2268783. Chinese-Cuban coffee shop. Delicious, inexpensive soups for less than $1.

$ **Exterminator Chili,** 305 Church St. at Walker St., II, B1, ☎ (212) 2193070. This is a 1950s-style luncheonette which caters to a young crowd. Open daily 11am-11pm.

$ **Thailand Restaurant,** 106 Bayard St. at Baxter St., II, BC1-2, ☎ (212) 3493121. Unpretentious decor, excellent Thai cooking and attentive service. Open daily: 11:30am-11:30pm.

SoHo, Greenwich Village, East Village, Lower East Side.

$$$$ **Chanterelle,** 89 Grand St. at Greene St., II, B1, ☎ (212) 9666960. Excellent French *nouvelle cuisine*, one of New York's most select restaurants. Reservations necessary. Closed Sun and Mon. AE, MC, V.

$$$$ **Coach House,** 110 Waverly Pl., III, B3, ☎ (212) 7770303. American cuisine. A longstanding institution in Greenwich Village. Closed Mon and Aug.

$$$$ **Gotham Bar & Grill,** 12 E. 12th St. between Fifth Ave.-University Place, III, C2-3, ☎ (212) 6204020. This is a former warehouse which was converted into an elegant restaurant. Reservations recommended. AE, CB, DC, MC, V.

$$$$ **John Clancy's,** 181 W. 10th St. at Seventh Ave., III, B3, ☎ (212) 2427350. Fish and shellfish are specialities. Reservations recommended. Open daily 6-11:30pm. AE, CB, DC, MC, V.

$$$$ **Provence,** 38 MacDougal St. at Prince St., II, B1, ☎ (212) 4757500. Provençal cuisine. The restaurant has diligent, attentive waiters, excellent food and an attractive garden. Reservations recommended well in advance. Closed Mon.

$$$$ **La Tulipe,** 104 W. 13th St. at Ave. of the Americas, III, B2, ☎ (212) 6918860. This is a discreet French restaurant with a charming garden and excellent cuisine. Reservations recommended. Open Tues-Sun 6-10pm. AE, CB, DC, MC, V.

$$$ **The Black Sheep,** 344 W. 11th St. at Washington St., III, B3, ☎ (212) 2421010. A popular French restaurant. Reservations recommended. Open daily 6pm-midnight. AE, CB, DC, MC, V.

$$$ **Cent'Anni,** 50 Carmine St. between Bleecker-Bedford Sts., III, B3, ☎ (212) 9899494. Northern Italian cuisine. The pasta and veal chops are highly recommended. Open Mon-Sat to 11:30pm, Sun to 10:30pm. AE.

$$$ **Indochine,** 430 Lafayette St., III, C3, ☎ (212) 5055111. Excellent Vietnamese cuisine in a decor of bamboo and green plants.

$$$ **J.S. Vandam,** 150 Varick St. at Vandam St., II, B1, ☎ (212) 9297466. The atmosphere is a popular bar scene and, after 10pm, it becomes very lively.

$$$ **Minetta Tavern,** 113 Minetta Lane at MacDougal St., III, B3, ☎ (212) 4753850. Italian cuisine. This is one of the oldest pubs in the Village. AE, CB, DC, MC, V.

$$$ **Old Homestead,** 56 Ninth Ave., III, B2, ☎ (212) 2429040. The oldest steak house in New York. AE, CB, DC, MC, V.

$$$ **Quatorze,** 240 W. 14th St. between Seventh-Eighth Aves., III, B2, ☎ (212) 2067006. Charming French brasserie. Reservations recommended. Open Mon-Fri noon-2:30pm, 6-11:30pm, Sat and Sun 6-11:30pm.

$$$ **Raoul's,** 180 Prince St. between Sullivan-Thompson Sts., II, B1, ☎ (212) 9663518. Friendly atmosphere and delicious French food. Reservations recommended. AE, MC, V.

$$$ **La Ripaille,** 605 Hudson St. between 12th-Bethune Sts., III, B3, ☎ (212) 2554406. Relaxed and comfortable atmosphere in this French restaurant. Reservations recommended. Open Mon-Sat 5:30-11:30pm. AE, MC, V.

$$ **Acme Bar & Grill,** 9 Great Jones St., III, B3, ☎ (212) 4201934. Cajun cuisine. A typically American decor with one of the best jukeboxes in town.

$$ **Amazonas,** 492 Broome St. between Broadway-Wooster St., II, B1, ☎ (212) 9663371. Brazilian decor and music. Reservations recommended. Open Sun-Thurs 5-11:30pm, Fri and Sat to 1:30am. AE, CB, DC, MC, V.

$$ **Amsterdam's Grand Bar and Rotisserie,** 454 Broadway between Grand-Howard Sts., II, B1, ☎ (212) 9256166; 428 Amsterdam Ave. at 80th St., V, AB3, ☎ (212) 8741377. Rotisserie specialities include chicken, duck and fish. AE, CB, DC, MC, V.

$$ **Bayamo,** 704 Broadway between 4th St.-Washington Pl., III, C3, ☎ (212) 4755151. Chinese-Cuban cuisine.

$$ **Bernstein on Essex Street,** 135 Essex St., II, C1, ☎ (212)

473 3900. Kosher restaurant. Open Sun-Tues to 1am.

$$ **La Bohème,** 24 Minetta Lane between Bleecker and W. 3rd Sts., III, C3, ☎ (212) 473 6447. A relaxed, friendly bistro serving French cuisine and pizza.

$$ **Broome Street Bar,** 363 West Broadway at Broome St., II, B1, ☎ (212) 925 2086. Good hamburgers in a pleasant neighbourhood restaurant.

$$ **Café Loup,** 18 E. 13th St. between Fifth Ave.-University Pl., III, C2, ☎ (212) 255 4746. A charming French bistro. Open daily. AE, CB, DC, MC, V.

$$ **Central Falls,** 478 West Broadway between Houston-Prince Sts., II, B1, ☎ (212) 475 333. Part piano bar, part gallery.

$$ **Chez Brigitte,** 77 Greenwich Ave. at Seventh Ave., III, B3, ☎ (212) 929 6736. Good Italian and French food in counter-style restaurant. Reservations recommended.

$$ **Cinco de Mayo,** 349 West Broadway between Broome-Grand Sts., II, B1, ☎ (212) 226 5255; 45 Tudor City Pl., IV, C3, ☎ (212) 661 5070. Very good Mexican cuisine. Reservations recommended. Open daily noon-midnight. AE, CB, DC, MC, V.

$$ **Cornelia Street Cafe,** 29 Cornelia St. between Bleecker-W. 4th Sts., III, B3, ☎ (212) 989 9318. An agreeable place for lunch or brunch, serving sandwiches and salads.

$$ **Cottonwood Cafe,** 415 Bleecker St. between Bank-11th Sts., III, B3, ☎ (212) 924 6271. Young clientele, pleasant atmosphere and good Tex-Mex food.

$$ **Cuisine de Saigon,** 154 W. 13th St. between Ave. of the Americas-Seventh Ave., III, B2, ☎ (212) 255 6003. Good Vietnamese food in an unpretentious place.

$$ **El Faro,** 823 Greenwich St. at Horatio St., III, B3, ☎ (212) 929 8210. Popular Spanish restaurant serving good paella. AE, MC, V.

$$ **5 & 10 No Exaggeration,** 77 Greene St., II, B1, ☎ (212) 925 7414. French-American cuisine. An Art Deco, 1940s decor, with piano music every night. Closed Mon. AE, MC, V.

$$ **Florent,** 69 Gansevoort St., III, A3, ☎ (212) 989 5779. This French restaurant is a favourite spot for artists and journalists. Good food and atmosphere. Open daily 6:30pm-2am.

$$ **Garvin's,** 19 Waverly Pl., III, BC3, ☎ (212) 473 5261. Simple American food and music. Reservations recommended. A pre-theater menu is available from 5-7pm. AE, CB, DC, MC, V.

$$ **Gulf Coast,** 489 West St. between 12th St.-West Side Highway, III, A3, ☎ (212) 206 8790. An old sailors' bar which has become a very fashionable Cajun and fish restaurant. Open daily 6pm-midnight.

$$ **Hawaii 5-0,** 121 Ave. A between 7th St.-St Mark's Pl., III, D3, ☎ (212) 420 8590. A Hawaiian restaurant serving delicious grilled fish. Reservations recommended.

$$ **Khyber Pass,** 34 St Mark's Pl. between Second-Third Aves., III, C3, ☎ (212) 473 0989. Among New York's Afghan restaurants, this one provides the best quality for the price.

$$ **Meridies,** 87 Seventh Ave. at Barrow St., III, B3, ☎ (212) 243 8000. Eclectic menu and outdoor dining area. Open Mon-Sat to midnight, Sun to 10pm.

$$ **Mie,** 196 Second Ave. at 12th St., III, C2-3, ☎ (212) 674 7060. An unpretentious Japanese restaurant. Open daily to midnight. AE, CB, DC.

$$ **New Deal Restaurant,** 152 Spring St. between Wooster St.- West Broadway, II, B1, ☎ (212) 431 3663. French and Californian cuisine in an Art Deco room, complete with bar and jazz. Open daily to 2am.

$$ **Princess Pamela,** 243 E. 10th St. at First Ave., III, C3, ☎ (212) 477 4460. Southern regional cuisine. There is a good jazz orchestra; come just for the music, if you like. No cover charge. Reservations recommended.

$$ **Prince Street Bar & Restaurant,** 125 Prince St., II, B1, ☎ (212) 228 8130. Indonesian restaurant with a wide selection of dishes. Very lively atmosphere.

$$ **Sabor,** 20 Cornelia St. between Bleecker-W. 4th Sts., III, B3, ☎ (212) 243 9579. A small Cuban restaurant. Reservations recommended. Open Sun-Thurs 6-11pm, Fri and Sat 6pm-midnight. AE, MC, V.

$$ **Sammy's Rumanian Jewish Restaurant,** 157 Chrystie St. near Delancey St., II, C1, ☎ (212) 673 0330; 673 5526; 475 9131. Serves generous portions of Rumanian and Balkan dishes.

$$ **Second Avenue Deli,** 156 Second Ave. at 10th St., III, C2-3, ☎ (212) 677 0606. Typical Jewish deli serving chicken soup, pastrami and blintzes.

$$ **Spring Street Natural,** 62 Spring St. at Lafayette St., II, B1, ☎ (212) 966 0290. One of New York's best vegetarian restaurants (also serves fish).

$$ **Sugar Reef,** 93 Second Ave., III, C2-3, ☎ (212) 477 8427. A trendy Creole and Cajun restaurant.

$ **Abyssinia,** 35 Grand St. at Thompson St., II, B1, ☎ (212) 226 5959. Comfort is not the strong point of this Ethiopian restaurant, but a glass of the mead is well worth the wait. The menu is sumptuous. Reservations recommended. Open daily 6-10:30pm.

$ **Arturo's,** 106 Houston St. at Thompson St., II, B1, ☎ (212) 475 9828. Specialities include pizzas cooked in wood-burning ovens. This is an old neighbourhood restaurant with a friendly family atmosphere. Live jazz. Reservations recommended.

$ **Caribe,** 117 Perry St. at Greenwich St., III, B3, ☎ (212) 225 9191. Creole cuisine.

$ **El Castillo de Jagua,** 113 Rivington St. between Essex-Ludlow Sts., II, C1, ☎ (212) 982 6412. Latin American restaurant with friendly and unique atmosphere.

$ **Chumley's** 86 Bedford St. at Barrow St., III, B3, ☎ (212) 675 4449. Delicious hamburgers in a former Prohibition speakeasy.

$ **De Robertis,** 176 First Ave. between 10th-11th Sts., III, C3, ☎ (212) 674 7137. Italian pastry shop open since 1904 where you can sip an espresso in the back room while watching the diverse East Village clientele.

$ **Dojo,** 24 St Mark's Pl. between Second-Third Aves., III, C3, ☎ (212) 674 9821. This Japanese-American restaurant offers good quality for the price.

$ **Elephant & Castle,** 183 Prince St., II, BC1, ☎ (212) 260 3600; 68 Greenwich Ave., ☎ (212) 243 1400. Omelettes, salads and sandwiches for a light lunch or brunch, but there is often a wait.

$ **Fanelli's Café,** 94 Prince St. at Mercer St., II, B1, ☎ (212) 226 9412. Italian food and hamburgers. One of New York's oldest bars, with a handsome black storefront and cut-glass door.

$ **Food,** 67 Prince St. at Wooster St., II, B1. This is a good place to stop for an inexpensive sandwich while visiting the SoHo galleries. The portions are generous but there is usually a line.

$ **Great Jones Street Café,** 54 Great Jones St. at the Bowery, III, C3, ☎ (212) 674 9304. Cajun and Southern cuisine. Colourful, noisy and small, this restaurant is fashionable and attracts a young crowd. Don't miss the delicious cornbread.

$ **Greene Street Café,** 101 Greene St. between Prince-Spring Sts., II, B1, ☎ (212) 925 2415. This is a good place for brunch. Reservations recommended.

$ **John's Pizzeria,** 278 Bleecker St., III, BC3, ☎ (212) 243 1680; 408 E. 64th St., IV, CD2. Some consider this the best pizzeria in New York, serving countless varieties of pizza.

$ **Katz's Restaurant,** 205 Houston St. at Ludlow St., II, C1, ☎ (212) 254 2246. This kosher-style restaurant is packed for lunch.

$ **Kiev Restaurant,** 117 Second Ave. at 7th St., III, C3, ☎ (212) 674 4040. This Ukrainian restaurant is popular with the late-night crowd. Open 24 hours.

$ **Mamun's Falafel,** 119 MacDougal St., II, BC3, ☎ (212) 674 9246. The oldest falafel shop in New York. Open to 5am.

$ **Odessa Restaurant,** 117 Ave. A between 7th-8th Sts., III, D3, ☎ (212) 473 8916. This former coffee shop is now a Ukrainian restaurant which serves delicious blintzes. It is a lively and charmingly old-fashioned place.

$ **Olive Tree Cafe,** 117 MacDougal St., III, BC3, ☎ (212) 254 3630. The falafels served by this Israeli restaurant are popular with New York University students.

$ **Omen,** 113 Thompson St. at Prince St., II, B1, ☎ (212) 925 8923. Japanese food served in a decor of wood and rice paper. Closed Mon. AE, CB, DC.

$ **Patisserie Lanciani,** 117 Prince St., II, BC1, ☎ (212) 477 2788; 271 W. 4th St., III, B3, ☎ (212) 929 0739. A beautifully decorated pastry shop which also serves lunch. Open daily noon-10pm. AE.

$ **Polonia,** 126 First Ave. between 6th-7th Sts., III, C3, ☎ (212) 674 9113. Polish coffee shop.

$ **Ratner's,** 138 Delancey St., II, C1, ☎ (212) 677 5588. A deli and pastry shop serving kasha, blintzes, gefilte fish, pickled lox. Not to be missed!

$ **Tamu,** 340 West Broadway at Grand St., II, B1, ☎ (212) 925 2751. This is a very good Indonesian restaurant housed in a former loft. Reservations recommended. Open Sat and Sun to midnight. AE, CB, DC, MC, V.

$ **Texarkana,** 64 W. 10th St. between Fifth Ave.-Ave. of the Americas, III, B3, ☎ (212) 254 5800. Excellent ambience in this Cajun restaurant. Open Sun-Fri 6pm-midnight, Sat 6pm-3:45am. AE, DC.

$ **Tortilla Flats,** 767 Washington St. at 12th St., III, A3, ☎ (212) 243 1053. This Tex-Mex restaurant stays open late and attracts a local clientele.

$ **Veniero's,** 342 E. 11th St. between First-Second Aves., III, C3, ☎ (212) 674 4415. This pastry shop and restaurant has great ambience.

$ **Veselka Coffee Shop,** 144 Second Ave. between 9th St.-St Mark's Pl., III, C3, ☎ (212) 228 9682. The menu is simple and the portions generous at this Polish/Ukrainian restaurant.

$ **Yonah Schimmel,** 137 Houston St., III, C3, ☎ (212) 477 2858. Jewish restaurant with delicious knishes and strudels.

Indian restaurants in the East Village

An Indian neighbourhood has recently grown up around 6th Street in the East Village. There are more than a dozen restaurants along the Curry Chasm, serving inexpensive Indian specialities. Most of the restaurants accept major credit cards, but it is best to confirm.

$ **Anar Bagh,** 338 E. 6th St., III, CD3, ☎ (212) 529 1937. One of the best Tandoori restaurants in the neighbourhood.

$ **Calcutta Restaurant,** 324 E. 6th St., III, CD3, ☎ (212) 982 8127. Most of the dishes are very spicy, but the chef will make them less so on request.

$ **Mitali,** 334 E. 6th St., III, CD3, ☎ (212) 533 2508. Wonderful decor. AE, MC, V.

■■■ MIDTOWN EAST

Hotels

▲▲▲▲ **Doral Tuscany,** 120 E. 39th St. at Park Ave., III, C1, ☎ (212) 686 1600. 128 rooms. ① AE, CB, DC, MC, V. Small, charming and discreet hotel with an efficient and helpful staff.

▲▲▲▲ **Grand Hyatt,** 42nd St. at Park Ave., near Grand Central Terminal, IV, C3, ☎ (212) 883 1234. 1400 rooms. ① ② ③ AE, CB, DC, MC, V. Opened in 1980, this hotel is decorated with marble and cascading plants. Sports club available with sauna and squash courts.

▲▲▲▲ **Helmsley Palace,** 455 Madison Ave. at 50th St., IV, C2, ☎ (212) 888 7000. 1050 rooms and suites. ① ② AE, CB, DC, MC, V. This luxurious hotel is very well situated near the Fifth Avenue museums and stores.

▲▲▲▲ **Inter-Continental,** 111 E. 48th St., IV, C3, ☎ (212) 755 5900. 777 rooms. ① AE, CB, DC, MC, V. Spacious and soundproof rooms; 24-hour room service. New York's oldest pharmacy, Caswell Massey, famous for its soaps and eaux de toilette, is situated in the same building.

▲▲▲▲ **Omni Berkshire Place,** 21 E. 52nd St. at Madison Ave., IV, C2, ☎ (212) 753 5800. 420 rooms. ① ② AE, CB, DC, MC, V. Situated near the Museum of Modern Art.

▲▲▲▲ **St Regis Sheraton,** 2 E. 55th St. at Fifth Ave., IV, C2, ☎ (212) 753 4500. 520 rooms. ① AE, CB, DC, MC, V. Constructed in the 1900s, this hotel remains one of the most beautiful in New York.

▲▲▲▲ **Sheraton Park Avenue,** 45 Park Ave. at 37th St., III, C1, ☎ (212) 685 7676. 175 rooms. ① AE, CB, DC, MC, V. The ambience is discreet. The bar is home to the only jazz club on this side of Park Avenue.

▲▲▲▲ **United Nations Plaza,** 1 United Nations Plaza at 44th St., IV, D3, ☎ (212) 355 3400. 289 rooms. ① ④ AE, CB, DC, MC, V. Sports facilities and sauna are available in this hotel located near the United Nations Headquarters. Good hotel restaurants.

▲▲▲▲ **Waldorf Astoria,** 301 Park Ave. at 50th St., IV, C3, ☎ (212) 355 3000. 1500 rooms. ① AE, CB, DC, MC, V. This luxurious Art Deco hotel was constructed in 1931 and was recently redecorated.

▲▲▲ **Doral Park Avenue,** 70 Park Ave. at 38th St., III, C1, ☎ (212) 687 7050. 200 rooms. ① AE, CB, DC, MC, V. This is a very quiet hotel situated near Grand Central Terminal.

▲▲▲ **Howard Hotel,** 127 E. 55th St. between Lexington-Park Aves., IV, C2, ☎ (212) 826 1100. 105 rooms. ① AE, DC, MC, V. Very well situated and comfortable hotel.

▲▲▲ **Loews Drake,** 440 Park Ave. at 56th St., IV, C2, ☎ (212) 421 0900. 650 rooms. ① ② AE, CB, DC, MC, V. Recently remodeled and expanded Pleasant bar.

▲▲▲ **Morgans,** 237 Madison Ave. at 37th St., III, C1, ☎ (212) 686 0300. 111 rooms. ① AE, MC, V. The staff is young and friendly. The outdoor restaurant is open for lunch only.

▲▲▲ **New York Helmsley,** 212 E. 42nd St. at Third Ave., IV, C3, ☎ (212) 490 8900. 790 rooms. ① ② ④ ★ AE, CB, DC, MC, V. This is a good hotel, near Grand Central Terminal.

▲▲ **Bedford,** 118 E. 48th St. at Fifth Ave., IV, C2, ☎ (212) 697 4800. 135 rooms. ① ★ AE, CB, DC, MC, V. Quiet and friendly family atmosphere.

▲▲ **Beekman Tower,** 3 Mitchell Pl. off First Ave. near 49th St., IV, C3, ☎ (212) 355 7300. 160 rooms. ① ② AE, CB, DC, MC, V. An apartment-hotel with studios or suites with kitchens. The piano bar offers a beautiful view over Midtown and the East River.

▲▲ **Elysee,** 60 E. 54th St. at Park Ave., IV, C2, ☎ (212) 753 1066. 110 rooms. ① AE, CB, DC, MC, V. The rooms in this small hotel are decorated in different styles, ranging from colonial to oriental.

▲▲ **Gramercy Park,** 2 Lexington Ave. at 21st St., III, C2, ☎ (212) 475 4320. 500 rooms. ① ⑤ AE, CB, DC, MC, V. This is a quiet, comfortable and old-fashioned hotel.

▲▲ **Helmsley Middletowne,** 148 E. 48th St. between Lexington-Third Aves., IV, C3, ☎ (212) 755 3000. 190 rooms. ★ AE, CB, DC, MC, V. The hotel consists primarily of suites with kitchen facilities. Rates are negotiable, depending on the length of stay.

▲▲ **Kitano,** 66 Park Ave. at 38th St., III, C1, ☎ (212) 685 0022. 100 rooms. ① AE, CB, DC, MC, V. Near Grand Central Terminal, this hotel combines Japanese and American influences. No room service.

▲▲ **Lexington Hotel,** 511 Lexington Ave. at 48th St., IV, C3, ☎ (212) 755 4400. 800 rooms. ① ② AE, DC, MC, V. A pleasant and well-situated hotel.

▲▲ **Loews Summit,** 569 E. 51st St. at Lexington Ave., IV, C2-3, ☎ (212) 752 7000. 760 rooms. ① ② AE, CB, DC, MC, V. A hotel with an international flair and very comfortable rooms.

▲▲ **Lombardy,** 111 E. 56th St., IV, C2, ☎ (212) 753 8600. 160 rooms. ① AE, CB, DC, MC, V. Situated near the Madison Avenue shops, this hotel offers good quality for the price and a friendly atmosphere.

▲▲ **Lyden House,** 320 E. 53rd St. between First-Second Aves., IV, CD2, ☎ (212) 888 6070. 133 suites. AE, CB, DC, MC, V. Elegant and spacious suites with kitchen facilities. Situated in a pleasant neighbourhood.

▲▲ **Plaza Fifty,** 155 E. 50th St. at Third Ave., IV, C3, ☎ (212) 751 5710. 206 rooms. AE, DC, MC, V. The hotel doesn't have a restaurant, but there are many places to eat in the neighbourhood.

▲▲ **The Roosevelt,** 45 E. 45th St. at Madison Ave., IV, C3, ☎ (212) 661 9600. 1050 rooms. ① AE, CB, DC, MC, V. Many tour groups stay at this tasteful and simply decorated hotel.

▲▲ **San Carlos,** 150 E. 50th St. at Lexington Ave., IV, C3, ☎ (212) 755 1800. 144 rooms. AE, CB, DC, MC, V. No restaurant or room service.

▲▲ **Shelbourne Murray Hill,** 303 Lexington Ave. at 37th St., III, C1, ☎ (212) 689 5200. 250 rooms. ① ② AE, CB, DC, MC, V. This is an elegant, unpretentious hotel with an attentive staff.

▲▲ **Tudor,** 304 E. 42nd St. at First Ave., IV, D3, ☎ (212) 986 8800. 550 rooms. AE, CB, DC, MC, V. This reasonably priced hotel is situated close to the United Nations Headquarters and Grand Central Terminal. The restaurant is scheduled to open soon.

▲ **Pickwick Arms,** 230 E. 51st St. at Lexington Ave., IV, C3, ☎ (212) 355 0300. 380 rooms. AE, DC, MC, V. This is a reasonably priced hotel.

Restaurants

$$$$ **Aurora,** 60 E. 49th St., IV, CD3, ☎ (212) 692 9292. Chef Gerard Panguad and decorator Milton Glaser created the reputation of this first-class French restaurant. Closed Sun. AE, CB, DC.

$$$$ **Brive,** 405 E. 58th St. at First Ave., IV, D2, ☎ (212) 838 9393. Delicious French cuisine. Reservations recommended. Closed Sun. AE, DC, MC, V.

$$$$ **Casual Quilted Giraffe,** 15 E. 55th St. between Fifth-Madison Aves., IV, C2, ☎ (212) 593 1221. American cuisine is served in this casual version of The Quilted Giraffe. Reservations recommended. Open Mon-Sat 11:30am-11:30pm. AE, MC, V.

$$$$ **Christ Cella,** 160 E. 46th St., IV, CD3, ☎ (212) 697 2479. This is one of New York's best steak houses. Closed Sun. AE, CB, DC, MC, V.

$$$$ **La Côte Basque,** 5 E. 55th St. between Fifth-Madison Aves., IV, C2, ☎ (212) 688 6525. This French restaurant is very fashionable. Closed Sun. AE, CB, DC, MC, V.

$$$$ **Le Cygne,** 55 E. 54th St., IV, CD2, ☎ (212) 759 5941. A French restaurant with impeccable service in a post-modern decor overflowing with flowers. Closed Sun. AE, CB, DC, MC, V.

$$$$ **The Four Seasons,** 99 E. 52nd St., IV, CD2, ☎ (212) 754 9494. This New York institution offers French-American cuisine along with newly created low-calorie menus. AE, CB, DC, MC, V.

$$$$ **Lutèce,** 249 E. 50th St. at Second Ave., IV, C3, ☎ (212) 752 2225. Recently remodeled, Lutèce serves classic French cuisine. Reservations recommended. Closed Sun. AE, CB, DC.

$$$$ **Palm,** 837 Second Ave. between 44th-45th Sts., IV, C3, ☎ (212) 687 2953; **Palm Too,** 840 Second Ave. at 45th St., IV, C3, ☎ (212) 697 5198. These restaurants specialize in delicious grilled steaks and fish. Closed Sun. AE, CB, DC, MC, V.

$$$$ **Sparks Steakhouse,** 210 E. 64th St. between Second-Third Aves., IV, C2, ☎ (212) 687 4855. This is a comfortable steak house with a complete wine cellar. Reservations recommended.

$$$ **Akbar,** 475 Park Ave., IV, C2-3, ☎ (212) 838 1717. This is one of New York's best Indian restaurants, popular for business lunches.

$$$ **Brazilian Pavilion,** 316 E. 53rd St. between First-Second Aves., IV, CD2, ☎ (212) 758 8129. The decor of this Brazilian restaurant is exotic. Reservations recommended. Closed Sun. AE, CB, DC, MC, V.

$$$ **Chez Vong,** 220 E. 46th St., IV, CD3, ☎ (212) 867 1111. An international crowd frequents this Chinese restaurant.

$$$ **Dardanelles East Ararat,** 1076 First Ave. at 58th St., IV, D2, ☎ (212) 752 2828. The ambience in this Armenian restaurant is unique. Reservations recommended.

$$$ **Huberts,** 102 E. 22nd St. between Park-Lexington Aves., III, C2, ☎ (212) 673 3741. The specialities of this French restaurant include fish and exotic dishes. Closed Sun. AE, MC, V.

$$$ **Le Périgord,** 405 E. 52nd St. at First Ave., IV, D3, ☎ (212) 755 6244. This established French restaurant offers delicious food, a complete wine list and a discreet ambience.

$$$ **Nanni's,** 146 E. 46th St. between Lexington-Third Aves., IV, C2, ☎ (212) 697 4161. Northern Italian cuisine.

$$$ **The Oyster Bar & Restaurant,** Grand Central Terminal, 42nd St. at Vanderbilt Ave., IV, C3, ☎ (212) 490 6650. Located in a vaulted, tiled setting in Grand Central Terminal, the Oyster Bar offers a remarkable variety of excellent fish dishes. Closed Sat and Sun. AE, CB, DC, MC, V.

$$$ **The Ritz Café,** 2 Park Ave. at 32nd St., III, C1, ☎ (212) 684 2122. The food is simple and well prepared; this is a good place for a Cajun meal. Reservations recommended. AE

$$$ **Smith & Wollensky,** 201 E. 49th St. at Third Ave., IV, C3, ☎ (212) 753 1530. Often crowded steak house. Reservations recommended. AE, CB, DC, MC, V.

$$$ **Union Square Café,** 21 E. 16th St. at Union Sq., III, C2, ☎ (212) 243 4020. A varied clientele frequents this establishment, which serves French and Italian cuisine. The menu is imaginative and the wine list complete. Reservations recommended. Closed Sun. AE, MC, V.

$$$ **Woods,** 24 E. 21st St. between Park Ave.-Broadway, III, C2, ☎ (212) 505 7868; 718 Madison Ave. between 63rd-64th Sts., ☎ (212) 688 1126; 148 W. 37th St., ☎ (212) 564 7340. American *nouvelle cuisine* restaurants serving salads, fresh vegetables and light desserts.

$$ **Albuquerque Eats,** 375 Third Ave. at 27th St., III, C1, ☎ (212) 683 6500. Texan cuisine and country music are offered here; the hamburgers are thick and served with tasty onion rings. This type of ambience is hard to find anywhere else in the neighbourhood.

$$ **Cedars of Lebanon,** 39 E. 30th St. between Park-Madison Aves., III, C1, ☎ (212) 725 9251. Middle Eastern cuisine with belly dancing after 10pm. Reservations recommended. AE, CB, DC, MC, V.

$$ **Tommy Maken's Irish Pavilion,** 130 E. 57th St. at Lexington Ave., IV, C2, ☎ (212) 759 9040. Irish pub-restaurant.

$$ **Xenia,** 871 First Ave. between 48th-49th Sts., IV, D3, ☎ (212) 838 1191. The Greek food is simple, fresh and well prepared. The garden makes it a sought-after place on summer evenings. Reservations recommended. AE, CB, DC, MC, V.

$ **Burger Heaven,** 9 E. 53rd St. between Fifth-Madison Aves., IV, C2, ☎ (212) 752 0340. The best hamburgers and milkshakes in New York — and it's cheap!

■ *MIDTOWN WEST*

Hotels

▲▲▲▲ **Dorset,** 30 W. 54th St. at Ave. of the Americas, IV, B2, ☎ (212) 247 7300. 400 rooms. ① AE, CB, DC. This is a quiet hotel situated near the Museum of Modern Art. Some of the rooms have kitchen facilities.

▲▲▲▲ **Essex House,** 160 Central Park South, IV, BC2 ☎ (212) 247 0300. 810 rooms. ① ② AE, CB, DC, MC, V. The top floors offer a stunning view.

▲▲▲▲ **Grand Bay Hotel at Equitable,** 152 W. 51st St. at Seventh Ave., IV, V2, ☎ (212) 765 1900. 178 rooms. AE, CB, DC, MC, V. The hotel opened in 1987; offers parking and sports club.

▲▲▲▲ **Helmsley Park Lane,** 36 Central Park South, ☎ (212) 371 4000. 640 rooms. ① ② AE, CB, DC, MC, V. The rooms of this elegant hotel overlook the park.

▲▲▲▲ **Marriott Marquis,** 1535 Broadway between 45th-46th Sts., IV, B3, ☎ (212) 398 1900. 1800 rooms. ① AE, CB, DC, MC, V. This hotel has revolving restaurants on the 50th floor and transparent elevators.

▲▲▲▲ **New York Hilton,** 1335 Ave. of the Americas at 53rd St., IV, B2, ☎ (212) 586 7000. 2130 rooms. ① AE, CB, DC, MC, V. Tour groups prefer this hotel and the busy lobby is lined with shops, bars and restaurants.

▲▲▲▲ **Parker Meridien,** 118 W. 57th St. at Ave. of the Americas, IV, B2, ☎ (212) 245 5000. 700 rooms, including 100 suites. ① ③ ④ AE, CB, DC, MC, V. This hotel combines old-world comfort with American efficiency. There are sports facilities and an excellent restaurant, the **Maurice.**

▲▲▲▲ **Plaza**, Fifth Avenue at 59th St., IV, C2, ☎ (212) 759 3000. 900 rooms. ① AE, CB, DC, MC, V. Recently remodeled, the Plaza is one of New York's great luxury hotels. Many of the rooms overlook Central Park.

▲▲▲▲ **Ritz-Carlton**, 112 Central Park South at Ave. of the Americas, IV, B2, ☎ (212) 757 1900. 300 rooms. ① AE, CB, DC, MC, V. Recently renovated, top-floor rooms offer a beautiful view of Central Park

▲▲▲▲ **St Moritz**, 50 Central Park South at Ave. of the Americas, IV, B2, ☎ (212) 755 5800. 800 rooms. ① ② AE, CB, DC, MC, V. One of New York's most pleasant hotels, it includes an outdoor café.

▲▲▲▲ **Sheraton Center**, 811 Seventh Ave. at 52nd St., IV, B2, ☎ (212) 581 1000. 1842 rooms. ① ★ AE, CB, DC, MC, V. Average hotel in a busy area.

▲▲▲ **Warwick**, 65 W. 54th St. at Ave. of the Americas, IV, B2, ☎ (212) 247 2700. 500 rooms. ① ② AE, CB, DC, MC, V. The facilities, including sports rooms, videos and large rooms with kitchenettes, the excellent service and the area make this hotel popular.

▲▲ **Algonquin**, 59 W. 44th St. between Fifth Ave.-Ave. of the Americas, IV, B3, ☎ (212) 840 6800. 200 rooms. ① AE, CB, DC, MC, V. The hotel has an old-fashioned charm and is one of the best in its category.

▲▲ **Days Inn**, 440 W. 57th St. between Ninth-Tenth Aves., IV, AB2, ☎ (212) 581 8100. 600 rooms. ① ② AE, CB, DC, MC, V. This hotel is used mainly by tour groups.

▲▲ **Diplomat**, 108 W. 43rd St. between Ave. of the Americas-Seventh Ave., IV, B3, ☎ (212) 921 5666. 220 rooms. AE, MC, V. Situated in the Times Square neighbourhood.

▲▲ **Holiday Inn Coliseum**, 440 W. 57th St. at Ninth Ave., IV, B2, ☎ (212) 581 8100. 600 rooms. ① ② ④ AE, CB, DC, MC, V. This is a motel with parking.

▲▲ **Milford Plaza**, 270 W. 45th St. at Eighth Ave., IV, B3, ☎ (212) 869 3600. 1310 rooms. ① ② AE, CB, DC, MC, V. Near the Theater District, the neighbourhood is rough after dark.

▲▲ **Ramada Inn of New York**, 790 Eighth Ave. at 48th St., IV, B3, ☎ (212) 581 7000. 365 rooms. ① AE, DC, MC, V. Despite the neighbourhood, this is a good family hotel.

▲ **Best Western Skyline Motor Hotel**, 725 Tenth Ave. at 49th St., IV, A3, ☎ (212) 586 3400. 231 rooms. ① ② ④ AE, CB, DC, MC, V. The rooms are pleasant ; the service is average.

▲ **Edison**, 228 W. 47th St. between Broadway-Eighth Ave., IV, B3, ☎ (212) 840 5000. 1000 rooms. ① ② AE, DC, MC, V. Average decor and basic service.

▲ **Gorham**, 136 W. 55th St., IV, BC2, ☎ (212) 245 1800. 160 rooms. AE, CB, DC, MC, V. This is a good hotel in its category.

▲ **Howard Johnson**, 851 Eighth Ave. at 51st St., IV, B2-3, ☎ (212) 581 4100. 300 rooms. ① ② . This motel chain offers standardized comfort at moderate rates.

▲ **Rio**, 132 W. 47th St. between Ave. of the Americas-Seventh Ave., IV, B3, ☎ (212) 382 0600. The lobby isn't much to look at, but the service is friendly.

▲ **Salisbury**, 123 W. 57th St. at Ave. of the Americas, IV, B2, ☎ (212) 246 1300. 320 rooms. AE, CB, DC, MC, V. This hotel, situated close to Carnegie Hall, offers moderate family rates.

▲ **Shoreham**, 33 W. 55th St. between Fifth Ave.-Ave. of the Americas, IV, BC2, ☎ (212) 247 6700. 68 rooms. ① AE, CB, DC, MC, V. No room service, but it has a very good restaurant, **La Caravelle**.

▲ **Westpark**, 308 W. 58th St. between Eight-Ninth Aves., IV, BC2, ☎ (212) 246 6440. 30 rooms. AE, MC, V. Situated in an area undergoing extensive renovation, the Westpark offers small apartments.

Chelsea

▲▲ **Chelsea Hotel**, 222 W. 23rd St. at Eighth Ave., III, B2, ☎ (212) 243 3700. 200 rooms. AE, CB, DC, MC, V. This hotel was once frequented by well-known writers but is now rather seedy.

▲▲ **New York Penta Hotel**, 401 Seventh Ave. at 33rd St., III, B1, ☎ (212) 736 5000. More than 1700 rooms. ① AE, CB, DC, MC, V. Located opposite Madison Square Garden and Penn Station, this hotel offers standard rooms and is good for groups.

▲▲ **Southgate Tower**, 371 Seventh Ave. at 31st St., III, B1, ☎ (212) 563 1800. 500 rooms. AE, CB, DC, MC, V. The decor leaves much to be desired, but the neighbourhood is active day and night.

Restaurants

$$$$ **Le Bernardin**, 155 W. 51st St. between Fifth Ave.-Ave of the Americas, IV, AB2, ☎ (212) 489 1515. Elegant seafood restaurant. Closed Sun.

$$$$ **Jean Lafitte**, 68 W. 58th Street at Ave. of the Americas, IV, B2, ☎ (212) 751 2323. It is often full at lunch; dinners tend to be less crowded. Reservations recommended. AE, CB, DC, MC, V.

$$$$ **Maurice,** Parker Meridien Hotel, 118 W. 57th St. between Ave. of the Americas-Seventh Ave., IV, B2, ☎ (212) 245 7788. Delicious French *nouvelle cuisine* in pleasant setting. Reservations recommended.

$$$$ **Palio's,** 151 W. 51st St. between Ave. of the Americas-Seventh Ave., IV, B2-3, ☎ (212) 245 4850. Northern Italian cuisine. Reservations recommended. Closed Sun. AE, CB, DC, MC, V.

$$$$ **Petrossian,** 182 W. 58th St. at Seventh Ave., IV, AB2, ☎ (212) 245 2214. The New York branch of the famous Parisian establishment opened in 1985. Salmon, foie gras and caviar are served on Lalique plates and Christofle flatware in a refined atmosphere. AE, CB, DC, MC, V.

$$$$ **Russian Tea Room,** 150 W. 57th St. between Ave. of the Americas-Seventh Ave., IV, AB2, ☎ (212) 265 0947. This is one of New York's landmarks, situated near Carnegie Hall. AE, CB, DC, MC, V.

$$$ **Café Un Deux Trois,** 123 W. 44th St. between Ave. of the Americas-Seventh Ave., IV, B3, ☎ (212) 354 4148. This French brasserie in the Theater District fills up before and after shows. The meals are light and delicious. Reservations recommended on weekends. Open late. AE, CB, DC, MC, V.

$$$ **Club '21',** 21 W. 52nd St. between Fifth Ave.-Ave. of the Americas, IV, AB2, ☎ (212) 582 7200. '21' was very famous in the 1950s Continental cuisine. Closed Sun. AE, CB, DC, MC, V.

$$$ **Lattanzi,** 361 W. 46th St. between Eighth-Ninth Aves., IV, B3, ☎ (212) 315 0980. This is the best and most lively northern Italian restaurant on Broadway. Specialities include Jewish-Italian dishes from Rome. Reservations recommended. Closed Sun. AE.

$$$ **Orso,** 322 W. 46th St. between Eighth-Ninth Aves., IV, B3, ☎ (212) 489 7212. Pizzas and pasta. Situated in the Theater District; the atmosphere is less hectic after 8pm when the shows start. Reservations recommended.

$$$ **Sardi's,** 234 W. 44th St. between Eighth-Ninth Aves., IV, B3, ☎ (212) 221 8440. Famous Continental-style restaurant catering to actors, directors and theater-goers. Reservations recommended. AE, CB, DC, MC, V.

$$$ **Trader Vic's,** The Plaza Hotel, Fifth Avenue at 59th St., IV, C2, ☎ (212) 355 5185. The service is friendly and the menu includes Indonesian, Chinese and Malaysian cuisine. AE, MC, V.

$$ **Cabana Carioca,** 123 W. 45th St. between Ave. of the Americas-Seventh Ave., IV, B3, ☎ (212) 730 8375. Brazilian cuisine in huge portions.

$$ **Chez Joséphine,** 414 W. 42nd St. between Ninth-Tenth Aves., IV, AB3, ☎ (212) 594 1925. The owner is Joséphine Baker's son. The cuisine is rather eclectic, with Californian grills, Italian pasta and French dishes.

$$ **Chez Napoléon,** 365 W. 50th St. between Eighth-Ninth Aves., IV, B3, ☎ (212) 265 6980. This French restaurant is small and friendly. Reservations recommended. AE, CB, DC, MC, V.

$$ **Darbar,** 44 W. 56th St. between Fifth Ave.-Ave. of the Americas, IV, BC2, ☎ (212) 432 7272. Elegant Indian cuisine. There are special prices for lunch and for meals before and after the theater. Reservations recommended. AE, CB, DC, MC, V.

$$ **Hard Rock Cafe,** 221 W. 57th St. between Seventh Ave.-Broadway, IV, B2, ☎ (212) 489 6565. For hamburgers and rock'n'roll in the midst of a noisy, lively crowd.

$$ **Jezebel,** 630 Ninth Ave. at 45th St., IV, B3, ☎ (212) 582 1045. Specialities include Southern-fried chicken, sweet potatoes and ribs. A pre-show menu is offered. Reservations recommended.

$$ **Joe Allen,** 326 W. 46th St. between Eighth-Ninth Aves., IV, B3, ☎ (212) 581 6464. Generous hamburgers and salads are served on red-and-white checked tablecloths in this friendly restaurant in the Theater District.

$$ **Lou G. Siegel,** 209 W. 38th St. between Seventh-Eighth Aves., IV, B3, ☎ (212) 921 4433. This is a good kosher restaurant in the heart of the Garment District.

$$ **Luchow's,** 1633 Broadway at 51st St., IV, B2-3, ☎ (212) 582 4697. The original of this German restaurant was on 14th Street for 100 years. AE, CB, DC, MC, V.

$$ **Rumpelmayer's,** 50 Central Park South at Ave. of the Americas, IV, B2, ☎ (212) 775 5800. Tea room and pastry shop, with sundaes, cakes and chocolates. It is a favourite with children.

$$ **Russian Samovar,** 256 W. 52nd St. between Broadway-Eighth Ave., IV, B2, ☎ (212) 757 0168. This is a good restaurant and the prices are lower than the Russian Tea Room. A pre-theater menu is served from 5-7pm. Reservations recommended. Open Tues-Sun to midnight. AE, MC, V.

$$ **Shezan,** 8 W. 58th St. at Fifth Ave., IV, C2, ☎ (212) 371 1414 or 1420. This Indo-Pakistani restaurant

has a decidedly contemporary decor. Closed Sun. AE, CB, DC, MC, V.

$ **Afghan Kebab House,** 764 Ninth Ave. between 51st-52nd Sts., IV, B2, ☎ (212) 307 1612. The kebabs are considered to be among the best in the city. This is a good place to know in this out-of-the-way neighbourhood.

$ **La Bonne Soupe,** 48 W. 55th St., between Fifth Ave.-Ave. of the Americas, IV, C2, ☎ (212) 586 7650. French-style bistro serving delicious and reasonable meals in a charming ambience. Open daily 10am-10pm.

$ **Carnegie Deli,** 854 Seventh Ave. between 54th-55th Sts., IV, B2, ☎ (212) 757 2245. One of the great New York delicatessens, with enormous sandwiches, delicious blintzes and cheesecakes.

$ **Christine's,** 344 Lexington Ave. between 39th-40th Sts., IV, C2-3, ☎ (212) 953 1920. Polish coffee shop for an inexpensive and quick meal.

$ **Museum of Modern Art,** 11 W. 53rd St. between Fifth Ave.-Ave. of the Americas, IV, C2, ☎ (212) 708 9480. Wonderful cafeteria-style restaurant in a lovely setting on the top floor.

$ **New York Delicatessen,** 104 W. 57th St. between Ave. of the Americas-Seventh Ave., IV, B2, ☎ (212) 541 8320. Situated near Carnegie Hall, this is a popular deli after a show and a good place to buy kosher sausages and pickles. Open daily 24 hours. AE, DC, MC, V.

$ **Verve Naturale,** 157 W. 57th St. between Ave. of the Americas-Seventh Ave., IV, B2, ☎ (212) 265 2255. This vegetarian restaurant serves delicious diet-conscious meals and fish dishes.

$ **Wolf's Restaurant & Deli,** 101 W. 57th St. between Fifth Ave.-Ave. of the Americas, IV, BC2, ☎ (212) 586 1110. A simple delicatessen.

$ **Woo Lae Oak of Seoul,** 77 W. 46th. between Fifth Ave.-Ave. of the Americas, IV, BC3, ☎ (212) 869 9958. Korean cuisine. Cook your own meat and vegetables on small barbecues.

Chelsea

$$$ **The Ballroom,** 253 W. 28th St. between Seventh-Eighth Aves., III, B1, ☎ (212) 244 3005. One of the more original places in New York to eat, complete with music in the piano bar. Reservations recommended for dinner. Closed Sun and Mon. AE, MC, V.

$$$ **Lola,** 30 W. 22nd St. between Fifth Ave.-Ave. of the Americas, III, BC2, ☎ (212) 675 6700. Creole cuisine.

$$$ **Roxanne's,** 158 Eighth Ave. at 18th St., III, B2, ☎ (212) 741 2455. Small American-style intimate neighbourhood restaurant. Closed Sun. MC, V.

$$$ **Sofi,** Fifth Ave. at 15th St. III, C2, ☎ (212) 532 5520. Mediterranean cuisine.

$$ **Cajun,** 129 Eighth Ave. at 16th St., III, B2, ☎ (212) 691 6174. One of New York's leading Cajun restaurants with Dixieland music and good quality for the price.

$$ **Claire,** 156 Seventh Ave. between 19th-20th Sts., III, B2, ☎ (212) 255 1955. Delicious seafood served in a tropical setting. Reservations recommended.

$$ **Merikien,** Seventh Ave. at 21st St., III, B2, ☎ (212) 620 9684. Japanese cuisine. Reservations recommended on weekends.

$$ **Miss Ruby's Café,** 135 Eighth Ave. between 16th-17th Sts., III, B2, ☎ (212) 620 4055. The menu changes every two weeks to feature a different American regional cuisine. Call ahead to check the evening's menu.

UPPER EAST SIDE

The Upper East Side is a delightful place for museum lovers. A walk up Fifth Avenue and along Central Park passes the Frick Collection, the Metropolitan Museum of Art and the Guggenheim. The hotels in this area are all luxurious.

Hotels

▲▲▲▲ **American Stanhope,** 995 Fifth Ave. at 81st St., V, C3, ☎ (212) 288 5800. 600 rooms, 1 AE, CB, DC, MC, V. This is one of the most luxurious of New York's 'small' great hotels, just across the avenue from the Metropolitan Museum of Art. The interior is decorated with American paintings and furniture and the rooms are richly furnished. There is a lovely outdoor café.

▲▲▲▲ **Carlyle,** 35 E. 76th St. at Madison Ave., IV, C1, ☎ (212) 744 1600. 500 rooms, including 60 suites. ① AE, CB, DC, MC, V. This is a dignified hotel that is the best in New York. The rooms are vast and room service is available 24 hours a day.

▲▲▲▲ **Lowell,** 28 E. 63rd St., IV, C2, ☎ (212) 838 1400. 60 apartments. ① AE, CB, DC, MC, V. This small, quiet hotel in the heart of one of New York's most fashionable neighbourhoods was a refuge for Scott Fitzgerald, Jean Cocteau and Dustin Hoffman. The apartments (studios or two rooms) are equipped with kitchens. Room service is available 24 hours a day. Rooms can be rented by the night, week, month or year.

▲▲▲▲ **Mayfair Regent,** 610 Park Ave. at 65th St., IV, C1-2, ☎ (212) 288 0800. 80 rooms and 119 suites. ① AE, CB, DC, MC, V. The atmosphere is British, the service impeccable. Rooms are generally rented by the year. One of New York's best restaurants, **Le Cirque,** is situated in the hotel.

▲▲▲▲ **Nº 10022 Lexington Avenue,** Lexington Ave. at 73rd St., IV, C1, ☎ (212) 697 1536. AE, CB, DC, MC, V. This hotel is almost invisible; it occupies an old building and is considered to be more a pied-à-terre than a hotel. The rooms are generally rented by the month or by the year, but shorter stays can be arranged, subject to room availability. It is decorated in the style of an English country manor.

▲▲▲▲ **Pierre Hotel,** 61st St. at Fifth Ave., IV, C2, ☎ (212) 838 8000. 235 rooms, including 67 apartments reserved for year-round occupants. ① AE, CB, DC, MC, V. The luxurious rooms are decorated with Chippendale furniture and marble bathtubs.

▲▲▲▲ **Plaza Athénée,** 37 E. 64th St., IV, C2, ☎ (212) 734 9100. 160 rooms, including 34 suites. ① AE, CB, DC, MC, V. Opened in 1984, it represents the summit of European refinement with Directoire-style furniture and Italian marble decor. Contains the marvelous French restaurant **Le Régence.**

▲▲▲▲ **Regency,** 540 Park Ave. at 61st St., IV, C2, ☎ (212) 759 4100. ① AE, CB, DC, MC, V. The hotel is very well situated and the service is excellent.

▲▲▲▲ **Sherry-Netherland,** 781 Fifth Ave. at 59th St., IV, C2, ☎ (212) 355 2800. ① AE, CB, DC, MC, V. The efficiency of the quasi-invisible and well-trained staff makes this a favourite with a highly select clientele.

▲▲▲▲ **Westbury,** 69th St. at Madison Ave., IV, C1, ☎ (212) 535 2000. 300 rooms, 40 suites. A, AE, CB, DC, MC, V. Handsome hotel with light and spacious rooms.

▲▲▲ **Golden Tulip Barbizon,** 140 E. 63rd St. at Lexington Ave., IV, C2, ☎ (212) 838 5700. 360 rooms. ① AE, CB, DC, MC, V. This very British and comfortable hotel has a competent and serious staff and a pleasant bar.

▲▲▲ **Lyden Garden,** 215 E. 64th St. between Second-Third Aves., IV, C2, ☎ (212) 355 1230. 133 suites. AE, CB, DC, MC, V. The comfortable rooms have kitchen facilities.

▲▲▲ **Surrey,** 20 E. 76th St. at Madison Ave., IV, C1, ☎ (212) 288 3700. 115 apartments. AE, CB, DC, MC, V. This is a quiet and comfortable hotel. There is an excellent restaurant, **Les Pléiades,** and an outdoor café in the summer.

▲▲ **The Mark,** 25 E. 77th St. between Fifth-Madison Aves., IV, C1, ☎ (212) 744 4300. 150 rooms and suites. AE, CB, DC, MC, V. This new hotel near the Whitney Museum of American Art offers good quality for the price. The rooms are light and equipped with kitchenettes.

Restaurants

$$$$ **An American Place,** 2 Park Ave. at 32nd St., IV, C2-3, ☎ (212) 517 7660. This American-style restaurant is very much in fashion at the moment. Reservations recommended. Closed Sun. AE, CB, DC, MC, V.

$$$$ **Arcadia,** 2 E. 62nd St. between Fifth-Madison Aves., IV, C2, ☎ (212) 223 2900. The French-style façade frames this very small but wonderful American restaurant. There is outdoor seating in the summer. Reservations recommended. Closed Sun. AE, CB, DC.

$$$$ **Le Cirque,** 58 E. 65th St. between Madison-Park Ave., IV, CD2, ☎ (212) 794 9292. Famous French restaurant. Reservations recommended. Closed Sun.

$$$$ **Jams,** 154 E. 79th St. at Lexington Ave., IV, C3, ☎ (212) 772 6800. American *nouvelle cuisine.* Reservations recommended. AE, CB, DC.

$$$$ **L'Omnibus,** 608 Madison Ave. at 61st St., IV, C2, ☎ (212) 980 6988. French brasserie. Reservations recommended.

$$$$ **Les Pléiades,** Surrey Hotel, 20 E. 76th St. between Fifth-Madison Aves., IV, C1, ☎ (212) 535 7230. French cuisine in a subdued decor. Reservations recommended.

$$$$ **Trastevere I & II,** 309 E. 83rd St. between First-Second Aves., V, D3, ☎ (212) 734 6343; 155 E. 84th St. between Lexington-Third Aves., V, C3, ☎ (212) 744 0210. Southern Italian cuisine.

$$$ **Arizona 206,** 206 E. 60th St. between Second-Third Aves., IV, C2, ☎ (212) 838 0440. American *nouvelle cuisine* in a western decor. Reservations recommended.

$$$ **Auntie Yuan,** 1191 First Ave. between 64th-65th Sts., IV, D1-2, ☎ (212) 744 4040. This chic Chinese restaurant is decorated in gold-and-black lacquer. Reservations recommended. AE.

$$$ **Bistro Bamboche,** 1582 York Ave. between 83rd-84th Sts., V, D3, ☎ (212) 249 4002. High-quality French cuisine. Reservations recommended.

$$$ **Demarchelier,** 808 Lexington Ave. between 62nd-63rd Sts., IV, C2, ☎ (212) 223 0047. French bistro.

The New York Deli, with one of the most beautiful Art Deco storefronts in the city.

$$$ **Erminia**, 250 E. 83rd St. between Second-Third Aves., V, D3, ☎ (212) 8794284. This is a country-style Tuscan trattoria. The food is grilled over wood fires. AE.

$$$ **Fu's**, 1395 Second Ave. between 72nd-73rd Sts., IV, D2, ☎ (212) 5179670. One of New York's best Chinese restaurants.

$$$ **Hulot's**, 1007 Lexington Ave. between 72nd-73rd Sts., IV, C1, ☎ (212) 7949800. French bistro.

$$$ **Ruč**, 312 E. 72nd St. between First-Second Aves., IV, D1, ☎ (212) 6501611. A good Czech restaurant with outdoor dining in summer.

$$$ **Sam's Café**, 1406 Third Ave. at 80th St., V, C3, ☎ (212) 9885300. Opened by Mariel Hemingway, most people come for a glimpse of the star. Reservations recommended.

$$$ **Il Vagabondo**, 351 E. 62nd St. between First-Second Aves., IV, D2, ☎ (212) 8329221. Southern Italian cuisine.

$$ **Bangkok House**, 1485 First Ave. at 78th St., V, D3, ☎ (212) 2495700. Thai cuisine in a family atmosphere. Reservations recommended. Open daily 5-11pm. AE, CD, DC, MC, V.

$$ **The Boathouse Café**, 74th St. at East Central Park Dr., IV, C1, ☎ (212) 5172233. Coffee and sandwiches with a beautiful view of the park.

$$ **Csarda**, 1477 Second Ave. between 77th-78th Sts., IV, CD1, ☎ (212) 4722892. Hungarian family restaurant. AE.

$$ **Délices Guy Pascal**, 1231 Madison Ave. at 80th St., V, C3, ☎ (212) 2895300. Pastry shop and tea room.

$$ **Friday's**, First Ave. at 63rd St., IV, D3, ☎ (212) 8328512. Beer and hamburgers.

$$ **Il Giardinetto**, 1319 Third Ave. between 75th-76th Sts., IV, C1, ☎ (212) 7449555. Northern Italian cuisine in a subdued decor. Reservations recommended for dinner.

$$ ≥ **1 Kitchen**, 1464 Second Ave. between 76th-77th Sts., IV, CD1, ☎ (212) 5706700 or 6701. This is part of a Chinese fast-food chain.

$$ **Pamir Afghan Restaurant**, 1437 Second Ave. between 74th-75th Sts., IV, CD1, ☎ (212) 7343791. Delicious Afghan food.

$$ **Red Tulip**, 439 E. 75th St. between York-First Aves., IV, D1, ☎ (212) 7344893. Authentic Hungarian gypsy music accompanies average food. Reservations recommended.

$$ **Sala Thaï**, 1718 Second Ave. at 89th St., V, D3, ☎ (212) 4105557.

The food is worthy of a Bangkok restaurant. AE, CB, DC.

$$ Serendipity, 225 E. 60th St. between Second-Third Aves., IV, C2, ☎ (212) 838 3531. Salads, sandwiches, ice cream and desserts.

$$ Vašata, 339 E. 75th St., IV, CD1, ☎ (212) 650 1686. Authentic Czech cuisine in a friendly atmosphere. Closed Mon. AE, CB, DC, MC, V.

$ Harper's Restaurant & Bar, 1303 Third Ave. between 74th-75th Sts., IV, C1, ☎ (212) 472 8636. Salads and hamburgers.

$ Istanbul Cuisine, 303 E. 80th St. between First-Second Aves., V, D3, ☎ (212) 744 6903. This is one of the few Turkish restaurants in New York.

$ Jackson Hole Wyoming, 1633 Second Ave. at 85th St., V, D3, ☎ (212) 737 8788; 521 Third Ave. at 35th St., III, C1, ☎ (212) 679 3264.

The generous hamburgers will satisfy any appetite.

$ J.G. Melon, 1291 Third Ave. at 74th St., IV, C1, ☎ (212) 650 1310. Salads and hamburgers.

$ Succès La Côte Basque, 1032 Lexington Ave. between 73rd-74th Sts., IV, C1, ☎ (212) 535 3311. This is a pleasant tea room and pastry shop.

Harlem

$$ Copeland's, 549 W. 145th St., VI, C3, ☎ (212) 234 2356. Southern cooking in the heart of Harlem.

$$ La Famille Restaurant, 125th St. at Fifth Ave., VI, C3, ☎ (212) 534 9909. Southern-style cuisine. The restaurant is upstairs, with jazz or salsa music at the bar downstairs. There is a permanently festive atmosphere here.

$$ Sylvia's, 328 Lenox Ave. between 126th-127th Sts., VI, C3, ☎ (212) 534 9414. Southern-style cuisine. Braised chicken and excellent desserts.

▬ UPPER WEST SIDE

This is a lively neighbourhood, very much in vogue at the moment. There are a multitude of chic boutiques and restaurants catering to young professionals and their families.

Hotels

▲▲ Ansonia, 2109 Broadway at 73rd St., IV, A1, ☎ (212) 724 2600. The Ansonia is a charming hotel.

▲▲ Empire Hotel, 44 W. 63rd St. at Broadway, IV, B2, ☎ (212) 265 7400. 600 rooms. AE, CB, DC, MC, V. Situated opposite Lincoln Center.

▲▲ Mayflower, 15 Central Park West at 61st St., IV, B2, ☎ (212) 265 0060. 400 rooms. ① AE, CB, DC, MC, V. This hotel has been recently remodeled. Some of the rooms overlook Central Park.

▲ Esplanade 305 West End Avenue at 74th St., IV, A1, ☎ (212) 874 5000. AE, DC. V. Reserve well in advance because most of the rooms are rented on a semi-permanent basis. The rooms have kitchen facilities.

▲ Excelsior, 45 W. 81st St. at Central Park West, V, B3, ☎ (212) 362 9200. 300 rooms. ① Near the Museum of Natural History.

▲ Milburn, 242 W. 76th St. between Broadway-West End Ave., IV, A1, ☎ (212) 362 1006. The hotel does not have a restaurant, but there are many in the neighbourhood.

Restaurants

$$$ Café des Artistes, 1 W. 67th St. at Central Park West, IV, AB1,

☎ (212) 877 3500. This is one of the liveliest French restaurants on the West Side, with an attractive 1900s decor. AE, CB, DC, MC, V.

$$$ Café Luxembourg, 200 W. 70th St. at Amsterdam Ave., IV, B1, ☎ (212) 873 7411. This popular French restaurant occupies a former swimming pool. AE, MC, V.

$$$ Memphis, 320 Columbus Ave. between 75th-76th Sts., IV, B1, ☎ (212) 496 1840. An appetizing selection of Cajun dishes.

$$$ Tavern on the Green, in Central Park at W. 67th St., IV, B1, ☎ (212) 873 3200. Six restaurants in a lovely setting. Specialities include seafood. Open to 1am.

$$ Conservatory, Mayflower Hotel, 15 Central Park West at 61st St., IV, B2, ☎ (212) 581 0060. The food is tasty and light. Reservations recommended for brunch. AE, CB, DC, MC, V.

$$ Délices Guy Pascal, 2245 Broadway at 80th St., V, A3, ☎ (212) 874 5400. Pastry shop and snack bar located next to the famous **Zabar's** shop.

$$ Ernie's, 2150 Broadway between 75-76th Sts., IV, A1, ☎ (212) 496 1588. This establishment caters to a young crowd who come more for the ambience than the food.

$$ The Ginger Man, 51 W. 64th St. at Broadway, IV, AB2, ☎ (212) 399 2358. This is the oldest restaurant in the Lincoln Center area, with American cuisine and live jazz on weekends.

$$ **Sarabeth's Kitchen,** 423 Amsterdam Ave. at 79th St., V, AB3, ☎ (212) 496 6280. Sarabeth prepares her own jams, pastries and scones, which are on sale in the restaurant.

$$ **Siam Cuisine,** 410 Amsterdam Ave. at 80th St., V, AB3, ☎ (212) 874 0105. Many New Yorkers consider this their favourite Thai restaurant. Reservations recommended. AE, CB, DC, MC, V.

$$ **Sidewalkers,** 12 W. 72nd St. between Central Park West and Columbus Ave., IV, B1, ☎ (212) 799 6070. Seafood specialities.

$$ **Silverbird,** 505 Columbus Ave. at 84th St., V, B3, ☎ (212) 877 7777. Near the Museum of Natural History,

this is the only Navaho restaurant in New York. Both the food and atmosphere are unique.

$ **Charles Green Tree Restaurant,** 1034 Amsterdam Ave. between 111th-112th Sts., V, B1, ☎ (212) 864 9106. Hungarian pastry and cuisine.

$ **Museum Cafe,** 366 Columbus Ave. at 77th St., V, B3, ☎ (212) 799 0150. This is a café-pub serving hamburgers and salads.

$ **Rosita's — El Ideal,** 2825 Broadway at 111th St., V, B1, ☎ (212) 866 3244. Puerto Rican food — delicious tropical fruit milkshakes and rice and bean dishes. Open daily 24 hours.

▬ BROOKLYN

Restaurants

$$$ **River Cafe,** 1 Water St., ☎ (718) 522 5200. Situated at the foot of the Brooklyn Bridge, this restaurant offers an unrivalled view of Manhattan and the Statue of Liberty. Outdoor seating in summer. Reservations recommended.

$$ **Gage and Tollner,** 372 Fulton St., ☎ (718) 875 5181. This restaurant opened in 1879 and has retained its old-fashioned charm. Seafood is a speciality. There is a pianist Fri and Sat. Closed Sun.

$$ **Peter Luger,** 178 Broadway, ☎ (718) 397 7400. This is considered one of the best steak houses in New York. The portions are enormous. Reservations recommended. Open daily 6-10pm.

$ **Junior's,** 386 Flatbush Ave., ☎ (718) 852 5257. Typical American cuisine. Famous for its cheesecake. Open Fri and Sat to 3am.

▬ QUEENS

Restaurants

$$$$ **The Water's Edge,** 44th Dr. at the East River, ☎ (718) 482 0033. This fish restaurant occupies a barge near the Queensboro Bridge and offers a panoramic view of Manhattan.

$$ **La Détente,** 23-03 94th St. between 22nd-23rd Aves., ☎ (718) 458 2172. This friendly Haitian restaurant is located near LaGuardia Airport.

Reservations recommended.

$$ **Taygetos,** 30-11 30th Ave., ☎ (718) 726 5195. This Greek restaurant is one of the friendliest and liveliest in Astoria.

$ **Cho Sun Ok,** 136-73 Roosevelt Ave. between Main-Union Sts., ☎ (718) 762 8960. Korean cuisine. You cook your own food here.

▬ RESTAURANTS OPEN AFTER MIDNIGHT

$ **Empire Diner,** 210 Tenth Ave. at 22nd St., III, A2, ☎ (212) 243 2736. During the day, it is relaxed and friendly, a good place to bring kids. During summer months, the outdoor tables are always crowded. Open all night, it attracts a diverse mixture of late-night people.

$ **Kiev Restaurant,** 117 Second Ave. at 7th St., III, C3, ☎ (212) 674 4040. Ukrainian cuisine. This is a popular place with the Downtown night crowd. Open 24 hours.

$ **Lox Around the Clock,** Ave. of the Americas at 21st St., III, B2, ☎ (212) 691 3535. Former butcher shop that is usually crowded. The brunch is very good. Open 24 hours.

$ **Mamun's Falafel,** 119 MacDougal St., III, BC3, ☎ (212) 674 9246. New York's oldest falafel restaurant. Open to 5am.

$ **Market Diner,** 572 Eleventh Ave. at 43rd St., III, B2, ☎ (212) 244 6033; 256 West Street, III, A3, ☎ (212)

695 6844. Clientele includes police-men and taxi drivers.

$ **Moondance Diner,** 80 Ave. of the Americas between Grand-Canal Sts., II, B1, ☎ (212) 226 1191. One of the best diners in town. The setting and ambience are very pleasant and the brunch is excellent. Open daily.

$ **New York Delicatessen,** 104 W. 57th St. between Ave. of the Americas-Seventh Ave., IV, B2, ☎ (212) 541 8320. This deli, with beautiful spiral staircases, is close to Carnegie Hall. Open daily 24 hours. AE, DC, MC, V.

$ **Ray's Famous Pizza,** 8 W. 11th St. at Ave. of the Americas, III, B3, ☎ (212) 243 2253 ; 72nd St. and Columbus Ave., IV, B1, ☎ (212) 877 4405. Some say this is the best pizza in New York. Open all night.

$ **Sarge's Deli,** 548 Fifth Ave. between 36th-37th Sts., III, C1, ☎ (212) 679 0442. Open 24 hours. AE.

▬ RESTAURANTS CLASSIFIED BY TYPE OF CUISINE

Abbreviations used to indicate neighbourhoods:
Chinatown: China.
East Village: E.Vil.
Financial District: Fin.Dist.
Greenwich Village: G.Vil.
Little Italy: Lit.It.
Lower East Side: Low.E.S.

Tribeca: Trib.
World Trade Center: W.T.C.
Midtown East: Mid.E.
Midtown West: Mid.W.
Upper East Side: U.E.S.
Upper West Side: U.W.S.

Afghan

$$ **Khyber Pass,** Low.E.S.
$$ **Pamir,** U.E.S.
$ **Afghan Kebab House,** Mid.W.

American

$$$$ **American Harvest,** W.T.C.
$$$$ **An American Place,** U.E.S.
$$$$ **Arcadia,** U.E.S.
$$$$ **Casual Quilted Giraffe,** Mid.E.
$$$$ **Christ Cella** (steaks), Mid.E.
$$$$ **Coach House,** G.Vil.
$$$$ **The Four Seasons** (French-American), Mid.E.
$$$$ **Gotham Bar & Grill** (French-American), Chelsea
$$$$ **Jams,** U.E.S.
$$$$ **Palm, Palm Too** (steaks), Mid.E.
$$$$ **Sparks Steakhouse,** Mid.E.
$$$$ **Windows on the World** (French-American), W.T.C.
$$$ **Arizona 206,** U.E.S.
$$$ **Baton's,** G.Vil.
$$$ **Club '21',** Mid.W.
$$$ **Flutie's** (fish and steaks), Fin.Dist.
$$$ **Morgan Williams** (French-American), Fin.Dist.
$$$ **Old Homestead,** G.Vil.
$$$ **River Café,** Brooklyn
$$$ **Roxanne's,** Chelsea
$$$ **Sam's Café,** U.E.S.
$$$ **Sardi's** (Italian-American), Mid.W.
$$$ **Smith & Wollensky** (steak), Mid.E.
$$$ **Tavern on the Green,** U.W.S.
$$$ **Woods,** Mid.E.
$$ **Albuquerque East,** Chelsea
$$ **Amsterdam Grand Bar & Rotisserie,** SoHo and U.W.S.
$$ **The Boathouse Café,** U.E.S.
$$ **Bridge Café,** (hamburgers, sand-wiches), China.
$$ **Broome Street Bar** (hamburgers), SoHo

$$ **Central Falls,** SoHo
$$ **Conservatory,** U.W.S.
$$ **Cornelia Street Café,** G.Vil.
$$ **Ernie's,** U.W.S.
$$ **5 & 10 No Exaggeration** (French-American), SoHo
$$ **Fraunces' Tavern Restaurant,** Fin.Dist.
$$ **Friday's** (hamburgers), U.E.S.
$$ **Garvin's,** G.Vil.
$$ **The Ginger Man,** U.W.S.
$$ **Hard Rock Café,** Mid.W.
$$ **Harry's at Hanover Square** (steaks), Fin.Dist.
$$ **Joe Allen,** Mid.W.
$$ **Meridies,** G.Vil.
$$ **Miss Ruby's Café,** Chelsea
$$ **Mortimer's,** U.E.S.
$$ **New Deal Restaurant,** SoHo
$$ **Peter Luger** (steaks), Brooklyn
$$ **Sarabeth's Kitchen** (pastry), U.W.S.
$$ **Serendipity,** U.E.S.
$ **Burger Heaven,** Mid.E.
$ **Elephant & Castle,** SoHo, G. Vil.
$ **Empire Diner,** Chelsea (see 'Restaur-ants open after midnight')
$ **Food** (sandwiches), SoHo
$ **Greene Street Café,** SoHo
$ **Jackson Hole Wyoming** (hamburgers), U.E.S.
$ **J.G. Melon** (hamburgers), U.E.S.
$ **Junior's,** Brooklyn
$ **Lox Around the Clock,** Chelsea (see 'Restaurants open after midnight')
$ **Market Diner,** G.Vil. and Chelsea (see 'Restaurants open after mid-night')
$ **Moondance Diner,** SoHo (see 'Restaurants open after midnight')
$ **Museum Café** (hamburgers), U.W.S.
$ **Patisserie Lanciani** (French-American), SoHo

American Southern cooking

$$ La Famille Restaurant, Harlem
$$ Jezebel's, Mid. W.
$$ Princess Pamela, Low.E.S.
$$ Sylvia's, Harlem

Cajun

$$$ Memphis, U.W.S.
$$$ The Ritz Café, Mid.E.
$$ Acme Bar & Grill, G.Vil.
$$ Bon Temps Rouler, Trib.
$$ Cajun, Chelsea
$$ Gulf Coast, G.Vil.
$$ Sugar Reef, E.Vil.
$ Great Jones Street Café, E. Vil.
$ Texarkana, G.Vil.

Chinese

$$$ Auntie Yuan, U.E.S.
$$$ Chez Vong, Mid.E.
$$$ Fu's, U.E.S.
$$ Bayamo (Cuban-Chinese), G.Vil.
$$ HSF, Chin.
$$ ≠1 Kitchen, U.E.S.
$$ Phoenix Garden (Cantonese), China.
$$ Siu Lam Kung, China.
$ Dai Sai Kai Restaurant (Cuban-Chinese), Lit.It.
$ Sun Lok Kee Rice Shop Inc., Lit.It.

Creole and Antillean

$$$ Lola, Chelsea
$ Caribe, G.Vil.
$ El Castillo de Jagua, Low.E.S.

Czechoslovakian

$$$ Ruč, U.E.S.
$$$ Vašata, U.E.S.

Delicatessen

$$ Second Avenue Deli, E.Vil.
$ Carnegie Deli, Mid.W.
$ Katz's Restaurant Deli, Low.E.S.
$ New York Delicatessen, Mid.W. (see 'Restaurants open after midnight')
$ Ratner's, Low.E.S.
$ Sarge's Deli, Mid.E. (see 'Restaurants open after midnight')
$ Wolf's Restaurant & Deli, Mid.E.

Ethiopian

$ Abyssinia, SoHo

Falafels

$ Mamun's Falafel, G.Vil. (see 'Restaurants open after midnight')
$ Olive Tree Café, G.Vil.

Fish

$$$$ John Clancey's, G.Vil.
$$$$ The Water's Edge, Queens
$$$ The Oyster Bar & Restaurant, Mid.E.
$$$ Sweets, Fin.Dist.
$$ Claire, Chelsea
$$ Gage and Tollner, Brooklyn

$$ Hawaii 5-0 (Hawaiian), E.Vil.
$$ Sidewalkers, U.W.S.
$$ Vincent's Clam Bar, Lit.It.

French

$$$$ Aurora, Mid.E.
$$$$ Le Bernardin, Mid.W.
$$$$ Brive, Mid.E.
$$$$ Chanterelle, SoHo
$$$$ Le Cirque, U.E.S.
$$$$ La Côte Basque, Mid.E.
$$$$ La Cygne, Mid.E.
$$$$ Jean Lafitte, Mid.W.
$$$$ Lutèce, Mid.E.
$$$$ Maurice, Mid.W.
$$$$ Montrachet, SoHo
$$$$ L'Omnibus, U.E.S.
$$$ Bistro Bamboche, U.E.S.
$$$ The Black Sheep, G.Vil.
$$$ Café des Artistes, U.W.S.
$$$ Café Luxembourg, U.W.S.
$$$ Café Un Deux Trois, Mid.W.
$$$ Demarchelier, U.E.S.
$$$ Huberts, Mid.E.
$$$ Hulot's, U.E.S.
$$$ J.S. Vandam, SoHo
$$$ Odéon, Trib.
$$$ Le Périgord, Mid.E.
$$$ Les Pléiades, U.E.S.
$$$ Quatorze, Chelsea
$$$ Raoul's, SoHo
$$$ La Ripaille, G.Vil.
$$$ Sofi (French-Italian), Mid.W.
$$$ Union Square Café (French-Italian), Mid.E.
$$ La Bohème (pizzeria), G.Vil.
$$ Café Loup, G.Vil.
$$ Chez Brigitte, G.Vil.
$$ Chez Joséphine, Mid.W.
$$ Chez Napoléon, Mid.W.
$$ Délices Guy Pascal (pastry shop), U.E.S. and U.W.S.
$$ Florent, G.Vil.
$ La Bonne Soupe, Mid.W.
$ Succès La Côte Basque (pastry shop), U.E.S.

German

$$ Luchow's, Mid. W.
$$ Rumpelmayer's (pastry shop), Mid.W.

Greek

$$ Dimitri's, U.W.S.
$$ Taigetos, Queens
$$ Xenia, Mid.E.
$ Z, Mid.E.

Haitian

$$ La Détente, Queens

Hungarian

$$ Csarda, U.E.S.
$$ Red Tulip, U.E.S.
$ Charles Green Tree Restaurant, U.W.S.

Indian

$$$ Akbar, Mid.E.
$$ Darbar, Mid.W.

$$ Mitali, E.Vil.
$$ Shezan (Indian-Pakistani), Mid.W.
$ Anar Bagh, E.Vil.
$ Calcutta Restaurant, E.Vil.

Indonesian

$$ Prince Street Bar & Restaurant, SoHo.
$ Tamu, SoHo

Irish

$$ Tommy Maken's Irish Pavilion, Mid.E.

Italian

$$$$ Palio's (northern Italian), Mid.W.
$$$$ Trastevere I & II (southern Italian), U.E.S.
$$$ Barocco, SoHo
$$$ Cent'Anni (northern Italian), G.Vil.
$$$ Ecco (northern Italian), Trib.
$$$ Erminia, U.E.S.
$$$ Lattanzi (northern Italian), Mid.W.
$$$ Minetta Tavern, G.Vil.
$$$ Nanni's (northern Italian), Mid.E.
$$$ Orso, Mid.W.
$$$ Salta in Bocca (northern Italian), Mid.E.
$$$ Il Vagabondo (southern Italian), U.E.S.
$$ Ancora, U.W.S.
$$ Angelo's (southern Italian), China.
$$ Costa Azzurra (northern Italian), China.
$$ Gianni's (northern Italian), Fin.Dist.
$$ Il Giardinetto (northern Italian), U.E.S.
$ Arturo's (pizzeria), SoHo
$ De Robertis, E.Vil.
$ John's Pizzeria, G.Vil. and U.E.S.
$ Ray's Famous Pizza, G.Vil. and U.W.S. (see 'Restaurants open after midnight')
$ Venerio's (pastry shop), E.Vil.

Japanese

$$ Meriken, Chelsea
$$ Mie, G.Vil.
$ Dojo (Japanese-American), E.Vil.
$ Omen, SoHo

Jewish

$$$$ Bernstein on Essex Street, Low. E.S.
$$ Lou G. Siegel, Mid.W.
$$ Sammy's Rumanian Jewish Restaurant, Low.E.S.

Korean

$ Cho Sun Ok, Queens
$ Woo Lae Oak of Seoul, Mid.W.

Latin-American

$$$ Brazilian Pavilion, Mid.E.
$$ Amazonas (Brazilian), SoHo
$$ Cabana Carioca (Brazilian), Mid.W.
$$ Sabor (Cuban), G.Vil.

Middle Eastern

$$$ Dardanelles East Ararat (Armenian); Mid.E.
$$ Cedars of Lebanon, Mid.E.
$ Istanbul Cuisine (Turkish), U.E.S.

Native American

$$ Silverbird, U.W.S.

Polish

$ Christine's, Mid.W.
$ Polonia (coffee shop), E.Vil.
$ Veselka (Polish-Ukrainian coffee shop), E.Vil.

Polynesian

$$$ Trader Vic's, Mid.W.

Russian and Ukrainian

$$$$ Petrossian, Mid.W.
$$$$ Russian Tea Room, Mid.W.
$$ Russian Samovar, Mid.W.
$ Kiev Restaurant, E.Vil. (see 'Restaurants open after midnight')
$ Odessa Restaurant (Ukrainian), E.Vil.

Spanish

$$$ The Ballroom, Chelsea
$$ El Faro, G.Vil.

Tex-Mex and Mexican

$$ Cinco de Mayo, G.Vil.
$$ Cottonwood Cafe, G.Vil.
$ Exterminator Chili, Trib.
$ Tortilla Flats, G.Vil.

Thai

$$ Bangkok House, U.E.S.
$$ Sala Thaï, U.E.S.
$$ Siam Cuisine, U.W.S.
$ Thailand Restaurant, China.

Vegetarian

$$ Spring Street Natural, SoHo
$ Verve Naturale, Mid.W.

Vietnamese

$$$ Indochine, G.Vil.
$$ Cuisine de Saigon, G.Vil.

▬ BARS AND NIGHTCLUBS

Bars

Bars are generally open until 4am.

Art Café, 151 Second Ave. at 9th St., III, C3. East Village. This is a friendly neighbourhood meeting place for local artists.

Brewsky's, 41 E. 7th St., III, C3,

☎ (212) 614 9318. Greenwich Village. 270 kinds of beer.

Brownie's, Ave. A, between 10th-11th Sts., III, D3. East Village. The crowd becomes a cosmopolitan mix after 5 pm.

B. Smith's, 771 Eighth Ave. at 17th St., IV, B3, ☎ (212) 247 2222. Midtown West.

Café Un Deux Trois, 123 W. 44th St., ☎ (212) 354 4148. See 'Midtown West-Restaurants $$$'.

Chumley's, 86 Bedford St., ☎ (212) 675 9449. See 'Greenwich Village-Restaurants $'.

5 & 10 No Exaggeration, 77 Greene St., ☎ (212) 925 7414. See 'SoHo-Restaurants $$'

Jim McMullen's, 1341 Third Ave. at 76th St., IV, C1, ☎ (212) 861 4700. Upper East Side. Very fashionable crowd.

Life Café, 343 E. 10th St. at Ave. B, III, D3, ☎ (212) 477 8791. East Village. This is a meeting place for local artists.

Magoo's, Ave. of the Americas near Walker St., II, B1, ☎ (212) 226 9919. Tribeca. Painters and sculptors occasionally exchange their work for meals here.

Manhattan Brewing Co., 40/42 Thompson St., II, B1, ☎ (212) 219 9250. SoHo. American and British food.

McSorley's Old Ale House, 15 E. 7th St., III, C3, ☎ (212) 473 9148. Greenwich Village. This is an institution in the Village.

Memphis, 329 Columbus Ave., ☎ (212) 496 1840. See 'Upper West Side-Restaurants $$$'..

Odéon, 145 West Broadway, ☎ (212) 233 0507. See 'Tribeca-Restaurants $$$'.

P. J. Clarke's, 915 Third Ave. at 55th St., IV, C2, ☎ (212) 355 8857. Midtown East. A New York institution.

Save the Robots, 25 Ave. B at 2nd St., III, D3. Lower East Side. Popular with the late-night crowd.

SoHo Kitchen & Bar, 103 Greene St., II, B1, ☎ (212) 925 1866. SoHo. Pizza and wine.

Wine Bar, 422 West Broadway, II, B1, ☎ (212) 431 4790. SoHo. A pleasant bar that serves French, Italian and Californian wines.

Le Zinc, 139 Duane St. at West Broadway, II, B2, ☎ (212) 732 1226. See 'Downtown-Restaurants $$$'.

Piano bars

Beekman Tower, 3 Mitchell Pl., ☎ (212) 355 7300. See 'Midtown East - Hotels★★'.

Broadway Baby, 407 Amsterdam Ave. between 79-80th Sts., V, AB3, ☎ (212) 724 6868. Upper West Side. Waiters and waitresses sing requested songs.

Café Carlyle, 35 E. 76th St., ☎ (212) 570 7189. See 'Upper East Side - Hotels★★★★'.

Marty's East, 209 E. 56th St., IV, C2, ☎ (212) 935 7676. Midtown East. This is a chic and expensive piano bar.

Mrs. J's Sacred Cow, 228 W. 72nd St., IV, AB1, ☎ (212) 873 4067. Upper West Side. An inexpensive restaurant with music by well-known jazz pianists.

Nickels, 227 E. 67th St., IV, C1, ☎ (212) 794 2331. Upper East Side. Good jazz piano and reasonably priced.

One Fifth, 1 Fifth Ave. at 8th St., III, BC3, ☎ (212) 260 3434. Greenwich Village. Good music in Art Deco room.

Live music

Angry Squire, 216 Seventh Ave. at 23rd St., III, B2, ☎ (212) 242 9066. Chelsea. AE, CB, DC.

Apollo Theater, 253 W. 125th St., VI, B3, ☎ (212) 749 5838. Harlem. Some of the most famous Black musicians have performed in this legendary, recently restored theater.

The Blue Note, 131 W. 3rd St. at Ave. of the Americas, III, B3, ☎ (212) 475 8592. Greenwich Village. This club presents the most famous names in jazz.

The Bottom Line, 15 W. 4th St. at Mercer St., III, C3, ☎ (212) 228 7880. Greenwich Village. The selection ranges from rock or rhythm and blues to jazz.

Carlos I, 432 Ave. of the Americas at 9th St., III, B3, ☎ (212) 982 3260. Greenwich Village. Traditional and avant-garde jazz. AE, CB, DC, MC, V.

The Cat Club, 76 E. 13th St. between Broadway-Fourth Ave., III, C2, ☎ (212) 505 0090. Greenwich Village. This is a popular place that features rock groups.

CBGB and OMFUG, 315 Bowery at Bleecker St., III, C3, ☎ (212) 982 4052. Greenwich Village. Punk rock.

Fat Tuesday's, 190 Third Ave., at 17th St., III, C2, ☎ (212) 533 7902. Midtown East. Some of the greatest names in jazz play here. AE, MC, V.

Folk City, 130 W. 3rd St. at Ave. of the Americas, III, B3, ☎ (212) 254 8449. Greenwich Village. Folk music.

The Lone Star Café, 61 Fifth Ave. at 13th St., III, C2, ☎ (212) 242 1664. Greenwich Village. Country and western. AE, CB, DC, MC, V.

Michael's Pub, 211 E. 55th St. between Second-Third Aves., IV, C2, ☎ (212) 758 2272. Midtown East. Jazz. Closed Sun. AE, DC, MC, V.

Roulette's, 228 West Broadway at White St., II, B1, ☎ (212) 219 8242. Experimental jazz and avant-garde rock.

S.O.B.'s, 204 Varick St. at Houston St., II, B1, ☎ (212) 243 4940. SoHo.

Brazilian music, food and ambience, AE, CB, DC, MC, V.

Sweet Basil, 88 Seventh Ave. South at Bleecker St., III, B3, ☎ (212) 2421785. Greenwich Village. This small club offers a varied selection of high-quality jazz. AE, MC, V.

Sweetwater's, 170 Amsterdam Ave. between 68th-69th Sts., IV, AB1, ☎ (212) 8734100. Upper West Side. Good jazz, soul and pop, as well as a restaurant. AE, CB, DC, MC, V.

Tramps, 125 E. 15th St., III, C2, ☎ (212) 7775077. Midtown East. Some of the best blues singers in the world.

Twenty-Twenty, 20 W. 20th St., III, BC2, ☎ (212) 6279800. Chelsea. This is a new supper club serving Cajun cuisine.

The Village Gate, 160 Bleecker St. between Thompson-Sullivan Sts., III, B3, ☎ (212) 4755120. Greenwich Village. Jazz, rock and salsa. AE, MC, V.

Village Vanguard, 178 Seventh Ave. South at 11th St., III, B3, ☎ (212) 2554037. Greenwich Village. Open since 1935, this has been called the Carnegie Hall of jazz clubs.

Nightclubs

Heartbreak, 179 Varick St., II, B1, ☎ (212) 6912388. Tribeca. One of the most popular discotheques.

Limelight, 47 W. 20th St., III, C2, ☎ (212) 8077850. Chelsea. Installed in a former church, this is a well-known singles spot.

Nell's 246 W. 14th St. between Seventh-Eighth Aves., III, B2, ☎ (212) 6751567. Chelsea. A fashionable club in an elegant setting.

Palladium, 126 E. 14th St., III, C2, ☎ (212) 4737171. Midtown East. One of the largest clubs in Manhattan.

Tunnel, 27th St. at Twelfth Ave., III, A1, ☎ (212) 2446444. Midtown West. Old docks were converted into this very trendy spot.

▬▬ SHOPPING

The Visitors Bureau (2 Columbus Circle, ☎ 212 3978222) offers a Visitors Shopping Guide. You can also consult the Yellow Pages or the Consumer Assistance Service (☎ 212 5770111). Most of the department stores are concentrated in Midtown Manhattan, from 34th Street to 59th Street. The designer shops are mainly located on Madison Avenue and the Upper West Side, while the best deals are to be found on the Lower East Side.

Department stores

Alexander's, Lexington Ave. at 59th St., IV, C2, ☎ (212) 5930880. Low-budget items. Check the prices here before buying elsewhere. Open Mon-Sat 10am-7pm, Sun noon-5pm. AE, MC, V.

B. Altman & Co., Fifth Ave. at 34th St., III, C1, ☎ (212) 6897000. This is the spot for traditional brand names. Open Mon-Sat 10am-6pm, Thurs to 8pm. AE, MC, V.

Barneys, 106 Seventh Ave. at 17th St., III, B2, ☎ (212) 9299000. Wide selection of European and American designer clothes for men and women. Open Mon-Fri 10am-9pm, Sat 10am-8pm.

Henri Bendel, 10 W. 57th St., IV, C2, ☎ (212) 2471100. Variety, good taste and imagination attract a select clientele. Open Mon-Sat 10am-6pm, Thurs to 8pm. AE, MC, V.

Bergdorf Goodman, Fifth Ave. at 57th St., IV, C2, ☎ (212) 7537300. Tradition and elegance reign in this depart-

ment store. Open Mon-Sat, 10am-6pm, Thurs to 8pm.

Bloomingdale's, 1000 Third Ave. at 59th St., IV, C2, ☎ (212) 3555900. Major American and European designers, children's department and wide selection in its many departments. Open Mon-Sat 10am-6:30pm, Sun noon-6pm.

Bonwit Teller, 4 E. 57th St. between Fifth-Madison Aves., IV, C2, ☎ (212) 5933333. Bonwit Teller sells high-quality women's fashions. Open Mon-Sat 10am-7pm, Sun noon-5pm. AE, MC, V.

Lord & Taylor, Fifth Ave. at 38th St., IV, C3, ☎ (212) 3913344. Traditional and conservative clothing, as well as sports and household goods departments. Open Mon-Sat 10am-6pm, Thurs to 8pm. AE.

Macy's, Broadway at 34th St., III, B1, ☎ (212) 6954400. This is one of the largest department stores in the world. Open Mon-Sat 9:45am-6:45pm, Sun 11am-6pm. AE.

Saks Fifth Avenue, Fifth Ave. at 50th St., IV, C3, ☎ (212) 7534000. Elegant, expensive clothes, essentially for women. Open Mon-Sat 10am-6pm, Thurs to 8pm. AE, CB, DC.

Shopping centers

These centers include several floors of high-quality boutiques, restaurants, bars or coffee shops.

Herald Center, 34th St. at Broadway, III, B1, ☎ (212) 2442555. Open Mon-Sat 9am-9pm.

The Market, in the Citicorp Center, 54th St. at Lexington Ave., IV, C2, ☎ (212) 559 2319. Open Mon-Sat 9am-9pm.

Trump Tower, 725 Fifth Ave. between 56th-57th Sts., IV, C2. Open Mon-Sun from 9am.

Food stores

Aphrodisia, 282 Bleecker St. between Ave. of the Americas-Seventh Ave., III, B3, ☞ (212) 989 6440. Greenwich Village. This is a herbalist shop with medicinal plants and aphrodisiac teas. Open Mon-Sat 11am-7pm, Sun noon-5pm.

Balducci's, 424 Ave. of the Americas between 9th-10th Sts., III, B3, ☎ (212) 673 2600. Greenwich Village. Smoked fish, bread and cheese. Open Mon-Sat 7am-8:30pm, Sun 7am-6:30pm.

D & G Bakery, 45 Spring St. between Mulberry-Mott Sts., II, BC1, ☎ (212) 226 6688. Little Italy. Be sure to arrive before 10:30am or there may not be any bread left! Open daily 8am-2pm.

International Grocery Store, 529 Ninth Ave. between 39th-40th Sts., IV, B3, ☎ (212) 279 5514. Midtown West. This grocery store specializes in Indian products. Open Mon-Sat 8am-6pm.

Italian Food Center, 186 Grand St. at Mulberry St., II, BC1, ☎ (212) 925 2954. Little Italy. Large selection of olive oils and pasta. Open daily 8am-7pm.

Kam Man Food Products, 200 Canal St. between Mott-Mulberry Sts., II, C1, ☎ (212) 571 0330. Chinatown. This is the largest store selling Chinese products on the East Coast. Open daily 9am-9pm.

Old Denmark, 133 E. 65th St. between Lexington-Park Aves., IV, C1, ☎ (212) 744 2533. Upper East Side. Danish specialities. Open Mon-Sat 9:30am-5:30pm.

Orwasher's Bakery, 308 E. 70th St. between First-Second Aves., IV, D1, ☎ (212) 288 6569. Upper East Side. Delicious homemade bread and rolls. Open Mon-Sat 7am-7pm.

Raoul's Butcher Shop, 179 Prince St., II, B1, ☎ (212) 674 0708. SoHo. This shop is run by a Belgian couple, but the sausage and meat are cut 'à la française'. Good pasta and prepared dishes.

Zabar's, 2245 Broadway between 80th-81st Sts., V, A3, ☎ (212) 787 2000. Upper West Side. Caviar, smoked fish, cheese, tea and coffee. You can find almost anything at Zabar's. Open Mon-Fri 8am-7:30pm, Sat 8am-midnight, Sun 9am-4pm.

Antique shops

Depression Moderne, 135 Sullivan St.

at Houston St., II, B1, ☎ (212) 982 5699. The furniture is arranged so as to recreate a 1930s setting. Open Mon-Sat 10am-7pm.

Fifty-50, 793 Broadway between 10th-11th Sts., III, C3, ☎ (212) 777 3208. Furniture from the '30s, '40s and '50s with such prestigious names as Eames, Noguchi and Knoll. Open Mon-Sat 10am-7pm.

Mood Indigo, 181 Prince St., II, B1, ☎ (212) 254 1176. Interesting selection of 1930s glass, Bakelite radios and furniture. Open Mon-Sat 10am-6pm.

Shoe stores

The first place to look for shoes is along 8th Street in the Village, between Fifth Avenue and Avenue of the Americas, or between Broadway and West Broadway, south of Canal Street.

Adler Shoe Shop, 6 E. 46th St. at Fifth Ave., IV, C3, ☎ (212) 687 8810. New York chain store. Open Mon-Sat 10am-6pm.

Church English Shoes, 428 Madison Ave. at 49th St., IV, C3, ☎ (212) 755 4313. Open since 1873, Church makes men's shoes to order. Open Mon-Sat 10am-6pm.

J. Sherman Shoes, 121 Division St. between Orchard-Ludlow Sts., II, C1, ☎ (212) 233 7898. Men's shoes sold at unbeatable prices. Open daily 10am-6pm.

El Vaquero, 908 Madison Ave., IV, C1, ☎ (212) 737 8730. Original women's shoes. Open Mon-Sat 10am-7pm.

Records

Colony Record, 1619 Broadway at 49th St., IV, B3, ☎ (212) 265 2050. The store motto is 'We have it or we can get it'. Open Mon-Sat 10am-6pm.

Finyl Vinyl, 89 Second Ave. between 5th-6th Sts., III, C3, ☎ (212) 533 8007. Music from the 1950s and '60s. Open Mon-Sat noon-8pm, Sun 1-8pm.

Footlight Records, 113 E. 12th St., III, C2-3, ☎ (212) 533 1572. Specializes in Broadway scores.

Gryphon Records Shop, 606 Amsterdam Ave. at 99th St., V, B2, ☎ (212) 874 1588; **Gryphon Annex,** 220 W. 80th St. at Broadway, V, A3, ☎ (212) 496 7011. Hard-to-find jazz and classical music. The annex specializes in film and Broadway scores.

J & R Music World, 23-33 Park Row, II, BC2, ☎ (212) 732 6800 or 349 8400. Low prices and a seemingly unlimited choice.

Jazz Record Center, 133 W. 72nd St. at Broadway, Suite 204, IV, AB1, ☎ (212) 877 1836. The Center buys and sells all types of jazz records. Open Mon-Sat 10am-6pm.

Midnight Records, 255 W. 23rd St. between Ave. of the Americas-Seventh Ave., III, B2, ☎ (212) 675 2768. Re-releases, imports and original records. Open Mon-Sat 10am-7pm.

Music Masters, 25 W. 43rd St., IV, C3, ☎ (212) 840 1958. Opera and rare records.

Nostalgia and All That Jazz, 217 Thompson St. between W. 3rd-Bleecker Sts., III, B3, ☎ (212) 420 1940. Primarily jazz, but also musical comedies. Open daily from 11am.

Record Mart, 1470 Broadway, IV, B2, ☎ (212) 840 0580. This store has the largest selection of Caribbean and Latin American music in New York.

Sam Goody, 666 Third Ave. at 43rd St., IV, C3, ☎ (212) 986 8480; W. 51st St. and Ave. of the Americas. All types of music. Open Mon-Sat 10am-7pm.

Tower Records, 692 Broadway at 4th St., III, C3, ☎ (212) 505 1500; 1975 Broadway at 66th St., IV, B1, ☎ (212) 946 2500. If you look hard enough, you will find it here. Open daily to midnight.

Electronic and photographic equipment

It's a good idea to shop around before making any purchases. The competition is fierce and most stores will make every attempt to sell you their products. It may take more time, but the effort spent discussing and bargaining may result in real savings in the end. Check the equipment, packaging, guarantees and terms of payment. Try these two neighbourhoods for electronic and photographic items: 32nd Street, between Avenue of the Americas and Seventh Avenue, and 45th and 47th Streets, between Fifth Avenue and Avenue of the Americas.

You can also consult *The Village Voice* or *The New York Times* for special offers. Take advantage of the competition; for example Crazy Eddie will reimburse your purchase price if you can find the same item at a lower price elsewhere. Stores are generally open seven days a week and accept credit cards.

Camera World, 104 W. 32nd St. at Ave. of the Americas, III, B1, ☎ (212) 563 8770. This is Willoughby's main competition. The prices are low. Open Mon-Sat 10am-6pm.

Crazy Eddie, 212 E. 57th St., IV, C2, ☎ (212) 980 5134; 405 Ave. of the Americas, III, B3, ☎ (212) 242 1126. Open Mon-Sat from 10am.

47th Street Photo, 115 W. 45th St., IV, B3; 67 W. 47th St. between Fifth Ave.-Ave. of the Americas, IV, BC3, ☎ (212) 260 4410. This store offers some of the lowest prices in New York. You must know exactly what you want, because orders are taken from a catalogue. Open Mon-Thurs 9am-4pm, Fri 9am-2pm, Sun 10am-4pm.

Grand Central Cameras, 420 Lexington Ave. at 44th St., IV, C3, ☎ (212) 986 2270. Efficient and friendly service. Open Mon-Sat 10am-6pm.

Hirsch Photo, 699 Third Ave. at 44th St., IV, C3, ☎ (212) 557 1150. Low prices. Open Mon-Fri 8:30am-5:45pm, Sat 10am-4pm.

Willoughby's, 110 W. 32nd St. between Ave. of the Americas-Seventh Ave., III, B1, ☎ (212) 564 1600. The best known and one of the more expensive stores for photographic equipment. Open Mon-Wed and Fri 9am-5pm, Thurs 9am-8pm, Sat 9am-6:30pm, Sun 10:30am-5:30pm.

Jewelry

Fifth Avenue is home to the most famous jewelers, including **Cartier, Bulgari** and **Tiffany's.** Diamond Row on West 47th Street is New York's diamond center.

Jaded, 1048 Madison Ave. at 80th St., V, C3, ☎ (212) 288 6631. The material is beautiful and the price is not too high. Open Mon-Sat 10am-6pm.

Robert Lee Morris, 409 West Broadway between Prince-Spring Sts., II, B1, ☎ (212) 431 9405; 456 West Broadway, II, B1, ☎ (212) 673 2000. Silver, copper and gold jewelry in an original decor. Open daily 11am-7pm.

Don't forget the reproductions sold in the **Metropolitan Museum of Art Gift Shop.**

Toys

Complete Strategist, 11 E. 33rd St. at Fifth Ave., III, C1, ☎ (212) 685 3880. Open Mon-Sat 10:30am-6pm, Thurs to 9pm. 320 W. 57th St. between Eighth-Ninth Aves., IV, B2, ☎ (212) 582 1272. Open Mon-Sat 11am-8pm, Sun noon-5pm. Specialists in war, science fiction and strategy games.

F.A.O. Schwartz, GM Building, Fifth Ave. between 58th-59th Sts., IV, C2, ☎ (212) 644 9400. This is a palace among toy stores. There are three floors of games, dolls, stuffed animals, electric trains and robots. Open Mon-Sat 10am-6pm.

Go Fly a Kite, 153 E. 53rd St., in the Citicorp Center, IV, C2, ☎ (212) 308 1666; 1201 Lexington Ave., IV, C1, ☎ (212) 472 2623. Kites of all shapes, colours and materials, as well as porcelain dolls and beautiful stuffed animals. Open Mon-Fri 10:30am-

7:30pm, Sat 10:30am-5:45pm, Sun noon-5:45pm.

Second Childhood, 283 Bleecker St. between LaGuardia Pl.-Thompson St., III, BC3, ☎ (212) 989 6140. This store specializes in antique toys. Open Mon-Sat 11am-6pm.

B. Shackman & Co., 85 Fifth Ave. at 16th St., III, C2, ☎ (212) 989 5162. Specializes in miniatures: doll houses, antique Victorian games. They sell beautiful post cards and Christmas decorations. Open Mon-Fri 9am-5pm, Sat 10am-4pm.

Toy Balloon, 204 E. 38th St. at Third Ave., III, C1, ☎ (212) 682 3803. Balloons in all sizes, colours and materials. Open Mon-Fri 9am-5:30pm.

Books

Adler's Foreign Books, 28 W. 25th St., III, C2, ☎ (212) 691 5151. Foreign-language books.

Complete Traveller, 199 Madison Ave., IV, C3, ☎ (212) 679 4339. Guide books and maps.

The Enchanted Forest, 85 Mercer St. between Broome-Spring Sts., II, B1, ☎ (212) 925 6677. For children and adults who love fairy tales. Also hand-made wooden toys. Open daily noon-7pm.

Forbidden Planet, 821 Broadway at 12th St., III, C2-3, ☎ (212) 473 1576. Open Mon-Sat 10am-7pm, Sun 11am-6pm; 277 E. 59th St. at Third Ave., IV, C2, ☎ (212) 751 4386. Open Mon-Sat 10am-9pm, Sun noon-9pm. This is the temple of science fiction. Part of the store is devoted to comic books and gadgets.

Gotham Book Mart, 41 W. 47th St., IV, BC3, ☎ (212) 719 4448. Poetry, drama, literature and art books. This is New York's oldest bookstore.

Hacker Art Books, 54 W. 57th St., IV, BC2, ☎ (212) 757 1450. Rare editions and art books.

Herlin Jean-Noel, 68 Thompson St. between Broome-Spring Sts., II, B1, ☎ (212) 431 8732. Catalogues from exhibits and contemporary art books.

Librairie de France, 115 Fifth Ave. at 19th St., III, C2, ☎ (212) 673 7400; 610 Fifth Ave. at Rockefeller Center, IV, C2, ☎ (212) 581 8810. This is the only French bookstore in New York. Open Mon-Sat 10am-6pm.

Murder Ink, 271 W. 87th St. at West End Ave., V, A3, ☎ (212) 362 8905. Specializes in mysteries.

New York University Bookstore, 18 Washington Pl., III, BC3, ☎ (212) 598 2255. You can find anything and everything here.

A Photographer's Place, 133 Mercer St., II, B1, ☎ (212) 431 9358. Everything concerning photography.

Rizzoli, 454 West Broadway, II, B1, ☎ (212) 674 1616; 712 Fifth Ave., IV, C2-3, ☎ (212) 391 3711; 31 W. 57th St., IV, C2, ☎ (212) 759 2424. One of the major art publishers.

Shakespeare & Co., 2259 Broadway at 81st St., V, A3, ☎ (212) 580 7800. Open daily 10am-midnight.

Strand Bookstore, 828 Broadway at 12th St., III, C2-3, ☎ (212) 473 1452. The Strand is one of the largest second-hand bookstores in the world. Open Mon-Sat 9:30am-6:30pm, Sun 11am-5pm.

Three Lives and Co., 154 W. 10th St., III, BC1, ☎ (212) 741 2069. An excellent selection of literature and art books.

Clothing

Banana Republic, 205 Bleecker St. at Ave. of the Americas, III, B3, ☎ (212) 473 9570. Open Mon-Sat 10am-9pm, Sun noom-6 pm; 87th St. and Broadway, V, A3, ☎ (212) 874 3500. Open Mon-Sat 10am-7pm, Sun 1-5pm. Banana Republic offers everything for safaris, including maps, colonial helmets, T-shirts.

Betsey Johnson, 130 Thompson St., II, B1, ☎ (212) 420 0169; 251 E. 60th St. between Second-Third Aves., IV, C2, ☎ (212) 319 7699. Innovative women's clothes. Open Mon-Sat 10am-7pm.

Billy Martin's, 812 Madison Ave. at 68th St., IV, C1, ☎ (212) 861 3100. Cowboy boots, leather belts, leather gloves and belt buckles. Open Mon-Sat 10am-8pm.

Brooks Brothers, 346 Madison Ave. at 44th St., IV, C3, ☎ (212) 682 8800. The men's store for classic clothing. Open Mon-Sat 9:15am-6pm.

Canal Jeans, 504 Broadway at Spring St., II, B1, ☎ (212) 226 1130. Low-price new and second-hand pants and jeans, T-shirts. Open daily 10am-8pm.

Charivari, 2307 Broadway between 83rd-84th Sts., V, A3, ☎ (212) 873 1424. High-fashion clothing. Open Mon-Sat 10am-7pm.

Charivari for Men, 2339 Broadway between 83rd-84th Sts., V, A3, ☎ (212) 873 7242. Sophisticated clothing. Open Mon-Sat 10am-7pm.

Fiorucci, 125 E. 59th St. between Lexington-Park Aves., IV, C2, ☎ (212) 751 5638. Original women's fashions.

Julie, Artisans Gallery, 687 Madison Ave. at 61st St., IV, C2, ☎ (212) 688 2345. Women's clothes made with unusual materials and creative designs. Open daily from 10am.

Norma Kamali, 113 Spring St., II, B1, ☎ (212) 334 9696. One of the most famous designer shops in New York. Open Mon-Sat 10am-6pm.

Parachute, 121 Wooster St., II, B1, ☎ (212) .925 8630; 309 Columbus Ave., IV, B1, ☎ (212) 799 1444. Cement, columns and concrete provide an austere background for the white, gray and black clothes. Open daily from 11am.

Paragon, 867 Broadway at 18th St., III, C2, ☎ (212) 255 8036. A wide selection of clothes for every type of sport. Open Mon-Fri 10am-8pm, Sat 10am-7pm, Sun 11am-6pm.

Piaffe, 841 Madison Ave. at 70th St., IV, C1, ☎ (212) 744 9911. This store specializes in petite sizes. Open Mon-Sat 10am-6pm.

Ralph Lauren, 867 Madison Ave. at 72nd St., IV, C1, ☎ (212) 606 2100. Everything for the fashionable dresser.

Reminiscence, 74 Fifth Ave. at 13th St., III, C2, ☎ (212) 243 2292. The 1950s clothes attract a young clientele. Open Mon-Sat 10am-7pm.

Second-hand clothing

Antique Boutique, 712-714 Broadway at Washington Pl., III, C3, ☎ (212) 460 8830. A large selection of men's and women's clothes. Open Mon-Fri 10:30-9pm, Sat to 10pm, Sun noon-8pm.

Harriet Love, 412 Broadway at Spring St., II, B1, ☎ (212) 966 2280. This was one of the first second-hand shops. The clothes are in excellent condition. Open Tues-Sat noon-5pm, Sun 1-4pm.

Trash & Vaudeville, 4 St Mark's Pl. between Second-Third Aves., III, C3, ☎ (212) 982 3590 or 777 1727; 170-172 Spring St., II, BC1, ☎ (212) 226 0590. Amusing clothes. Open Mon-Thurs noon-8pm, Fri 11:30am-8pm, Sat 11am-8pm, Sun 1-4pm.

Unique Clothing Warehouse, 718 and 726 Broadway at 8th St., III, C3,

☎ (212) 674 1767. Unique items. Open Mon-Sat 10am-9pm, Sun noon-8pm.

Miscellaneous

Dell & Dell, 19 W. 44th St. at Fifth Ave., IV, C3, ☎ (212) 575 1686. For emergency repairs of broken eyeglasses, Dell & Dell will fix them on the spot. You can also purchase new frames. Open Mon-Fri 9am-6pm, Sat 9am-1pm.

James II, 15 E. 57th St., IV, C2, ☎ (212) 752 6166. English Victorian porcelain, silver frames and generally high prices. Open Mon-Sat 10am-5pm. Closed Sat during the summer.

The Last Wound-Up, 290 Columbus Ave. at 74th St., IV, B1, ☎ (212) 787 3388. This store sells marvellous music boxes. Open Mon-Sat 10am-6pm.

Maxilla & Mandible, Ltd, 78 W. 82nd St. at Columbus Ave., IV, B3, ☎ (212) 724 6173. Situated near the Museum of Natural History, the windows of this shop display animal skeletons, vertebrae, teeth and skulls. Open daily 11am-7pm.

Mythology, 370 Columbus Ave. between 78th-79th Sts., V, B3, ☎ (212) 874 0774. This interesting shop located behind the Museum of Natural History sells books and toys. Open Mon-Sat 10am-6pm.

Star Magic, 743 Broadway, III, C3, ☎ (212) 228 7770. Interesting gadgets and machines. Open daily 10am-7pm.

Think Big, 390 West Broadway, II, B1, ☎ (212) 925 7300. The key word here is 'oversized'. Open Mon and Tues 11am-6pm, Wed-Fri 10am-8pm, Sat 11am-8pm.

Urban Archeology, 137 Spring St., II, B1, ☎ (212) 431 6969. Here you can find such treasures as barbershop signs, wooden Indians, Prohibition-style or western bars, bathtubs and an unimaginable assortment of plumbing material. Open daily 10am-7pm.

SUGGESTED READING

Abbot Berenice. *New York in the Thirties*. Reprint of 1939 ed. (Dover, 1973).

Bayles, W. H. *Old Taverns of New York* (Gordon Pr., 1977).

Birmingham, Stephen. *Life at the Dakota: New York's Most Unusual Address* (Random House, 1979).

Black, Mary. *Old New York in Early Photographs 1853-1901* (Dover, 1973).

Botkin, Benjamin A. *New York City Folklore, Legends, Tall Tales, Anecdotes, Stories, Sagas, Heroes, Characters, Customs, Traditions and Sayings*. Reprint of 1956 ed. (Greenwood, 1976).

Breslin, Jimmy. *Queens: People and Places* (Zoetrope, 1984).

Caro, Robert A. *The Power Broker: Robert Moses and the Fall of New York* (Random House, 1975).

Ellison, Ralph. *Invisible Man* (Random House, 1972).

Finney, Jack. *Time and Again* (Simon & Schuster, 1986).

Fitzgerald, Scott F. *The Great Gatsby* (Macmillan, 1925).

Gardner, Deborah Jane. *New York Art Guide* (Robert Silver Associates, 1987).

Gayle, Margot, and Gillon, Edmund, Jr. *Cast-Iron Architecture in New York* (Dover, 1974).

Goldberger, Paul. *The City Observed: A Guide to the Architecture of Manhattan* (Random House, 1979).

James, Henry. *Washington Square* (Penguin, 1984).

Janowitz, Tama. *Slaves of New York* (Washington Square Press, 1987).

Jenkins, S. *The Greatest Street in the World: The Story of Broadway* (Gordon Pr., 1977).

Lewis, David. *When Harlem Was in Vogue* (Knopf, 1981).

Liebling, A. J. *Back Where I Come From* (1938).

Kazin, Alfred. *New York Jew* (Random House, 1979).

McInerney, Jay. *Bright Lights, Big City* (Random House, 1987).

Mitchell, Joseph. *The Bottom of the Harbor* (1960).

Morris, James. *The Great Port: A Passage Through New York* (1969).

Morris, Jan. *Manhattan '45* (Oxford University Press, 1987).

Orkin, Ruth. *A World Through My Window* (Harper & Row, 1978).

Riis Jacob. *How the Other Half Lives* (Hill & Wang, 1975).

Rossner Judith. *Looking for Mr. Goodbar* (Pocket Books, 1983).

Runyon, Damon. *First to Last and On Broadway*.

Sanders, Ronald, and Gillon, Edmund V. *The Lower East Side: A Guide to Its Jewish Past with 99 Photographs* (Dover, 1980).

Simon, Kate. *Fifth Avenue: A Very Special History* (Harcourt Brace Jovanovich, 1979).

Sloan, John. *New York Etchings 1905-1949* (Dover, 1978).

Starr, Roger. *Rise and Fall of New York City* (Basic, 1985).

Stern, Zelada. *The Complete Guide to Ethnic New York* (St. Martin's Press, 1980).

Still, Bayrd. *Mirror for Gotham: New York as Seen by Contemporaries from Dutch Days to the Present*. Reprint of 1956 ed. (Greenwood Pr.).

Federal Writers Project. *WPA Guide to New York City* (Pantheon, 1982).

Watson, E. B. *New York Then and Now* (Dover, 1976).

Wharton, Edith. *The Age of Innocence* (Scribners, 1983).

White, E. B. *Here Is New York* (Harper & Row, 1949).

White, N., and Willensky, E. (ed.). *AIA Guide to New York* (Harcourt Brace Jovanovich, 1988).

Wolfe, Tom. *The Bonfire of the Vanities* (Bantam, 1988).

Yeadon, David. *Nooks and Crannies: A Walking Tour Guide to New York City* (Scribners, 1979).

INDEX